# GENDER, POWER, AND VIOLENCE

## PRAISE FOR *GENDER, POWER, AND VIOLENCE*

"Angela J. Hattery and Earl Smith present a comprehensive intersectional analysis of how sexual and intimate partner violence is supported by institutional structures—an analysis that is necessary if we are to truly end the epidemic of violence and the devastating impact of its concomitant trauma." —**Claire N. Kaplan**, PhD, program director, Gender Violence and Social Change and Men's Leadership Project, University of Virginia

"This book contributes to the literature on sexual and gender-based violence by examining the institutions in which these phenomena occur and the power structures that justify and facilitate this type of violence. The authors attempt to situate violence within the context of power and oppression. This analysis is timely and necessary in order to understand interpersonal violence from a macro perspective. Written in an accessible and engaging manner, this book will be a useful tool for students and laypersons alike who seek to understand the complexities of gender-based violence and who wish to prevent future occurrences of violence and harm." —**Karen Holt**, PhD, assistant professor of criminal justice, Michigan State University

"This is a compelling, accessible, and polemical interrogation of rape culture and gender-based violence in U.S. institutions. Rather than simply describing male abuse of power the authors end each chapter with potential strategies and solutions for each institution, ending with a 'call to arms' in the final chapter to change institutional practices to change society." —**Jennifer Marchbank**, professor, gender, sexuality, and women's studies, Simon Fraser University

"In an analysis that is both broad and incisive, *Gender, Power, and Violence* provides a fresh vantage point on an epidemic that is anything but new. Zooming out from individual victims and perpetrators to the institutions where gender-based violence is rampant, Hattery and Smith connect the dots, arguing compellingly that these structures have the power to either perpetuate or address a devastating social problem." —**Lauren B. Cattaneo**, associate professor, George Mason University

"This book is a must-read for anyone who is interested in understanding the power dynamic of institutional gender-based violence and the role of institutions in perpetuating sexual violence." —**Keith Labelle**, PhD, assistant director of bystander intervention training, University of Rhode Island

# GENDER, POWER, AND VIOLENCE

## RESPONDING TO SEXUAL AND INTIMATE PARTNER VIOLENCE IN SOCIETY TODAY

*Angela J. Hattery and Earl Smith*

ROWMAN & LITTLEFIELD
*Lanham • Boulder • New York • London*

Published by Rowman & Littlefield
An imprint of The Rowman & Littlefield Publishing Group, Inc.
4501 Forbes Boulevard, Suite 200, Lanham, Maryland 20706
www.rowman.com

6 Tinworth Street, London SE11 5AL, United Kingdom

British Library Cataloguing in Publication Information Available

**Library of Congress Cataloging-in-Publication Data**

Names: Hattery, Angela, author. | Smith, Earl, 1946- author.
Title: Gender, power, and violence : responding to sexual and intimate
    partner violence in society today / Angela J. Hattery and Earl Smith.
Description: Lanham : Rowman & Littlefield, [2018] | Includes bibliographical
    references and index.
Identifiers: LCCN 2018040485 (print) | LCCN 2018041983 (ebook) | ISBN
    9781538118184 (electronic) | ISBN 9781538118177 (cloth : alk. paper)
Subjects: LCSH: Intimate partner violence. | Sex crimes. | Sex
    crimes—Prevention.
Classification: LCC HV6626 (ebook) | LCC HV6626 .H3249 2018 (print) | DDC
    362.82/92—dc23

LC record available at https://lccn.loc.gov/2018040485

♾️™ The paper used in this publication meets the minimum requirements of
American National Standard for Information Sciences—Permanence of Paper
for Printed Library Materials, ANSI/NISO Z39.48-1992.

Printed in the United States of America

To Earl: This one is personal. #MeToo. We can't underestimate the power of men who stand up as allies and use their voices and their platforms to combat sexual and intimate partner violence and child sexual abuse. From the depths of my heart, thank you for being one of those men. Thank you for your courage. And your support.

To Angela: Personal it is. Our analysis of intimate partner violence, of sexual assault, of discrimination taking place in the gender queue will resonate far and wide. It is important.

To Emma: From the day you were born, I hoped and prayed and worked so that you and your friends would live in a world that valued your bodies and kept you safe from violence. We aren't there yet, but I'm proud of you for the work you do every day to support women and children in their quest to heal from trauma and reach their full potential. It matters. I know. Love, Mom.

To Travis and Porter: Be allies. To your mom, your sister, your wife, and all of the women in your lives. I can guarantee you that there is nothing more powerful or meaningful that you can do in this life. Love, Mom.

To Daniel and Aziz: Live life to the fullest. You earned it! Love, Dad.

# CONTENTS

PREFACE      ix

ACKNOWLEDGMENTS      xiii

1   INTRODUCTION      1

2   THEORY, HISTORY, AND TERMINOLOGY      5

3   FRATERNITIES      23

4   THE MILITARY      55

5   PRISONS      83

6   SPORTSWORLD      109

7   THE CATHOLIC CHURCH      151

8   HOLLYWOOD, WASHINGTON, AND THE #METOO MOVEMENT      183

9   A CALL TO ACTION      199

APPENDIX      217

NOTES      225

BIBLIOGRAPHY      235

INDEX      241

# PREFACE

We wrote the initial draft of the manuscript *Gender, Power, and Violence* in the summer of 2015. For a variety of reasons that were beyond our control, the book that should have hit bookstores in the late fall of 2106 languished in production. We were, of course, discouraged, but we could not then have predicted what we now know—a blessing in disguise! The #MeToo movement not only provided us with many more cases to interrogate, but inspired us to add an additional set of institutions—politics and the entertainment industry— into our analysis. An analysis that started with five institutions, expanded to seven, *precisely* in response to what we were seeing in the news, on Facebook, and in our Twitter feeds. We interrogate, in much more depth than journalistic accounts are able to provide, the myriad ways in which violence against women is a tool deployed in all types of institutions, from workplaces to sports to the military to entertainment and in all the other spaces that women inhabit.

As difficult a topic as sexual violence is, especially when the bodies bearing the scars are women and children, as sociologists we appreciate the opportunity to lend our analysis and perspective to the brave voices of op-ed writers, columnists, bloggers, and others who are informing the public about powerful figures in politics, athletics, the military, the entertainment industry, and elsewhere who perpetrate violence on the bodies of women and children. We believe that our analysis compliments and extends much of what is offered by journalists.

We have been researching sexual and intimate partner violence for decades. Most of the women whose stories we tell in our book *African American Families*, which was published in 2007, had no agency; no power; and, perhaps most importantly, no widespread recognition inasmuch as none of the men they were accusing were known to anyone outside of their families and communities. These women suffered in silence. They were "invisible." Few besides us were interested in hearing, let alone telling, their stories. In many ways, the work we had been doing for decades was catapulted into the spotlight with the #MeToo movement. In essence, when you strip away the sparkling lights of Hollywood from people like Harvey Weinstein or Bill Cosby or take a closer look at men like Al Franken walking the halls of the Capitol building or of Ray Rice and countless other men who inhabit the global institution we refer to as SportsWorld, the story is not much different from those that we told in *African American Families*, stories of regular people living otherwise unextraordinary lives. The stories that we tell in this book are likely, however, to resonate differently with our readers. Why? Not because the violence is any different or because the pain is any more or less, but because you may feel like you know the perpetrators, men like Bill Cosby, or you may actually know men just like the ones we profile in this book, men you work with who routinely sexually harass women in the office. The stories in this book may hit very close to home.

The #MeToo movement has had an impact similar to the Black Lives Matter movement. For most women, as empowering as #MeToo is, it was not revolutionary. Women have been experiencing sexual and intimate partner violence since the beginning of time. What #MeToo did was force men to look at what women have always known. That sexual and intimate partner violence is part of the landscape in which women live. Similarly, Black people have been dealing with police violence in their communities for centuries, yet it took the protests in Ferguson, Missouri, and Baltimore to put this issue on the map—at least on the map that white people consult. These two recent social movements have sparked citizen engagement not seen in the United States since the large-scale modern civil rights movement of the1960s. And, that is fantastic! We hope that folks reading our book will be moved to action if they are not already involved.

What is revolutionary is that as a result of #MeToo and Black Lives Matter, suddenly individuals who wanted to tell their stories of police brutality or sexual harassment didn't have to rely on daily newspapers like the *New York Times* or *USA Today*. Ordinary people—not just academics or journalists—could post their own tweets, Facebook videos, and Instagram accusations online and open up the previously invisible world of sexual harassment to millions. And this online testimony forced a response.

This new development in both #MeToo and Black Lives Matter allows us to "seize the moment." We, too, are seizing the moment to offer an in-depth and more nuanced analysis of the systemic way that sexual and intimate partner violence impacts women in so many institutions in which they are simply trying to make a living.

In the weeks and months when we were putting the finishing touches on this book, two institutions we've interrogated for many years, SportsWorld and the Catholic Church were once again in the news, both for hiding and failing to hold accountable serial, sexual predators. Larry Nassar was accused of sexually assaulting more then 250 athletes in his capacity as team physician. He was convicted and ultimately sentenced to prison for hundreds of years. He will die in prison. Simultaneously, the attorney general of the Commonwealth of Pennsylvania convened a grand jury that returned a report indicating that more than three hundred priests serving in Pennsylvania had sexually abused more than one thousand children. More than one thousand.

Our book answers the question why. Why these cases continue to happen and why they continue to become part of public discourse, in the media, in our courtrooms, and on social media.

As difficult as it is to open up our Facebook feeds and see so many women we know and even more we don't personally know declaring #MeToo, it is this social movement that opens the door for our book, so many years in the writing, and allows us to enter the dialogue in a way that expands and deepens the conversation.

# ACKNOWLEDGMENTS

Every book we write is influenced by others who contribute their ideas, critiques, and support.

This book has had an interesting editorial journey, and we are especially grateful to our editor at Rowman & Littlefield, Kathryn Knigge, who believed in yet another one of our ideas and helped us to shape the manuscript and move the book through the process so that it can get to the reading public and inspire thoughtful analysis and probably some critique.

We are grateful to Nancy Xiong and David Corwin in the Women and Gender Studies Program at George Mason University, who supported us by allowing us to focus on this book for two summers while they kept the Women and Gender Studies Center open and the program flourishing.

We would like to acknowledge the work of Mary Ann Vega, George Mason alum (BA 2015 and MAIS 2018), who worked with us for several years—as a student in our classes; as a student researcher funded by the undergraduate research office, OSCAR; and as a master's student. Mary Ann has studied sexual and intimate partner violence right alongside of us and her work has challenged us, especially when it comes to sexual violence on college campuses.

We would like to thank Om Arvind, Spenser Rush, Alex Nowakowski, and Kendra Coleman, undergraduate research assistants at George Mason University, who assisted us with research and created many of the amazing data visualizations that we include in the book. They also contributed their talents to preparing ancillary materials that can be used by instructors and book clubs who adopt the book.

## ACKNOWLEDGMENTS

We are grateful to Lyla Byers, newly minted MA in Women and Gender Studies at George Mason University, who stepped in at the end of the project and contributed significantly to the discussion of #MeToo, and who helped develop the case studies of Bill Cosby, Harvey Weinstein, and Larry Nassar. Thanks to Cameron Shaw who jumped in during the final hours and graciously assisted with the index. A thankless job.

We thank Jennifer Hammat and Courtney Diener, our colleagues at George Mason University, who helped us navigate the intricacies of campus sexual assault, Title IX, and campus conduct processes.

We are grateful to our careful, and anonymous reviewers who encouraged us to clarify our arguments and include even more resources so that this book would be as accurate and comprehensive as possible.

Thank you to so many scholars who contributed to the development of the ideas and arguments we put forth in this book; their work is cited.

Finally, our biggest debt of gratitude is to all of the folks who let us into their lives so that we could learn more about the impact of sexual and intimate partner violence as well as child sexual abuse on real people's lives. To the women and men we interviewed in North Carolina and Minnesota: we hope we have done justice to your experiences. We know that by allowing us to share your stories you are helping others.

As with any book, we are grateful for the input of others, but any errors remain our responsibility.

# 1

# INTRODUCTION

Now, should we treat women as independent agents, responsible for themselves? Of course. But being responsible has nothing to do with being raped. Women don't get raped because they were drinking or took drugs. Women do not get raped because they weren't careful enough. Women get raped *because someone raped them*.

—Jessica Valenti, *The Purity Myth*

People should know that sexual abuse of children is not just happening in Hollywood, in the media, or in the halls of Congress. This is happening everywhere; wherever there is a position of power, there seems to be potential for abuse. I had a dream to go to the Olympics, and the things that I had to endure to get there, were unnecessary, and disgusting. . . . Our silence has given the wrong people power for too long, and it's time to take our power back.

—McKayla Maroney, gymnast, victim of Larry Nassar

Sexual and intimate partner violence is part of the landscape that women and children live with.

We've been troubled by the high levels of sexual and intimate partner violence that women and children are subjected to and we have devoted much of our professional careers to trying to better understand what factors shape who will be perpetrators, who will be victims, and how an organization will respond (or not) when it is reported. We've spent nearly two decades researching various aspects of gender-based violence (GBV) and written three books and countless academic articles based on the research we conducted with women and men living with both sexual and intimate partner violence. We've spent the last several decades living and working on college campuses, and we know firsthand the stories of fraternity brothers and athletes who were accused of sexual violence—as well as the fallout experienced by their victims. We've done research with people who are incarcerated or were formerly incarcerated and we have heard firsthand about the sexual violence both men and women experience while they are locked up. But, despite all of this exposure to gender-based violence in our work, even we didn't see the patterns emerge until we proposed to teach a new course to first-year students (formerly known as "freshmen") on a college campus where we were working.

This was around 2004.

Though it had been bubbling near the surface for a few years, the sexual abuse that rocked the Catholic Church to its foundation received massive attention in 2002 when the *Boston Globe* broke story after story of children being sexually abused by priests in the local diocese. Similarly, though rape on college campuses had been a concern for many years, Peggy Sanday's book, *Fraternity Gang Rape*, which was published originally in 1994 and again in 2007 and later the film *The Hunting Grounds*, which debuted in 2015, were the first exposures many people had to the phenomenon. Similarly, there had always been cases of athletes accused of rape and intimate partner violence being reported on outlets like ESPN, though typically the coverage focused on the speculation that athletes were falsely accused, not on the violence they were perpetrating. The more we read and researched and watched the news, the more we realized that what was missing from the analysis was an interrogation of the role that *institutions* play in perpetuating gender-based violence. And the course we proposed was our first attempt to try to make these connections. Over time, we added two additional institutions to our analysis: prisons and the military, both of which have extraordinarily high rates of gender-based violence and both of which have endured public airings of this violence and of the institutional mishandlings of it.

And then came 2017 and #MeToo. Almost no institution has been immune to this movement, including our academic discipline of sociology. And, so, no book on gender-based violence could be either. That being said, there was no way for us to include every single institution with #MeToo testimonials, so we decided to analyze two additional institutions that received the most media attention: the entertainment industry and politics. We take, then, as our focus, the phenomena of gender-based violence and child sexual abuse in seven social institutions: college fraternities; the military; prisons; athletics (what we refer to as SportsWorld); the Catholic Church; and taken together in one chapter, politics and entertainment.

We found that in each iteration of teaching this course, our students were mesmerized by both the epidemic of sexual violence in each institution and by the similarities among these disparate institutions that, at first glance, seem to have very little in common. The more we taught the class, the more we saw the similarities across institutions, and the more we all became convinced that it is a set of unique structures across these institutions that leads to high rates of gender-based violence.

## WHY THESE PARTICULAR INSTITUTIONS?

At first glance these institutions may seem to be completely unrelated. Yet, in fact, this set of institutions has three things in common:

1. They share a set of organizational structures that allow gender-based violence and/or violence against children to be perpetuated.
2. They have high rates of violence being perpetrated against women and/or children.
3. They have a culture of complicity that allows the abuse to continue without any intervention.

As one of the authors (Smith) has argued across three editions of his text *Race, Sport and the American Dream* (2007, 2009, 2014), SportsWorld is a microcosm of society. Everything that is present in the larger society is present in SportsWorld, including racism, sexism, homophobia, and class wars, as well as, unfortunately, GBV, sexual and intimate partner violence, and child sexual abuse. And the same is true of each of the institutions we analyze in this book. This book elucidates the similarities and differences among the various institutions and their structures, with particular focus on the gender-segregated or nearly segregated nature of each. Further, this book seeks to draw attention to violence in these institutions but also to demonstrate the features of each institution that make violence, and more importantly its cover-up, commonplace. Finally, this book exposes the reader to intersectional theory as a framework for understanding individual and institutionalized violence, particularly gender-based violence and child sexual abuse.

When violence is analyzed using an intersectional framework (which is discussed at length in chapter 2), several important patterns quickly appear and rise to the top. There are, for example, many important differences in the ways that violence is gendered. Men perpetrate far more violence than women, and most of it they perpetrate upon each other via war, gang violence, gun violence, and the types of violence that unfold in the sports arena. In these cases, there are important race and class differences as well, both in terms of who the victim of the violence is and who the perpetrator is. Minority men are more likely to be killed in homicides (they are also more likely to be the perpetrator); white men are more likely to be serial killers, and minority men are more likely to be killed in war—though white men most often wage these wars, most often against poor countries populated by nonwhite people. Certain forms of violence, for example sexual and intimate partner violence, are particularly interesting because they almost always involve both men and women. But almost always, men are the perpetrators and women are the victims.

It's really hard to think about the kinds of sexual and intimate partner violence that we are going to explore in this book. The stories of the women and children we will share are tragic. They make our hearts hurt. Even today, after listening to stories for more than two decades, it still hurts to hear Evie describe her experiences as a child prostitute: *"You can't imagine what it's like to have to sit on the laps of men when you are a ten-year-old. I hadn't even learned to ride a bike yet."*

And, yet, what if we don't listen? What if we don't have the courage to ask difficult questions? What if we don't hold our beloved institutions to a standard that demands accountability when women and children's bodies are ravaged by violence? To be silent is to fail the stories of the women and children we unpack here. To be silent is to be complicit with the very institutions that allowed rapists, child molesters, and physically abusive men to hide—and worse, to continue abusing until in some cases the number of victims reached the thousands.

But we can do more than listen. And, you can do more than read this book. And we hope you will. We will devote time in the final chapter to a discussion of what you can do, in your own life, in your community, and in the institutions you inhabit. We will provide practical suggestions and a resource guide where you can find more ways to address the issues we interrogate here. But for now, the first thing you can do is open your minds and hearts to learning everything you can about gender-based violence and child sexual abuse and the role that these institutions play in perpetuating it. Let's begin with some basics so that we are all on the same page.

# 2

# THEORY, HISTORY, AND TERMINOLOGY

We believed, and continue to believe, that much public and academic discourse still largely ignores the interrelationships between the different manifestations of violence and the construct of gender. Since the social construction of our gender greatly informs how we act, how we react, and how we function in the world, it seems crucial that we begin an inquiry into how our notions of gender influence the perpetration and the experience of violence.

—Paula Ruth Gilbert and Kim Eby, *Violence and Gender*

I think that if rape is inevitable, relax and enjoy it.

—Legendary men's college basketball coach,
Bobby Knight, 1988

Victims of gender-based violence (or GBV, as we frequently refer to it in this book) are all around us. They are our mothers, our daughters, our sisters, our wives, and girlfriends; they are our teachers and doctors; and they wait on us in restaurants and clean our houses. If you can't identify one girl or woman you know who has been a victim of GBV, then it's probably the case that no woman has ever trusted you enough to share this with you.

And, if you are not moved by the sheer volume of girls and women who are victims of GBV, it is important to note that the impact of the abuse doesn't stop with the victim herself. Everyone in her life, whether they know about the abuse or not, will be affected; she may suffer from mental health issues such as depression or anxiety, she may self-medicate with alcohol or drugs; she may develop an eating disorder—a common strategy to become "invisible" to the next potential perpetrator. All of these behaviors impact her personal life, her work life, and her education.

But it's not just the personal impact, whether you are aware of the victims around you or not, sexual victimization and intimate partner violence (IPV) are costly financially as well. The Centers for Disease Control estimates that IPV costs $8.3 billion annually in lost productivity, health care, law enforcement and court services, and wages. The national cost of sexual violence is estimated at $127 billion, $34 million more than the criminal victimization with the next highest costs. The total cost of sexual violence includes costs associated with tuition lost, wages lost, associated mental health costs, the costs associated with addiction, and for college victims, the lost earning potential associated with dropping out or changing majors.[1] Gender-based violence takes a costly toll on our citizens, whether we ourselves are victims or not.

## WHAT IS GENDER-BASED VIOLENCE?

*Gender-based violence* is a term used to focus our attention on the fact that certain forms of violence, specifically sexual and intimate partner violence, are *gendered*. The term replaces the term *violence against women*, which was previously the preferred umbrella term for rape and domestic violence. There is some renewed debate among feminist scholars about these terms. For example, Michael Messner argues that though there is power in adopting the term *gender-based violence* because it is inclusive of violence perpetrated not only against women but also against boys, gay men, and other members of LGBTQ+ communities, he worries that dropping the use of the term "violence against women" can be a convenient way to decenter women in the debate. He argues that because the vast majority of the violence we are talking about here, sexual and intimate partner violence, is perpetrated by men against *women*, the term *violence against women* keeps our attention focused on the gendered aspects of the violence.[2]

We choose to use the term *gender-based violence* for the reasons Messner cites; it opens up the conversation about violence against boys, men, and members of LGBTQ+ communities, and this is critically important. But we also use this term because it allows us to focus the conversation on the fact that the *perpetrator has a gender as well,* and it is typically male; using the term *gender-based violence* is a constant reminder that the most important predictor of who will be a victim is gender, and the most important predictor of who will be the perpetrator is also gender.

That said, we are constantly vigilant regarding Messner's second claim that removing the word "women" from the discussion of violence has the potential to decenter women. We are clear throughout this text that violence is gendered: perpetrated primarily by men against women and this is a result not only of patriarchy but also of the very structures of the institutions we will explore, most notably the fact that they are gender segregated: run by men for men. And when women venture inside, they are subjected to sexual and intimate partner violence—acts that are tolerated, encouraged, and covered up. In these contexts, it is the gendered nature of the institutions themselves and the need to police the transgression—that is, a woman's attempt to enter the institution—that leads to rates of GBV that are epidemic. Lastly, because we are using this umbrella term, we note that when we intend to focus *specifically* on one form of violence—sexual violence or intimate partner violence—we will make those distinctions clear.

Though our focus in this book is on the United States, we would be remiss if we failed to note that GBV is a worldwide epidemic. The World Health Organization reported in 2015 that worldwide, one in three women will be the victim of some act of GBV. The prevalence of GBV varies geographically, with a "low" of 23 percent in the United States and Canada to a high of nearly 40 percent in the Middle East, North Africa, and the African continent.

So how can we explain the epidemic rates of gender-based violence worldwide and in the United States? As sociologists, we employ the theoretical lens

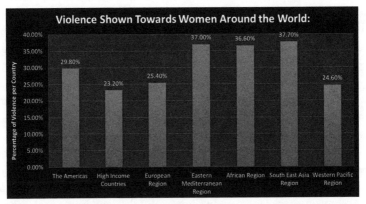

**Figure 2.1. Violence against women globally. World Health Organization. 2015. "Violence Against Women: Prevalence," Domestic Violence World Statistics 2015.**

of intersectionality in order to provide a framework for interrogating sexual and intimate partner violence and child sexual abuse.

## THEORETICAL FRAMEWORK: INTERSECTIONAL THEORY

Intersectional theory is built on the assumption that there are multiple systems of oppression that independently and collaboratively create complex systems of stratification that produce inter-locking systems of inequality. Black feminist scholar Patricia Hill Collins refers to this as the Matrix of Domination.

A core tenet of intersectional theory is the assumption that every system of domination has a counter system of privilege. In other words, every privilege that is received is a direct result of an act of oppression. Men's ability to dominate the leadership and command of the United States military is a direct result of the policies that, up until recently, banned women from gaining the combat experience required for promotion to certain ranks.

Sometimes it is useful to consider an illustration that is disconnected from the topic we are considering. This strategy prevents us from conflating the theory with the particulars of the issue. So, let's consider an example from the area of health care. We know that African American men die prematurely: seven or eight years earlier than their white counterparts. Generally, a discussion of this gap in life expectancy focuses on the reasons why African American men die early, for example because they are more likely to hold jobs that involve physical labor, they are more likely to live in poverty, they are more likely to lack access to health care, they experience racial discrimination, and the stresses associated with being an African American man. Yet, an intersectional framework forces us to ask the opposing question: Why is it that white men live so much longer? When we pose the question this way, we realize that the gap is also created by the fact that white men tend to have more access to white-collar employment and the best-quality health care. In addition, their affluence affords them the ability to pay for the "dirty" work in their lives to be taken care of by others, mostly by African American men and women. The intersection of race and social class creates *simultaneously* a disadvantage for African American men and an advantage for white men. When we dig deeper into this question of life expectancy, we see that there are significant gender differences as well. Specifically, not only do women live longer than men, but the racial gap is significantly smaller for women than for men. In short, our understanding of racial disparities in health and illness are improved when we layer these explanations together: focusing not only on gender or race, but on the ways in which they interact to produce outcomes that vary by both statuses. And this is the case when we interrogate the patterns of GPV in the United States and in these institutions.

In her latest text, published in 2016, Patricia Hill Collins, along with her coauthor Sirma Bilge, extends the concept of intersectionality as an analytical tool beyond the concept of Matrix of Domination.[3] They argue that in order to utilize intersectionality to understand contemporary social issues we must understand that intersectionality is comprised of several core ideas: relationality, social context, power, inequality, and social justice. In other words, when examining any phenomenon, we must focus our attention on the social context in which it exists, the ways in which inequality is structured and distributed, which groups put the current structures in place (power) and how they benefit from the current structures (relationality). Lastly, intersectionality is not merely an analytical tool; it is a call to action (social justice). Once the Matrix is revealed, what are those with power going to do about it? There are at least two choices: We can do nothing and allow social inequality to not merely exist but also expand; or we can identify strategies that will result in the dismantling of the structures that create the social inequality and work toward relations that are more equitable.

## THE IMPORTANCE OF LANGUAGE

How we talk about things matters. Words matter. Just as is the case with the debate on using the term *gender-based violence* as opposed to *violence against women*, there is a debate among scholars and activists over the use of the term *victim* as opposed to *survivor*. In the 1980s, advocates in the anti-rape movement began calling for the adoption of the term *survivor* to recognize the fact that victims had survived their experience with violence and that they were continuing to survive. The term *survivor* was also argued to be a more empowering term, releasing victims from the status of victimhood. And, for many years we employed the term *survivor* for all of the aforementioned reasons. More recently, anti-violence advocates are calling for a return to the use of the term *victim* for many of the same reasons that we are using the term *gender-based violence* as opposed to *violence against women*; the term *victim* is a constant reminder that a crime has been perpetrated against a woman or girl and that the crime was intentional. The comparison can be made, for example, to those who survive cancer or a hurricane, neither of which targets people because of their identity. In contrast, women are targeted for intimate partner violence, and sexual violence in particular, simply *because they are women*. In order to keep the focus on the fact that sexual and intimate partner violence are crimes that are deliberately perpetrated by men on women's bodies and in some cases boys and men, we intentionally use the term *victim*. Language matters.

One of the things we find most difficult when we teach classes and give talks in public forums about sexual and intimate partner violence is language. Americans live in a world of contradictions when it comes to sex. Sexualized images of women and children are everywhere, when we turn on the TV, when we open up applications on our smart phone, or when we check out with our groceries at the local store. But Americans hate talking about sex. Americans would rather talk about anything else than sex. But, when we talk about sexual violence and child sexual abuse, we have to talk about sex and sex organs and sex acts. And we have to talk about the ways in which these sex acts are forms of violence. When we teach in our classrooms and talk in public forums about sexual violence and child sexual abuse, we insist that these things be called for what they are, and we don't shy away from using language that many Americans are uncomfortable with. And we hold ourselves to the same standard in this book. If we don't say what it is, exactly what it is, we can't address it.

Sexual violence includes everything from unwanted touching to sexual intercourse (oral, anal, and vaginal) to sexual harassment. In a court of law, sexual violence is often referred to as "sexual assault." *Rape* is the more generalized term that many people use when they are referring to sexual violence. College campuses have carefully selected the term *sexual misconduct* to label everything from sexual harassment to sexual assault. As we will discuss at length in the next chapter, college campuses steer clear of legal definitions in order to make it crystal clear that when some is found "responsible" (not "guilty") of sexual misconduct, they have violated the norms of the campus community, not necessarily committed a crime, even though it is often the case that they have, in fact, committed a crime. The strongest response campuses can take to sexual misconduct is expulsion. They cannot incarcerate "responsible" parties. Nor do they want to. As we shall see, they would prefer not to be involved in the criminal justice system at all.

*Child sexual abuse* (CSA) is an umbrella term that includes all kinds of unwanted, nonconsensual sexual contact, including unwanted touching and sexual intercourse (oral, anal, and vaginal), but it also includes actions like exposing children to pornography, taking sexualized pictures of children, and child prostitution.

Child sexual abuse is in some ways a bit more complex than sexual violence experienced by adults precisely because, according to the law, children under a legally designated age are not able to consent to sex with anyone, *even if the children believe that the sexual activity is wanted.*

Oftentimes, victims of child sexual abuse report "consenting," especially when the person abusing them is a family member or close friend, like a teacher or coach. Both young girls and boys, in particular those who are abused over a long period, often develop a belief—fueled by the abuser—that they have a "special relationship." Childhood victims almost always know something is "wrong" about the abuse, but they may construct an ideology of consent that is consistent with the "special relationship" rationale. One of the women we interviewed, Veta, described her first sexual experience. Veta was sixteen, and her "partner" was a forty-two-year-old married man by whom she would become pregnant. In discussing the awkwardness of the age difference, Veta recalled telling her parents she was pregnant, and when they insisted that she bring the father of her child home so they could meet him, she found herself introducing her parents to a man who was not only married to someone else but was also *older than they were*!

For us the distinction between child sexual abuse and statutory rape is about power, rather than an "age line" drawn in the sand. Though most states began revising their statutory rape laws in the early 2000s in order to deal with cases involving a sixteen-year-old "perpetrator" and a fifteen-year-old "victim" who had consensual sex, technically, all that is required to demonstrate statutory rape in a court of law is sex between someone of majority age and someone of minority age. We find that child sexual abuse is often more nuanced. For example, Veta's case qualified as statutory rape, clearly, but what about sex between a very experienced twenty-five-year-old and sixteen- or seventeen-year-old with no sexual experience? Under statutory rape laws, this would not be illegal, but that doesn't mean it isn't ethically or morally problematic. Sexual violence is rooted in power, and in this case the power vacuum in knowledge and experience may be used to engage in sexual activity without clear consent.

Intimate partner violence (IPV*)* refers to the physical, emotional, psychological, and sexual abuse that takes place between intimate partners. These partners may be married, in a long-term committed relationship, or simply dating. They may be living together or not living together. They may be separated or even divorced. They may be heterosexual or be in a same-gender relationship. IPV occurs between two people who claim/claimed to love each other. Intimate partner violence can take many forms, it can be physical, emotional or psychological, or sexual. Physical abuse can range from a slap or a push, to kicking, biting, punching, or hitting with an object. Victims of physical abuse often sustain cuts, bruises, and lacerations, they frequently sustain broken bones, and in extreme cases they experience violence that hospitalizes them.

Emotional/psychological abuse refers to abuse that is designed to belittle and humiliate the victim. It is the most common form of abuse; it coexists with all other forms of abuse. And, many victims report that it is as painful as physical violence.[4] Quite often emotional or psychological abuse is verbal; and ranges from name calling to verbal assault—berating someone for a mistake or for doing something the "wrong way." Emotional or psychological abuse often involves public humiliation; for example, women often reported that their husband or boyfriend called them names in front of their friends. Or a man invites friends over to watch a sports event and berates his wife or girlfriend for not providing proper food or enough beer. Public humiliation frequently involves calling one's wife or girlfriend names or referring to her as "dumb" or saying "she doesn't know anything" in a public setting, such as when shopping or doing business at a bank.

Sexual abuse refers to any forced, coerced, or undesired sexual behavior. People often find it difficult to imagine sexual abuse inside of a sexually intimate relationship. How can you force someone to have sex who has had sex with you many times before, perhaps hundreds or thousands of time? Just as in non-intimate relationships where girls and women experience sexual violence, intimate partners engage in sexual violence, too, by using power to engage in unwanted sexual activity. Although courts often struggle with sexual violence cases inside of an otherwise consenting relationship—indeed until the early 1990s it was legal to rape your wife—sexual violence is sexual violence, regardless of the relationship between the perpetrator and the victim.

One of the most common forms of intimate partner violence is stalking, especially among teens. Stalking can include tapping phone lines, hacking into email accounts, and following the victim as she travels to work or school, on errands and so forth. Stalking can also involve harassment, including incessant phone calls or text messages—often hundreds per day—or banging on the door for hours demanding to be let in to her home.

At the extreme end of the range of behaviors that fall under the umbrella of intimate partner violence is intimate partner violence homicide, which simply refers to the most severe outcome of physical violence, the death of the victim. Intimate partner violence homicide can be immediate, as with a gunshot or stabbing, or it can result from a severe beating, which may take place in minutes or over a span of hours.

## STATISTICS ON GENDER BASED VIOLENCE

The statistics on various forms of GBV are highly contested among the public, though most experts agree that all forms of sexual and intimate partner violence and child sexual abuse are grossly underreported; it is estimated that only about 10 percent of all GBV and child sexual abuse is reported. Although all forms of GBV and CSA are underreported, most experts from research scholars to government agencies like the Centers for Disease Control report remarkably stable measures of violence over time.

One in five women report being raped, and many more experience sexual violence or harassment that falls short of the legal definition. Most women (80 percent) know the person who sexually violated them.

One in five girls and one in twenty boys experience child sexual abuse, 12.3 percent of girls and 27.8 percent of boys were raped *when they were ten years old or younger*.

Approximately 25 percent of women and 13.8 percent of men have experienced severe physical violence by an intimate partner (e.g., hit with a fist or something hard, beaten, slammed against something) at some point in their lifetime. Black and Native American women experience the highest rates of lethal and near lethal violence, including being shot, stabbed, beaten unconscious and so forth.

Approximately fifteen hundred women are murdered every year by their intimate or ex-intimate partners, and intimate partner homicide accounts for *half* of all female homicide.[5]

It is estimated that more than half of all women experience emotional, psychological, and sexual abuse by their partners and 15 percent of women and 6 percent of men report being stalked.

It is important to pause for a minute and allow these statistics to become real and not just numbers on a page. Forty-four million women living in the United States, our mothers, our daughters, our spouses, even ourselves, are victims of sexual and intimate partner violence. Victims of violence are all around us. If you think you don't know someone who is a victim, let us be clear, you do. She just hasn't told you yet. Perhaps because her perpetrator is a member of one of the institutions that we interrogate in this book.

## WHAT ARE INSTITUTIONS?

When most readers think of institutions, they think of organizations that have some level of bureaucracy and some physical space; for example, we think of prisons, schools, churches, banks, the Capitol building in Washington, D.C. For a sociologist, all of these are institutions, but so are many other things. Sociologists consider institutions to be any system that has a defined set of norms that organize social life. For example, the family is an institution, education is an institution, and the entities we are focused on in this book—fraternities, the military, SportsWorld, the Catholic Church, Hollywood, politics, and prisons—are all institutions, even though not all have a defined physical space. So, what is it about the specific organizations examined in this book that makes them institutions?

1. Each institution has a set of norms that dictate social behavior for members of the institution.
2. Each institution has a set or sets of rules, a hierarchical structure, and some sort of system of internal justice that regulates the behavior of members.
3. Each institution is gender segregated.
4. Each institution socializes its members and demands a high level of loyalty.

It is important to note the role that loyalty plays, namely, that the institution is more important than the individual. Often loyalty is reinforced by the implementation of some sort of uniform or dress code that minimizes individual differences and maximizes the importance of the institution. For example, not only do sport teams require their players to wear uniforms, but generally the team name is more prominent than the individual name, and in some cases the uniform doesn't include the individual player's name at all. Some institutions go so far as to control nearly every aspect of its members' lives. We call these institutions total institutions.

## TOTAL INSTITUTIONS AND QUASI-TOTAL INSTITUTIONS

Erving Goffman, in his 1961 groundbreaking work *Asylums: Essays on the Social Situation of Mental Patients and Other Inmates*, introduced the concept of a total institution. Goffman's concept of the total institution was developed based on this ethnographic research in mental health institutions, or what were at the time called insane asylums. Of the institutions we analyze in this text, only one, the US prison system, is a total institution. We consider the other institutions to be quasi-total institutions, since they have many, but not all, of the same structures as total institutions.

According to Goffman, a total institution is an institution whose primary mission is to control literally every aspect of members' daily lives; members are allowed to make very few decisions. For example, inmates wear uniforms, they eat the food that is served when it is served, and their access to showering is regulated, as is "yard time." The access that inmates have to the "free world"—vis-à-vis visits, phone calls, letters, and even access to TV and the internet—is monitored and highly controlled. In a true total institution, members are not allowed to leave voluntarily but must be officially dismissed, which is a significant difference between prisons and the other institutions that we examine.

Total institutions often have rigid hierarchies with very structured power relations. They also typically have internal systems of justice, which allows those in charge to make nearly every decision and with very little oversight.

Even in quasi-total institutions, when it comes to GBV and child sexual abuse, this hierarchy creates yet another layer of power, one that functions to create a climate wherein violence can be perpetrated, victims are afraid to report, and there are often few if any consequences for the people who committed the violence. In the military, it is common that women are raped by the very supervisors or commanders to whom they report. Women often believe they cannot say "no" to the sexual advances of a supervisor any more than they refuse any particular task they are assigned. Additionally, in the military, the reporting structure dictates that victims of rape report to their supervisor. When the supervisor is the rapist, reporting is impossible. Similarly, in SportsWorld, if a young man is being sexually abused by his coach, he may worry that if he refuses, he will see his playing reduced or, worse, he will be cut from the team. In Hollywood, the perpetrator may be the very person authorized to offer an acting contract, as was the case with Harvey Weinstein.

The military is very clearly a quasi-total institution. Much like prisons, nearly every aspect of daily life is controlled, especially for enlisted members, those living in the barracks, and those who are deployed. Military members, unlike prisoners, do not have their access to the civilian world monitored or controlled generally, though they may have limited access during deployments or when they are working on assignments that have require high levels of security clearance. Military members can leave, though without permission they would face a court martial.

The remaining five institutions do not meet the criterion of a quasi-total institution, but they each have features of total institutions that significantly shape the experiences of members. The Catholic Church impacts the daily lives of its members—in this case ordained members—in significant ways. Priests (and all ordained members) work and live where they are assigned, they receive whatever compensation the Church provides, including access to vehicles, and their personal lives are highly regulated, especially with regard to the vow of celibacy.

Fraternities, politics, Hollywood, and SportsWorld are the least regulated of all the institutions, but for most members, certain aspects of their lives are highly regulated. Members may be required to wear uniforms for certain events, they may have their access to food regulated, and many aspects of their time are dictated by others. For example, fraternity members are required to attend certain events. If they miss, they can be fined or even dismissed, depending upon the infraction. Similarly, both college and professional athletes are required to practice, travel, and compete as determined by the coach, and they too face fines and dismissal if they fail to show up for their scheduled events. Politicians at all levels, but especially at the federal level, work in an environment that is significantly constrained by rules and regulations, particularly those related to finances and ethics. Even in Hollywood, actors are members of unions, and access to top roles often requires absolute loyalty to the men who own and run the film companies. In addition to the controlling nature of these institutions, they all share a set of structures that shape the prevalence of and their response to sexual and intimate partner violence and child sexual abuse: They are gender segregated, they have internal systems of justice, and they have strong and active rape cultures that are characterized by, among other things, hypermasculine expectations for members' behavior.

The term *sex-segregated institution* generally refers to one that is overwhelmingly comprised of one gender. It need not be the case that the institution is 100 percent of one gender, but in most cases, sex-segregated institutions are 90 percent or more comprised of one gender. Though institutions can be segregated by any gender (for example all-women's colleges), our focus here is on institutions that are reserved for men. The institutions we are interrogating may not be sex segregated in terms of membership—though some, like prisons and the military, are—but rather in leadership, as with the Catholic Church or politics, or simply in day-to-day interactions, as in fraternities, Hollywood, and SportsWorld. What is important here is to note that sex segregation produces four unique patterns that can contribute to GBV: gender segregation, hypermasculinity, resistance to integration, and segregation in leadership.

## PATTERN ONE: SEGREGATED GENDERS

Sex-segregated institutions are just that, segregated, which means that there is very little if any routine contact among the genders. In institutions that are dominated by men, this means that they have few if any meaningful interactions with women as part of their daily routines. Again, the level of this varies from prisons and the military in which the number of mixed gender interactions may be almost none, to fraternities and SportsWorld, where men may interact with women, but these interactions generally occur in a context in which women have very limited roles—as cheerleaders or "little sisters." When men have few meaningful interactions with women, or when those interactions are framed by dominance and subordination, it is much easier to "other" women and engage in exploitation and violence against them.

## PATTERN TWO: HYPERMASCULINITY

Sex-segregated institutions are overwhelmingly hypermasculine. In other words, gender roles are rigidly proscribed—men fight or lead and women are there to serve men's needs—and traditional masculinity is the *only acceptable gender expression for men*. Sexual and intimate partner violence is often utilized as a way to establish or reestablish a hypermasculine identity. Our own research with men who batter was confirmed by a study published in 2015, which stated that in the context of a hypermasculine culture, men who feel inadequate or feel their masculinity is challenged will often engage in GBV as a strategy to demonstrate their masculinity: "Boys who experience stress about being perceived as 'sub-masculine' may be more likely to engage in sexual violence as a means of demonstrating their masculinity to self and/or others as well as thwarting potential 'threats' to their masculinity by dating partners."[6]

Why? Because perpetrating violence against women is a straightforward expression that serves two purposes: It confirms masculinity and it reinforces the inferiority of women. Though this will not be the focus of our discussion here, these same institutions tend to also be very intolerant of the presence of gay men and people who identify as non-binary and may enforce this intolerance with violence as well, including sexual violence.

Hypermasculinity is a hallmark of rape culture, an environment in which rape jokes are commonly told, victims are blamed for their own rapes, women are sexually objectified, and so on. We and many other feminists argue that the United States can be characterized as being a rape culture. We can turn on the TV and watch an episode of *Family Guy*, for example, and hear rape jokes being made. There is a change.org petition (https://www.change.org/p/stop-rape-jokes-on-family-guy) demanding the writers stop putting rape jokes into future episodes. Music videos feature women in provocative clothing and provocative postures whose sole purpose seems to be to serve the male artists.

Robin Thicke's song "Blurred Lines," which in 2013 peaked at number one in fourteen countries and has been critiqued for its normalizing of nonconsensual sex.

Rape culture is indeed everywhere, and the institutions we interrogate are proof of that. In fact, with the possible exception of the Catholic Church, the hypermasculine nature of the military, fraternities, SportsWorld, Hollywood, politics, and even prisons, exacerbates and intensifies rape culture. Even subcultures, like police departments, prosecutors' offices, and conduct hearing boards on individual college campuses can be rape cultures.

## PATTERN THREE: RESISTANCE TO INTEGRATION

A third pattern often seen in sex-segregated institutions where women are seeking to integrate, such as the military or the Catholic Church, is that men often perceive these attempts as transgressions that need to be policed. Integration of any sort has never been met without a fight, and most often, the fights involve violence. Think, for example, of the fire hoses, dogs, and National Guard troops and tanks that were deployed all over the Southern region of the United States as part of the enforcement of the landmark case *Brown v. Topeka Kansas Board of Education* that rendered segregation in public spaces unconstitutional. Though the battles of gender integration have not been on such a mass scale, the battle lines have been equally as guarded.

## PATTERN FOUR: SEGREGATION IN LEADERSHIP

The fourth pattern of sex segregation, concentrated among the leadership in organizations, plays a significant role in both the tolerance for and the lack of focus on preventing and intervening in cases of GBV and child sexual abuse. There are a variety of reasons for this, ranging from the lack of experience many men have with sexual and interpersonal violence, compared to women, to the culture of brotherhood that develops in sex-segregated institutions, which rises to the highest levels of leadership, demanding the protection of male members at any cost. Sex segregated institutions are typically hypermasculine, and to stand up to GBV or child sexual abuse may be defined as unmasculine. The tone the leadership sets is especially important in the Catholic Church, in which both men and women worship in the pews, but only men are allowed to lead.

## POWER

Often the elephant in the room in discussions of sexual and intimate partner violence is the issue of power—both its role in individual acts of violence as well as in institutional response to GBV and child sexual abuse when they occur. For many decades, feminist theorists and scholars have demonstrated that rape is not a crime of passion, but rather an act of power. As Catharine MacKinnon argues in her 1991 influential book, *Theorizing a Feminist Theory of the State*, the power that men have to rape women (and other men) is rooted in their position of dominance in a patriarchal society.

Intimate partner violence and child sexual abuse are also acts of violence that are rooted in power. Two of the most widely known and referenced family violence theorists Murray Straus and Richard Gelles identify a key pattern in family violence: the tendency for it to be perpetrated by people with power against those without power. Stronger, older people abuse younger, weaker people. Of course, this trend reverses when parents reach an elderly status and they become vulnerable to their adult children. People with more resources—parents, adult children, husbands—are more likely to be abusive toward those without resources—children, elderly adults, wives—than the reverse. Straus and Gelles also argue that people engage in abusive behavior because they can, and because it works. When a parent spanks a child, there are generally no consequences—"they can"—and it generally changes a child's behavior in the desired direction—"it works."

The same is true in intimate partner violence. The men we interviewed often said that they beat up their wives and girlfriends in order to make them behave the way they wanted them to. Henry said that when he came home from a long day at work and the house wasn't clean and there was no dinner on the table he wondered what his girlfriend, who was not employed and stayed at home full-time, was doing all day. His frustration often escalated to verbal and physical abuse. When we asked him to reflect on his reaction to the situation, he indicated that his intent was to discipline her so that she would behave the way he wanted her to. Our research, as well as that of Gelles and Straus, indicates that at least initially this type of violence does have an immediate effect. In order to stop the yelling or the hitting, women often do change their behavior immediately and for the short term in order to avoid additional violence. That said, violence is rarely effective in the long run, as victims of intimate partner violence typically reach their capacity for being the brunt of anger and seek a way to leave the relationship.

## INSTITUTIONAL POWER

Not only people have power. Institutions do as well. Institutions, through their leadership, establish norms and cultures that dictate members' behavior. For example, in SportsWorld there are often norms about handling injuries. Although the NFL now requires players to go through a concussion protocol before they are sent back out on the field, the media focus on concussions in the National Football League and in college football has revealed that in the past, players were typically sent back out on the field, despite having sustained a serious, perhaps life-threatening injury. This practice is consistent with the hypermasculine culture of football, where boys, from a very early age, are told not to cry and to play through the pain. Institutions also establish and enforce norms with regard to the roles that women should play. If an institution is resistant to integration by women, for example, then the institution will set the tone for how to treat women who attempt to integrate the institution. This "tone" may involve refusing to hire women, refusing women access to the resources they need, or in many cases sexually harassing and even raping women so that they will "voluntarily" exit the institution.

When it comes to power, institutions face a very real and often perplexing tension: the tension to do the morally correct thing—reducing rape—while meeting the interests of the institution. For example, colleges and universities make it clear in all of their promotional material and even in their mission statements, that the safety and success of their students is paramount. Yet one in five women on a college campus are raped while they are in the institution's care. Colleges and universities experience the tension between providing for the safety of their women students while simultaneously protecting the future careers of those students in the same community who are being accused of sexual violence. At the end of the day, with virtually no exception that we can find, colleges and universities resolve this tension by hiding rape statistics and utilizing a process of conduct board hearings that rarely find perpetrators responsible, which results in them remaining on campus, free to rape more victims.

Colleges and universities, the Catholic Church, the National Football League (NFL), fraternities, the military, Hollywood, political entities, and even prisons would prefer that rapes not be perpetrated by members in their institutions at all. But, as they are currently organized, none of these institutions can prevent rape. So, they do the next best thing—they actively hide instances of GBV so as to appear to be free from this violence. In doing so, they fail to hold perpetrators accountable, because to hold them accountable would be to admit there are perpetrators to begin with. By failing to hold perpetrators accountable and not removing them, the institution seems to give them license to continue, and thus the institution *ends up with more of what it wants less of.* We will return to this discussion in the final chapter, but suffice it to say that we believe that if institutions handled GBV directly and held perpetrators accountable, any short-term loss suffered in terms of reputation would quickly be replaced by the long-term gains of overall lower rates of GBV. Thus, institutions would be able to meet their moral and ethical obligations to keep their members safe and effect an overall rise in the respect of communities for these institutions.

## FINAL THOUGHTS

As we move into our interrogation of each institution, intersectional theory provides the framework for us to ask questions that interrogate both the disadvantage—gender based violence—and the benefit that is gained from either engaging in it personally or covering it up when it happens. This kind of analysis allows us to better identify power and its institutional nature. GBV in any institution is not a simple matter of a few bad apples or a few evil people. GBV, if not sanctioned outright, is tolerated and covered up by these institutions for reasons that have to do with their sex-segregated nature, the value they place on hypermasculinity, and their overall resistance to allowing women into the institution at all, and especially into the leadership.

Gender-based violence and child sexual abuse are, tragically, far too common experiences for women and children living in the United States. Despite gains that the United States has made in other areas of gender equality, for example in education, almost nothing has changed in the thirty years that we have been studying and researching these issues and advocating for reform. We believe that part of the reason for this lack of movement on such important issues is silence. Americans don't like to talk about sex, and they definitely don't want to talk, or learn, about sexual and intimate partner violence or child sexual abuse. But if we don't talk about it, and if we don't understand its root causes and the role that our beloved institutions play, then it will continue to harm those we care about the most. It will continue to be used as a way to deny women and girls access to their dreams: to fly jets or play basketball or enjoy socializing at a fraternity party. Which is where we begin.

# 3

# FRATERNITIES

> I used to say that I was attacked by my classmate, but I was raped by my college.
>
> —Classmate of one of the authors

Rape is one of the most underreported and disbelieved allegations on college campuses. And, unfortunately, the majority of the cases that are portrayed in the media—like the high-profile 2014 *Rolling Stone* article that focused on rape at the University of Virginia, a small part of which was discounted after the fact—fuel the belief that most women make up rape and that college women in particular cry rape after "regret sex." To read about the case that broke open the scandal of fraternity rape at the University of Virginia we recommend *Crash into Me: A Survivor's Search for Justice*, by Liz Seccuro. Much of "Jackie's" story in *Rolling Stone* was actually lifted from Seccuro's memoir, which occurred in the fraternity that "Jackie" said was the venue of her assault. In an interview with Carol Costello[1] on CNN in December 2014, Susan Patton, otherwise known as the "Princeton Mom," argued, "I believe she got really drunk and had sex with someone she regretted. To me that's not a crime, that's not rape. . . . That's a learning experience that has to do with making choices and taking responsibility for the choices you make." Costello responded several times with statements about not blaming victims, noting: "Rape is the only crime in which we turn the lens onto the survivor, the victim, and not onto the perpetrator. When someone gets shot, we don't ever ask them, 'Why didn't you get away from that bullet?'" This interchange illustrates both the reasons for underreporting and the ways in which rape allegations are often not believed, discounted as sexual mistakes rather than the violence they are.

In this chapter, we explore the role that fraternities and fraternity culture play in the larger context of rape on college campuses. We certainly would never argue that fraternities are solely responsible for creating the culture of GBV that we see on campuses or that fraternity brothers are the only perpetrators of this violence. But employing the concept of "fraternity" as used by anthropologist Peggy Reeves Sanday allows us to fine-tune our interrogation and understanding of the ways in which a fraternal culture works to perpetuate sexual and intimate partner violence and child sexual abuse, not only on college campuses but also in SportsWorld, the military, and the Catholic Church as well. As Sanday writes, quoting the Random House Unabridged Dictionary, "I use the word 'fraternity' in its broader sense to mean a group of persons associated *by or as if by ties* of brotherhood, or any group or class of persons having common purposes and interests."[2]

In this chapter, we focus specifically on the ways in which fraternities shape the climate on college campuses in ways that makes rape a predictable outcome. But, first a little bit about fraternities and their history in higher education.

## THE ROLE OF FRATERNITIES IN HIGHER EDUCATION

Before we begin our discussion, we want to make clear that unless otherwise specified, the discussion is limited to historically white fraternities. We do not mean to imply that historically black or Hispanic fraternities do not have these types of issues, but for a variety of reasons—including the different historical missions and purposes of nonwhite fraternities, differences in the presence nonwhite fraternities have on campuses, and the previous research on fraternities—our focus is on white fraternities.

Nicholas Syrett's book *The Company He Keeps: A History of White College Fraternities*[3] provides a detailed historical analysis of white fraternities, and we refer to his text in providing this overview. Interestingly, Syrett's interest in fraternities, as he states in the preface, stems, as does Sanday's, as does our own, from media reports and on-campus experiences with fraternities and rape, including gang rapes.[4] We recall, for example, on a campus where we taught, taking a morning walk on freshman move-in day and observing a sign hung from the pillars of a fraternity with a well-known reputation for rape: "Thank you, fathers, for bringing us your daughters." We were obviously outraged and sent an email to the college president. His response was simply to note that boys will be boys. This was not something he was worried about. For us, it was yet another visible symbol of the role that fraternities play in perpetuating not only rape, but also rape culture. Why? Because all of the statistics on rape on college campuses reveal that a women's highest risk for rape is during her first six weeks on campus. Thank you, fathers, for bringing us your daughters.

Syrett's analysis provides three key concepts for our discussion here. First, fraternities have not always had a reputation for rape. Second, fraternities, from their inception, hold masculinity among the most important qualities for young men and that rewards are handed down to the men who most embody masculinity. And, third, many men, especially those who may be "deficient" in traditional masculinity, might "over perform" masculinity to demonstrate their manliness to other men. And *it is men who are the only judges who matter.*

Syrett argues further that fraternities serve a variety of functions, including playing a critical role in defining hegemonic masculinity. Interestingly, not only do the fraternities hold their own members to these standards, but most students hold all men on campus to this standard. In the current context, hyper-masculinity is defined by a few key characteristics. At the core are two that will sound recognizable to any reader familiar with fraternities: the ability to drink excessive amounts of alcohol and the ability to have sex with as many women as possible. This is the campus culture that fraternities define and create. Is it any wonder, then, that rape is nothing short of epidemic on college campuses?

While not all rape on college campuses is perpetrated by fraternity members, we argue that fraternities establish a set of standards of masculinity and a campus culture—of excessive drinking and promiscuous sex—that fraternity and non-fraternity men adhere to and that encourage rape on college campuses. This fraternity culture and its hegemonic standards of masculinity are also pro-mulgated through other sources as well, especially via social media and "reality TV" shows that showcase this culture as the norm. Our society, including our universities, enables a rape culture such that the reality is that rape occurs on *all* college campuses, regardless of the *actual presence* of "Greek" fraternities.

## FRATERNITY CULTURE IN NON-FRATERNITY SETTINGS

Black fraternities have similar but also unique problems as compared to white fraternities. Lionized in the film *Drumline*, set at a fictional college in the South that could have been Morehouse or Florida A&M, the public perception of HBCUs is that even if the football team is not that good, if you attend a game you will be guaranteed a fabulous halftime show put on by the band. This is especially true for the Florida A&M marching band, which has also performed at Super Bowl football games, the Grammy Awards, and in inauguration parades.

Unfortunately, the bands at many HBCUs are also known for fraternity-style hazing. On November 19, 2011, in Orlando, Florida, the Florida A&M band prepared for the last game of the football season against Bethune-Cookman University. During a pregame hazing ritual known as "walking the gauntlet," Robert Champion was forced to walk the dark bus isle without his shirt on while his fellow band members beat on him with a drum mallet and other objects. Once he reached the back of the bus, touching the back door, he would then have "crossed over." But Robert Champion never made it. He was beaten to death, perhaps because he was perceived to be gay. He was only twenty-six. His death was ruled a homicide, and thirteen of his fellow band members were charged with felony hazing.

The band, which was suspended in 2012, was reinstated in 2014 after serving just twenty-one-months of suspension. Two members of the band faced criminal charges. Dante Martin was convicted and sent to prison with a sentence of seventy-seven months to six years. Jessie Baskin was jailed for only fifty-one weeks, less than one year, for his participation in the beating death of Robert Champion.

As this example demonstrates, fraternities—regardless of their name or the ethnicity of their members—behave in similar ways when they embrace a fraternity-like culture that glorifies masculinity and abhors anything feminine, including even the perception that one is gay.


## RAPE ON COLLEGE CAMPUSES

We've been studying rape on college campuses for more than twenty-five years, and the sad fact remains that very little has changed. Statistics on all forms of GVP are grossly underreported and rape on college campuses is no exception. That being said, a variety of different research studies conducted by independent scholars and national organizations, find nearly identical prevalence rates that have been remarkably consistent over more than twenty-five years A report issued by the U.S. Department of Justice in 2014 estimated that 18 percent, or one in five, or nearly one hundred ten thousand women are raped on college and university campuses each year.[5] Across the typical four years a student is enrolled in college, a half million of her female peers will be raped. Put another way, on the typical state university campus with twenty-five thousand students, there are likely hundreds of rapes per year. So, over the course of four years, thousands of rape victims walk the quad, sit in classes, and live in residence halls, all on the same campus as the men who raped them.

## One in Five

Given the one-in-five victimization statistic, one might conclude that 20 percent of all college men are rapists. In fact, the typical college rapist, just like the typical convicted rapists whom Diana Scully interviewed in prison, commits six rapes while he is in college. According to a 2015 study conducted by Jacquelyn Campbell,[6] a leading researcher on sexual and intimate partner violence, 5.6 percent of college men studied admitted to committing an act of sexual violence that met the *legal* definition of sexual assault. On a campus of twenty-five thousand students, assuming half of the students are men, we would expect to find nearly seven hundred rapists. As we will see when we discuss the internal system of justice on college campuses, the fact that most campuses don't expel a single student for sexual misconduct in a decade is very troubling indeed.

## Fraternities and Rape on College Campuses

There is much debate about whether it is true or not that certain subgroups of men are more likely to commit rape than others. In the college context the two groups that are most frequently labeled as "high risk" are fraternities and athletes. It is not surprising, then, that as we researched the various institutions that we wanted to analyze for this book both SportsWorld and fraternities were immediately obvious choices. So what do the data indicate? In a study published in 2007, John Foubert, Johnathan T. Newberry, and Jerry L. Tatum confirmed what previous research has shown: men who join fraternities are three times more likely to commit rape than men who do not join fraternities.[7] The question, then, is, are men who join fraternities more prone to commit rape, or is there something about fraternity culture that creates a type of hypermasculinity that results in rape and/or an environment that facilitates rape? Peggy Reeves Sanday's extensive ethnographic research on fraternities, published in her 2007 book *Fraternity Gang Rape*, provides a rich window into fraternity culture, and we rely on her research heavily in our discussion of fraternity rituals and culture.

CHAPTER 3

## Fraternity Culture

Fraternities inculcate members with a new set of shared values. Some of these values, at least as represented on paper, are noble:

> *Our Mission: Sigma Alpha Epsilon (SAE)*
> The mission of Sigma Alpha Epsilon is to promote the highest standards of friendship, scholarship and service for our members based upon the ideals set forth by our Founders and as specifically enunciated in "The True Gentleman."[8]

At first glance, Sigma Alpha Epsilon looks to be a group any parent would want their son to join. And, certainly there are many chapters of Sigma Alpha Epsilon and every other fraternity that focuses on providing leadership, scholarship, and service. But, unfortunately as demonstrated nearly every week in the news, it is often difficult to find much evidence of leadership training; there is much more evidence of values that are direct reflections of the hypermasculine values: a sense of superiority, excessive drinking and getting as much heterosexual sex as possible, all of which are reinforced clearly and powerfully during the pledging process and initiation rituals.

## Pledging Practices and Initiation Rituals

For those readers unfamiliar with fraternities and sororities, there are several phases to the membership process, recruitment, pledging, and initiation. Pledging serves at least two functions in fraternities: (1) it socializes new members into the values of the organization and builds their identity with the organization and (2) it provides a temporary servant class for the fraternity members. The socialization process involves teaching the pledges about both the formal and informal values of the institution. For example, pledges have to learn the history of the fraternity, important people and dates in the fraternity's history, the meanings of its symbols, and so on. Additionally, by being around the house—no pledge is allowed in the house without being escorted by a brother until he is initiated—he will learn the norms of the fraternity. For example, Sanday and others describe informal times when brothers may shoot pool or, conversely, watch porn together. Pledges will attend meetings during which announcements are made, which might include the logistics of getting a ticket for the weekend's football game or, as Sanday's informants learned, discussions of a brother's sexual prowess or failure. For a member in training, all of these experiences teach a pledge what is expected of him and what is valued.

In many fraternities, pledges also serve a more practical function: They perform undesirable tasks for the brothers. These tasks involve doing the brothers' laundry and cleaning the house. Other duties typically involve serving as the designated driver for the fraternity parties. Reportedly, one of the reasons that pledging on campuses where football is king takes place in the fall is because the pledges can be used to drive the brothers to and from the tailgate parties, which involve consuming large quantities of alcohol that take place before, during, and after the games. On other campuses, where fraternity houses—that may or may not be recognized by the university—are off campus, pledges fill the role of shuttle drivers, bringing women to the parties and taking them home after the parties are over. Because all of these chores are done together, a great deal of bonding takes place among the pledges, and their identities as members of the fraternity are cemented.

Pledging is a powerful process that socializes new members into the norms of the fraternity and transmits powerful values. In her study, *Fraternity Gang Rape*, Peggy Sanday was able to interview fraternity members about their initiation rituals. It is from these rituals that more is revealed about how rape culture is established in fraternities.

Fraternities consider the initiation ritual to be pivotal in cementing the brothers' identity as members of the fraternity and their loyalty to the house. In reading several of the examples Sanday provides, several themes emerge: (1) dying and rebirth, (2) a sense of elitism, (3) loyalty and identity, and (4) hypermasculinity.

## Dying and Rebirth in Rituals

In order to become a member of a fraternity, a man must shift his identity and allegiances away from his former life and toward the fraternity; he is leaving his old family and joining a new family. These kinds of rituals are not uncommon, especially in the institutions we are analyzing in this book. What is unique to the fraternity initiation are the rituals and the values that are transmitted. In many fraternities, the dying and rebirth rituals are quite elaborate. Pledges are almost always required to come to the house dressed in clothes that, unbeknownst to them, will eventually be destroyed and replaced with new robes. Often there are a series of tasks that are performed that culminate with the pledges being required to get into makeshift coffins where their former selves die and they are resurrected as brothers. Common among the fraternity rituals Sanday analyzed was the "dying" of any remnants of a "feminine" self. For example, pledges might be required to suck liquid out of balloon that is described as their mother's breastmilk. When they suck the liquid they find that it is milk that has been mixed with hot sauce and thus burns their mouths. As they spit the milk out, the brothers scream at the pledges telling them that they are mama's boys and not man enough to be a brother in this fraternity. They are then allowed to brush their teeth, offered a glass of cold water, and told that the uncomfortable ritual was required to help them break away from their mother.

## Elitism in Rituals

Fraternities are about exclusivity, and it is their exclusivity that gives them power on college campuses. Other than sport teams, fraternities are often the most powerful social forces on campus as they are frequently the primary or only reliable source for alcohol, the substance that fuels college social life. Fraternities have historically been a place for elite young men to develop leadership skills and social capital. Up until very recently, they were completely racially segregated, segregated by religion, and restricted to men from upper-middle- and upper-class families. For example, Sigma Alpha Epsilon (SAE) posts on their official website:

> Our Creed: "The True Gentleman"
> The True Gentleman is the man whose conduct proceeds from good will and an acute sense of propriety, and whose self-control is equal to all emergencies; who does not make the poor man conscious of his poverty, the obscure man of his obscurity, or any man of his inferiority or deformity; who is himself humbled if necessity compels him to humble another; who does not flatter wealth, cringe before power, or boast of his own possessions or achievements; who speaks with frankness but always with sincerity and sympathy; whose deed follows his word; who thinks of the rights and feelings of others, rather than his own; and who appears well in any company, a man with whom honor is sacred and virtue safe.—*John Walter Wayland*[9]

Today the majority of "white" fraternities remain exclusionary in terms of race and religion. Although they may have opened up more in terms of social class, which could be explained by the fact that colleges in general have become more accessible to middle-class families, the costs to join and participate remain a way to exclude men from less well-to-do families. In short, fraternities are a bastion of privilege: male privilege, white privilege, religious privilege, heterosexual privilege, and class privilege. And, like most spaces where privilege is concentrated, those who are members and those who are on the outside looking in attribute significant power to the group. As a result, many men desire to join fraternities, and they will endure almost anything in order to access that power, privilege, and sense of being elite.

Additionally, this position of power and privilege extends to the campus community. Many women want to attend fraternity parties and will do almost anything to be invited. Administrators are afraid to sanction fraternities, and in many cases they allow them more or less free rein. And those in the wider community who may live near fraternity houses will put up with the weekly vomit on the street on Sunday mornings, the noise on Saturday nights, and the endless movement of people and drinking paraphernalia—kegs, beer pong tables—in and out of the houses.

Several rituals are designed explicitly to develop and reinforce this sense of elitism: of the man himself, of his fraternity, and of fraternity life on his college campus. These rituals often involve endurance activities, including sleep deprivation, exercising to exhaustion, and exposure to harsh conditions. One fraternity member that Sunday interviewed described being forced to stay in a basement for an entire day, during which the temperature was controlled and oscillated between extremes by turning the furnace up to 100 degrees and then once the room reached 100, turning the air conditioning down to 50 degrees. Pledges were required to be in these conditions wearing dress slacks and button-down shirts, an outfit that is not suitable for either extreme and they were not allowed to take off or put on any clothing. As one can imagine, the fluctuation between sweating and freezing is terribly uncomfortable. (This type of ritual serves the dual function of soiling clothes that can then be discarded as part of a dying ritual.) Alumni whom the pledges don't know may be recruited to participate in this ritual as confederates who appear to "fail" and "quit." After the experience ends, the brothers praise the pledges for their strength and endurance, noting that not everyone survived (although of course at the end of the entire initiation the alumni are brought back and introduced to the pledges). These types of rituals are used to reinforce the sense of superiority among the pledges and the elite status of the fraternity they are joining.

## Loyalty and Identity in Rituals

Not so different from many of the other institutions that we are analyzing in this book, fraternities want to instill a strong sense of identity and loyalty in their members. Part of the ritualization of identity is adopting the term "brother" when referring to each other. "Brother" connotes family; blood is thicker than water; we belong together forever regardless of time and place. There are other aspects of the initiation ritual that help to build identity and a sense of community, including being given symbols—typically pins—that are worn at formal events, being dressed in a ceremonial robe after the death and rebirth ritual, and gaining access to the final secrets that only fully initiated members know, including the initiation ritual itself. As is typical with any team-building exercise, loyalty is typically built through a series of "trust" challenges. Pledges might be blindfolded, forced to stand on a box, and told to jump to the floor, which they are told is covered in shards of glass. Pledges will resist and are sometimes pushed by the brothers, only to land on bubble wrap. All of these kinds of trust activities teach the pledges that they can trust their brothers, who will never hurt them. It's not such a difficult leap, then, to understand how a fraternity brother can be asked to "trust" his brother who is taking an unconscious young woman upstairs to a bedroom. And he can be counted on to stand up for a brother who finds himself in trouble, even accused of rape.

## Hypermasculinity in Rituals

One of the core elements of fraternities is masculinity. And here masculinity means only white, heteronormative hypermasculinity. Parties are one of the central aspects of fraternity social life, not only because they provide an opportunity for socializing and fun, but also because they create opportunities for members to express hypermasculinity vis-à-vis excessive drinking and identifying women with whom one can have sex. The parties themselves, as well as the discussions after the parties, socialize pledges around the value the fraternity places on these two core aspects of masculinity. When there is evidence to substantiate the claim of a brother's masculinity, the message to pledges is even more potent. Sanday illustrates this with a story told to her by one of her student informants.

> When he woke up the next day, Ed was peevishly proud of having vomited all over the place. He went charging through the house waking up everyone. He kept telling everyone about vomiting. All of the brothers seemed proud of having vomited. When he woke up Jack, Jack said to Ed, "Hey, bro! You blew some chunks eh?"[10]

Vomit, then, becomes the "evidence" that a brother engaged in excessive drinking. And the reaction of the other brothers to this evidence ensures that the pledge who may be observing this exchange has a clear understanding of how he must demonstrate masculinity through excessive drinking if he is to be accepted into the fraternity.

Beyond the fact that rituals and behaviors like vomiting and posting pictures of naked women on Facebook (as fraternity brothers at Penn State did) communicate expectations of masculinity, fraternity culture is deeply rooted in the premise that men are superior to women. This deeply held value is critical to the development of rape culture in fraternities. Based on interviews with an informant, Bob described an initiation ritual that involves the pledges being treated like women, a ritual explicitly designed to reinforce women's inferior status.

Sanday relates a story told by Bob, who says that when the pledges arrived at the house for their initiation they were sprayed with a thick, red liquid and were forced to wear diapers. At one point, their diapers were removed and the brothers "ridiculed their genitals."[11] In a similar set of rituals described by Rick, a member of a different fraternity, pledges were told to wear jock straps under their clothes instead of underwear when they arrived for their initiation. The pledges were instructed to strip out of their clothes so that they were naked except for the jockstrap. Brothers pulled down the pledges' jockstraps and used basting brushes to apply Ben Gay to their scrotums. The jockstraps were then replaced and "thirty seconds later all of the pledges were writhing in pain." The brothers explained to the pledges why this ritual was necessary, "We're going to cleanse the weak, dependent, pussy out of you."[12] Bob and Rick both report that throughout the initiation rituals, which often go on for several hours, the brothers use derogatory language, calling the pledges "pussies," "pin-dicks", and so forth. The rituals and the language used communicate quite clearly to the pledges that masculinity is valued, femininity—and by extension women—is weak and inferior, and that a core element of masculinity is heterosexuality.

## RAPE CULTURE IN FRATERNITIES

Rape culture refers to a set of values and customs that minimize the impact of rape, that limit the definition of rape, and that relegate women to the status of sex objects whose only value is to serve men sexually. Fundamental to the concept of a rape culture is the belief that rape is in fact very uncommon and that in most cases of "actual rape" the victim deserves it. In rape culture, women are blamed for being raped regardless of the circumstances. For example, a woman who is raped while running in a park will be blamed for going running alone; a woman who is raped after being drugged at a fraternity party will be blamed for accepting a drink; girls as young as five years old have been blamed for being raped because they dressed "provocatively."

In general, the fraternity members Sanday studied argue that when women get raped they "ask for it." From their perspective, first and foremost they ask for it by coming to the parties. They also ask for it by accepting the alcohol the fraternity is happy to provide. They ask for it by dancing and flirting. In short, they ask for it by their very existence.

Rape culture also defines women as having very few functions in society other than as sex objects. They are to be viewed in pornography, to dance at football and basketball games, to serve as ring girls in boxing matches, and to just be sexually available whenever and however men demand them to be. The exceptions to this rule, of course, are some mothers and older women who are thought of as asexual.

As Syrett and Sanday argue, one of the defining features of fraternities is their exploitation of women as a strategy for demonstrating their heterosexual hypermasculinity. The women who hung around and even lived in the fraternity house during the summer Sanday conducted her research identified several categories of women:

> Regulars were women who attended every party but were not girlfriends of any of the brothers. In addition to "wenches," "regulars," and "bimbos" there was a strong inner circle of women who were girlfriends of the brothers. The girlfriends came to the parties to make sure their boyfriends didn't take up with any of the other women at the party. Girlfriends didn't like the regulars and made ugly remarks about their virtue. This would seem to be fairly normal jealous behavior if it weren't for the fact that many of the girlfriends had once been regulars themselves. The various types of women never bonded with one another, as their primary interest was in the brothers, which is the way that the brothers seemed to want it to be.[13]

In sum, rape cultures are built on the fundamental belief that women are inherently inferior to men and that their only real value is their sexual availability to men. In this context, then, it is not so difficult to understand how men create a rational explanation for rape: women ask for it. However, it is also true that men's sexual advances are sometimes rejected. If women's sexuality is defined as something that is generally and universally available to men at their discretion, then refusal becomes an anomaly that fraternity brothers cannot easily accept. In order to manage refusals, they employ a variety of strategies for getting reluctant or unwilling women to have sex.

## How the Fraternity Environment Facilitates Rape

Rape culture can be fueled by particular environmental arrangements and practices that facilitate rape, and many fraternities have structures that make them what some scholars call "rape prone." On many campuses, for a variety of reasons, fraternities are often the primary hub for social activity. Fraternity houses differ from traditional campus housing or residence halls, in several key ways that facilitate hosting parties: (1) they have space; (2) they are almost always unsupervised, since there are no university employees such as resident advisors (RAs) paid to enforce university policies; and (3) they are owned by their chapters not by the university.

So why aren't sororities the social hub of campuses or at least partners in sponsoring parties on campuses? Juliet Lapidos, in an opinion essay published in the *New York Times* in January 2015, poses this very question. In the wake of the *Rolling Stone* exposé on fraternities and rape at the University of Virginia, Lapidos considers the same question we do: Perhaps parties would be safer if sororities were allowed to host them. Lapidos cites the National Panhellenic Conference, the organization that governs historically white sororities, confirming that sororities are not allowed to host parties where alcohol is served unless these parties are cosponsored with a fraternity and held at a third-party location. In other words, sororities cannot host parties in their houses if they serve alcohol. Lapidos argues, as we do, that when fraternities control the party scene on campus, they hold all of the power, and this is especially dangerous for women.

> The ban also gives frats undue control over the party scene. It's frat members who get to mix the drinks, establish the "ambience" (sticky floors, dim lights, music loud enough to mask arguments or even cries of protest) and determine the guest list. If a frat member wants to bring a girl back to his bed, all he has to do is get her upstairs—not across campus in full view of other students, who could theoretically intervene if they saw anything suspicious. Yet undergraduate women keep attending frat parties because, as one freshman [said], "It's what we know."[14]

We add to this, that fraternity brothers also hold power because the house is their turf and it is familiar to them. Women who report being raped in fraternity houses often report that they didn't know where they were in the house and they didn't know how to get out. When we talk with sorority women in our classes they understand that they are vulnerable because the fraternity men hold all of the power and they hold none. In these conversations we ask them what would happen if they boycotted fraternity parties? Like union strikes, the power the women do hold is to refuse to participate in the scene the fraternities are creating. Their responses generally reflect the fear that union members express when they go on strike, that they will be replaced by "strikebreakers"—in this case, women who will continue going to the parties and whose status will rise as a direct result of their shrinking numbers. These conversations are terribly revealing in that they demonstrate that women's sense of worth is bound up so tightly with what men think about them that they choose to put their own safety at risk for fear of losing men's attention.

Another practice that fraternities sometimes engage in that contributes to their power and control in hosting parties is one that is seen on a campus where fraternity houses are not on campus. In order to get women to attend a party at an off-campus fraternity house, fraternities employ their pledges to shuttle women back and forth to campus.

It should be clear to the reader by now that women are an essential ingredient to a fraternity party because their presence as sex objects is a fundamental requirement for fraternity men seeking to demonstrate heterosexual hypermasculinity. As a result, it is standard practice nationally that fraternities require men to bring their own alcohol to the parties, but women drink for free. Similarly, fraternity shuttles are not available for men wanting to attend a fraternity party but are readily available for women. On college and university campuses around the United States, on any given night when fraternities are having parties, they put out notifications including the cell phone number to text for a pickup. A woman or group of women simply texts the number with their location and a pledge picks them up and delivers them to the fraternity house. When they are ready to leave, the pledges are there to shuttle them home. As a result, the women may have no idea where they are and are dependent on pledges to get home. Women who are raped at fraternity parties talk about escaping the fraternity house and having no idea how to get home. (And clearly no pledge is going to shuttle a woman home who is screaming that she's been raped.) Each individual action, hosting a party, supplying free alcohol, shuttling women to and from parties seems innocuous enough. But, when we analyze all of these practices together, it is clear that fraternities and their members hold all of the power in the social scene on campus and they engage in deliberate practices that facilitate rape.

## Manipulating Consent

In addition to creating an environment that is conducive to rape, fraternity brothers engage in specific behaviors designed to facilitate sexual activity.

Fraternity brothers argue that these strategies are just part of the sexual dance between men and women and if they result in a sexual encounter, that these encounters are consensual. We disagree. In fact, these strategies are designed to manipulate consent when it cannot be obtained ethically. Based on her research, Sanday identifies four strategies employed by the brothers: (1) riffing, (2) working a "yes" out, (3) rape baiting, and (4) pulling train.

## Riffing

According to Sanday's research:

> "Riffing" means talking your way into a situation. Some brothers were better riffers than others. There is a skill involved in being good at riffing, because it involves persuading someone to do something. There are many kinds of riffs. There is the "nice guy" riff, which means offering to walk a woman home when it is late at night. By being well mannered and almost chivalrous, the "nice guy" riffer hopes to induce the woman to invite him in.[15]

Sanday finds other evidence of riffing, including mentions on the message boards of "unconscious riff" and "corpse riff," both used in reference to a woman who reported being gang raped in the fraternity house.[16] The use of the term "riffing" implies that these strategies are deliberate and not simply a misunderstanding among two people or a "he said, she said" or "regret sex" scenario.

## Working a "Yes" Out

Sanday devotes an entire chapter in her book to "working a yes out," because it is such a common strategy employed by fraternity brothers. "Working a yes out" refers to encouraging or forcing a woman to consent to sex either through talking her into it or plying her with alcohol. Verbal coercion and the use of alcohol to get women to consent are common practices on college campuses. In fact, being plied with alcohol or drugs was the most common scenario reported by students who completed a campus climate survey. It's a story we hear all too often from students confiding in us and seeking help after they've been raped.

Sanday trained male student research assistants to interview fraternity brothers about a gang rape that had taken place on her campus and about sex and parties more generally. In dozens of these conversations, fraternity brothers talked about the difference between rape and "working a yes out," which is not, according to them, rape. In short, they limit the use of the term "rape" to obtaining sex by the use of physical force. Anything else, including deliberate actions like verbal persuasion and plying women with alcohol, either knowingly or unknowingly to the women, was not considered by them to be rape; it was labeled "seduction." "When asked about the difference between seduction and rape the brothers commented 'With rape, she never gives in. . . . With seduction, she might say no for awhile, but then she gives up and decides that she wants sex too. Physical forces is the difference."[17] Repeatedly, the brothers talked about the fact that women often had to be persuaded, that "no" didn't really mean "no." They even described times in which they didn't think they would ultimately be able to "work out a yes" and were surprised when the woman finally gave in.

The framework provided by Sanday's research is useful in providing a lens for better understanding the incident at Yale University in October 2010 when pledges of the fraternity Delta Kappa Epsilon walked across the Yale campus chanting "No Means Yes, Yes Means Anal." In the end, fraternity members apologized for using poor judgment, but based on Sanday's research, we suggest that this incident, which wasn't the first by the DKEs at Yale, was simply a public expression of a set of beliefs and ideologies that are widely held by fraternity members and expressed openly in fraternity houses. "No" never really means "no."

*Rape Baiting*

Rape baiting is a term that refers to strategies that one can employ to increase the probability that a man will have sex by the end of the evening, without regard to consent. In addition to the strategies already discussed, rape baiting also includes tactics for identifying potential victims. In Sanday's research, which was originally conducted in the late 1980s, she revealed a strategy that continues to be used today: marking women at parties based on the probability that a brother will be successful in "working a yes out." She quotes a fraternity member explaining the system: "The brothers marked women who came to their parties with something called power dots . . . white being the most difficult, then yellow, then blue, red and with black being the easiest. . . . I think the dots helped to mark women for other men so that they would know where to start."[18]

In 2014, a fraternity at the University of Wisconsin-Milwaukee was reportedly marking certain women's hands with a red "X" and targeting these women with date rape drugs that were mixed into their drinks. Women on many campuses across the United States report similar marking systems that are designed to target women for drugging or "working a yes out."

## Pulling Train

"Pulling train" refers to group sex, which may be consensual or not, involving one woman and several, sometimes as many as a dozen, men. Sanday argues, and we agree, that men who believe that a woman can physically have sex with multiple men one after the other are delusional and are operating in the scapegoat mentality. The "group sex" that Sanday describes as well as the incidents reported at Baylor University and the University of Minnesota are acts of gang rape, non-consensual sex forced by many men on one woman. The men, however, see pulling train differently, they conceive of this strategy as a way to facilitate sex for men who have never had it before. For a man who has not had sex and is not confident in his abilities to "work out a yes," by climbing into a "train" he takes advantage of the fact that his brothers have already done the hard work of getting the woman ready for sex and he can take advantage of this situation. Fraternity brothers are not alone in buying into the flawed ideology that once a woman has consented to sex with one member of a group—a fraternity or sports team—she has consented to sex with all of them. A jury was convinced in the trial of University of Minnesota basketball player Mitch Lee that the victim in the case could not have been raped by Lee because she had already consented to sex with his teammate a few minutes earlier.

## The Role of Premeditation

Sanday's research is important in many ways. Not the least among them was her training and use of student ethnographers who attended parties and even interviewed fraternity brothers. Sanday's student researchers found that fraternity brothers engaged in carefully scripted practices in order to prepare a woman for sex, consensual or not, depending on her interests. Early in the week when a party was planned, the brothers described identifying a "target." They tended to choose first-year women for the reasons we discussed, they were eager to enter the social scene, they were unfamiliar with the social norms, and they didn't know their way around yet. We can also assume that they weren't yet familiar with the various reputations of fraternity houses as being "rape" houses or "safe" houses. Men reported that they looked for these women in their classes, the dining hall, or just hanging out on campus. They started to "chat them up" and "made them feel special." By midweek they had invited their "target" to a party at the fraternity house that coming weekend. When their "targets" arrived they immediately got them a glass of whatever punch the brothers had concocted, typically a very sugary drink that hides the burn of the grain alcohol used to "spike" it; a drink often referred to as "jungle juice." Because the punch flavor hides the alcohol, it is easy to get very drunk very quickly. The brothers then reported moving on the target, putting their arms around her, dancing with her, kissing her, and as long as she didn't resist or as long as she seemed "into it" they steered her upstairs to a designated room.

Why a designated room? The brothers indicated that before the party started they cleared out a room of all identifiable things, posters, pictures, and so forth. This was to ensure that if she reported the rape and the police brought her to the house to show them what had happened she wouldn't be able to find the room where she was raped because while there had been nothing memorable or personal in it at the time, personal items were replaced *after* the party weekend. This strategy also reduces the likelihood that she can even identify the man who raped her because the designated room, unlike one's own room, did not contain any photographs or other visuals connected to the rapist. The men indicated that they then maneuvered the women to the bed and started engaging in sexual activity with them, fondling them, removing clothing, kissing them and so forth. If the woman complied, then they engaged in consensual sex. If not, the men reported that they attempted to "work a yes out" and if that failed, they used physical force and restraint in order to complete the sexual activity. As long as they had sex, consensual or not, they had met their obligation for heterosexual hypermasculinity. When asked if the brothers considered this rape, they indicated quite clearly that it was not rape, that "the women asked for it." They asked for it by coming to the party, because according to these men it is understood that parties are for drinking and sex, and by not only consenting to come to the party but by coming enthusiastically, they were looking for sex. We concede that there very well may be women who are coming to get drunk and have sex, but even if that is the case, consent doesn't work that way. Consenting to attend a party is not consenting to sexual behavior. According to the law, each individual sexual act must be consented to, even when one has had consensual sex in the past, otherwise the act is legally considered sexual assault. There is no such thing as "blanket" consent.

A phenomenon that garnered attention in the spring of 2017 is an example of the legal requirement of progressive consent. "Stealthing" refers to the case when a man and a woman are engaged in otherwise consensual sex and the man takes off his condom without the knowledge or consent of the woman. "Stealthing" meets the legal definition of rape, and men are being prosecuted for this form of sexual violence.

Perhaps more perplexing in this rationale is the belief that all women have agreed to the purpose of the party. We would argue that this is precisely why college men target first-year women and why the first six weeks on campus is the period of highest risk for sexual violence, because these women don't yet know the norms on campus and even less so those at a fraternity party. And even among those who do, Sanday suggests, "Party women who believe that their sexual activities are all in good fun do not, perhaps, realize the extent to which they play an important role in the formation and celebration of ties of brotherhood."[19]

A college student who has been raped can choose to make a report to the local police, which is very uncommon, or engage the campus reporting mechanism, which sets the internal systems of justice into motion.

## CAMPUS DISCIPLINARY SYSTEMS

There is considerable debate about the reliability of the internal systems of justice of colleges and universities to adjudicate sexual and intimate partner violence. One perspective is that men and women coming to campus are unprepared to handle the lax atmosphere of alcohol and sexual behavior away from their parents' watchful eye and that when rape occurs, it should be treated as a "teachable" moment for both the offender and the victim. Critics of this perspective argue that rape is a violent felony, and college campuses are the ones unprepared to deal with such behavior. Others argue that for all of the inadequacies of the college conduct system, victims are not necessarily treated more fairly by local law enforcement and prosecutors' offices. Still others argue that incarcerating men who rape women on college campuses only contributes unnecessarily to a system in which perpetrators are not given the tools to understand why their behavior is wrong and to learn about consent. Clearly, there are no easy answers here, but our discussion is meant to lay out the controversies so that the reader clearly understands the implications, both positive and negative, of the preference colleges and universities have for handling sexual and intimate partner violence internally.

There are many reasons why colleges and universities favor a sexual misconduct process (colleges and universities do not use terms such "rape" or "sexual assault"). From our perspective, some of these reasons are good and some are highly problematic.

To be clear, in many states, including in Virginia, where we live and work, Title IX guidelines require that *felony* sexual assaults be reported to local law enforcement. Though these systems are not mutually exclusive, it is not uncommon for schools to discourage victims from making a formal report to law enforcement.

**Table 3.1.   Pros and cons of an Internal Conduct Process on college and university campuses**

| Good Reasons | Problematic Reasons |
| --- | --- |
| Not all sexual misconduct can be easily prosecuted in court. | Colleges and universities have a vested interest in under-reporting for fear (we argue unfounded) of being ranked as unsafe. |
| Many victims would prefer not to have to testify in court, which might mean their parents find out. | Current best practices for conduct officers is to treat most conduct violations as "teachable" moments. |
| Many victims want the process over as quickly as possible. | Conduct officers and conduct board members are not necessarily trained to evaluate felony sexual assault, nor do many have any training with regard to the research on sexual assault on campuses. |
| Many victims want a consequence for the sexual assault, but may not want to see the offender go to jail. | Rarely are offenders suspended or expelled, and thus, they are free to commit more rapes. |
| Most cases of college rape involve alcohol and are difficult to prosecute. | |
| Many victims don't want their parents to know they were drinking or that they were previously sexually active. | |

For a variety of reasons, we recommend that all cases of rape on college campuses be reported to the local police and dealt with in the formal criminal justice system, but we understand all the reasons why victims would prefer—and we argue, should—have access to an internal conduct process. That said, because most victims don't know that conduct processes rarely result in removing the perpetrator from campus—indeed hundreds, perhaps thousands of campuses have never expelled a single perpetrator—they end up rarely satisfied with the process.

Unfortunately, there are no national-level statistics that capture the outcomes of campus misconduct hearings. Anecdotally, we know that additional Title IX requirements and additional Title IX training have resulted in more rapes being reported and more victims utilizing the campus process, but we are not able to estimate with any certainty the number or percentage of cases that result in a finding of responsibility and the expulsion of the perpetrator.

Around the time of the gang rape that Sanday analyzes, the early 1980s, colleges and universities began to receive reports from their women students that they had been raped. They almost always identified another student as the perpetrator. Thus, colleges and universities, and particularly those professionals who work in student affairs but also directors of women's centers or women and gender studies centers, identified a clear need to put policies into place to address rape on their campuses. There have been mostly positive revisions since the inception of these policies, and policies vary from institution to institution, but generally they share common features and a set of unique terms to describe both the individuals involved and the sexual acts.

*Sexual misconduct*: Any unwanted sexual activity, including "penetration."

*Hearing board*: A panel of university members, generally faculty and staff, but in some universities including students (a practice considered extremely problematic), that hears the cases. There is tremendous variation in terms of how members are selected and how much (or little) and what kinds of training they receive.

*Sanctions*: Typically sanctions range from required papers on sexual assault to suspension or expulsion, the latter of which are extremely rare.

*Complainant*: The accuser.

*Respondent*: The accused.

*Responsible employee:* After clarifications by the Department of Education in 2015, all campus employees, including faculty and staff, but also students when they are in an employee role, such as resident director, are required to report any violation of Title IX to the Title IX coordinator. The only exceptions are faculty and staff serving in confidential roles, such as in the rape crisis center or psychological services. We note that this is a controversial requirement, especially of faculty who teach courses like we do who routinely get disclosures of sexual and intimate partner violence during the course of the semester, in person but also in journals and even research papers.

Quite clearly, campus systems of justice are set up very differently from the criminal justice system. The reasons for these differences are many, but they reflect the reasons colleges and universities prefer to handle cases of sexual and intimate partner violence through an internal system. For example, the differences in the language reflect the fact that colleges and universities are not the criminal justice system, they cannot impose criminal justice sanctions including incarceration, and therefore they are careful not to use language like "rape," "sexual assault," "defendant," and so forth. Second, the system is meant to be transformative rather than strictly punitive; those who are found "responsible" (not "guilty") are most often assigned opportunities to learn more about sexual assault—writing research papers, attending trainings—rather than punished by suspension or expulsion. Many defend this system as one that is less stressful for victims, results in a faster resolution, and will therefore increase reporting.

All of these may be true. But, in fact, *reporting has not increased substantially* since the inception of these types of polices, and remains stuck at approximately 10 percent. Moreover, among those who do report, a tiny fraction, perhaps 10 percent, go through the conduct process. In the rare case that the conduct process is utilized, as we noted, it almost never results in any sort of real punishment. Thus, the very reason given for establishing this process, that it is a friendlier process for the victim, doesn't pan out when we examine the data. Of equal concern is the fact that reducing the prevalence of rape on campus is not *expressly articulated* as a goal of the process as it is with other conduct issues. Most conduct processes are expressly designed to reduce behavior that is detrimental to the campus community, for example, reducing underage drinking or plagiarism. In fact, failing to hold perpetrators accountable results in *a more dangerous campus community*.

Frankly, it is also insulting that colleges and universities treat felony rape in the same manner as plagiarism. Not only are they entirely different kinds of misconduct, but faculty and staff are trained to identify plagiarism and we understand the reasons it occurs, such as students' lack of understanding of what constitutes plagiarism, not giving themselves enough time to complete a project, and the ease of accessing papers via the internet. We also have effective strategies for reducing it. None of this can be said about rape. The vast majority of faculty and staff, including conduct officers on many campuses, are not trained to conduct the complex investigation that is necessary when a rape is reported. They often do not know how to evaluate the evidence, and they are not familiar with the vast research literature on rape in general and rape on college campuses in particular. It is quite simply absurd that rape on college campuses is dealt with using this process.

We are not the only people who make this critique. Many scholars of rape on college campuses, as well as those who serve rape victims in sexual assault services, evaluate the conduct process similarly.

But, is it better for victims of rape on college campuses to utilize the criminal justice system in their local communities? Not necessarily. As we will discuss at length in our discussion of rape by college athletes, even when victims report to local law enforcement, the cases are often referred back to the campus police anyway. In cases that involve high-profile students, the police often report that they are barred from conducting an investigation on the campus, and this is especially true if the accused is an athlete. Rape is a very difficult case to prosecute, and as a result, only about 4 percent of rapes ever result in a criminal sentence that includes jail time. We agree that locking up perpetrators without any required training to help them address their attitudes and behavior and return to the community better able to navigate consensual sexual encounters also does little good.

So, what should be done? We address this question at length in the final chapter, but suffice it to say here that first, sexual violence must be understood for what it is—violence, not regret sex or part of the college experience. In some cases, incarceration is appropriate, and we recommend that evidence-based, effective treatment programs for sex offenders be made not only available but mandatory for those convicted of sexual violence. On college campuses, we advocate for suspension and expulsion when perpetrators are found responsible. Victims of sexual violence deserve the freedom to complete their education free from further encounters with the perpetrator, and all students deserve a chance to be safe by removing the men who are perpetrating violence. This doesn't mean that the perpetrator can never come back or that he can't transfer. But we would advocate that he completes an effective, evidence-based treatment program before he is allowed anywhere near a college campus. This approach would effectively provide both the need for accountability (or punishment) and the educational approach that colleges and universities aspire to and indeed apply in other types of misconduct, including alcohol violations and plagiarism. Though there is still much work to be done, not the least of which is the development and testing of effective intervention and treatment programs for sex offenders, there is some reason for optimism.

During the Obama administration, both the Department of Education and the White House worked to develop policies and guidelines to assist universities in dealing with reports of sexual assault. For example, in September 2014 the White House launched the "It's on Us" campaign. The "Its on Us" campaign was dedicated to using the most up-to-date research in order to develop best practices and a tool kit for colleges and universities to utilize so that they could more effectively address rape on their campuses.

Most significant has been the utilization of Title IX as an avenue for addressing not only rape on college campuses, but the inadequate response of college administrators to reports of rape.

Passed in 1972, people most often associate Title IX with equity in sports, requiring that boys and girls and men and women have equal opportunities to participate in sports. For the first forty years or so after the passage of Title IX this was the case, it was used primarily as a legal remedy for girls and women who sought opportunities to play sports in elementary, middle, and high school and in college. Beginning in the early 2000s, women began to explore the use of Title IX as a legal remedy for addressing inequality in the response to sexual assault on college campuses. Catharine MacKinnon was one of the first scholars to argue that sexual harassment claims could be redressed using Title IX. In 1980, she advised a group of students at Yale to file a sexual harassment claim using Title IX. It was unsuccessful. Ironically, nearly 25 years later, in 2003, a Yale student argued successfully to a judge that sexual assault was a severe form of sexual harassment that was appropriately adjudicated using Title IX. Title IX does not ensure that girls and women will not be raped in educational institutions. What it does do is require that the educational institution where the rape takes place provide equal treatment to both parties. Additionally, when colleges and universities allow gender-based violence to persist, they create a hostile educational environment for women. Title IX claims, and there were 502 at the time we were completing this book, allege, for the most part, that when women report sexual assault to the appropriate university officials, they are not treated equally and their rights are not protected as carefully as those of the men they accuse of raping them. Title IX investigations, conducted by the Office of Civil Rights, generally take years to be resolved, and typically they result in colleges and universities having to invest in better prevention and intervention programs and to reorganize their conduct-hearing processes. They can also include fines. In 2012, the University of Montana was ordered to pay $12 million in fines.

All of that being said, the 2016 election of President Donald Trump and his appointment of Betsy DeVos as Secretary of Education, which oversees both the Office of Civil Rights and Title IX, has us extremely concerned. DeVos has made it abundantly clear that under her leadership, campus sexual assault policies will be required to be revised to focus more attention on the accused. In July 2017, DeVos invited men who had been accused of sexual misconduct on college campuses to share their experiences with her. Based on reporting, we know that the discussions centered on issues of a lack of "due process" in the adjudication process. Based on these conversations, the acting head of the Education Department's Office for Civil Rights, Candice Jackson, told the *New York Times*, "Rather, the accusations—90% of them—fall into the category of 'We were both drunk,' 'We broke up,' and six months later I found myself under a Title IX investigation because she just decided that our last sleeping together was not quite right."[20]

What is interesting to note is that, to our knowledge, DeVos has never invited victims of campus rape to talk about their experiences. And it is victims, and their allegations of mistreatment at the hands of campus officials, that account for the vast majority of the Title IX claims under investigation.

It is, of course, important that the Department of Education hear from all related parties and weigh all different perspectives; however, we feel that these new policies and the new approach by the Department of Education are, in effect, moving the discussion of sexual assault on college campuses back to the days when the victim of the sexual violence (usually a woman but at times also a man) was blamed for the crime. Furthermore, we speculate that the Office of Civil Rights will see both its budget and its staffing slashed, which will impede its ability to conduct investigations of the mishandling of rape on college campuses. If this comes to fruition, it will turn the Title IX clock back decades.

## CONCLUSION

Rape can have devastating consequences for victims, including acute and chronic mental health issues, self-medicating with alcohol or drugs, and difficulty establishing healthy sexual relationships. Although very little formal research has been done, anecdotally, those who work with rape victims on college campuses know that in addition to the aforementioned problems, rape victims often struggle academically and socially. For example, many rape victims report that their academic performance declines in the aftermath of the rape. This shows up as poor grades, dropped classes, transferring to other institutions, and lower graduation rates. Rape victims report a variety of causes for their decline in academic performance, including a host of problems brought on by mental health issues as well as a challenge that is unique to the institutions we are analyzing for this book: The perpetrator almost always remains on campus, and his presence may cause the victim to avoid locations where she might run into him, including in her classes. The question for us and for all scholars, activists, and student affairs professionals is how to make our campuses safe learning environments for all students.

Perhaps the most troubling thing about rape on college campuses is that not much has changed in the nearly thirty years that we have been studying it. The rate of rape has remained steady, first-year women are still the prime "targets" because they are the most vulnerable, and colleges and universities continue to insist that rape allegations be handled through the dean of students' office by professionals who often have very little training about sexual assault. Clearly what we are doing is not working.

## WHAT CAN BE DONE?

As most everyone who researches and/or works with sexual assault on college campuses is well aware, this is a complex problem that will require many different approaches; there are no simple or "one-stop shopping" solutions. We highly recommend *Five Things Student Affairs Professionals Should Know about Campus Gender-Based Violence* authored by Nancy Chi Cantalupo, one of the nation's leading experts on campus sexual assault, as a place to start our thinking about revising campus sexual violence policies. Cantalupo's report is a must-read for anyone interested in research-based best practices.[21] It is an excellent accompaniment to the "It's on Us" toolbox produced by the Obama White House. Cantalupo's recommendations provide a jumping-off point, to which we add our own unique suggestions.

### More Prevention Efforts

For obvious reasons, it is important to have prevention programs that are effective in preventing rapes from happening in the first place. For decades this approach centered on teaching young women not to get raped, for example, by using a "buddy system," not walking alone at night, and more recently not accepting a drink at a party from someone you don't know. There are many problems with this approach; first and foremost, they hold the victim accountable for being raped because they engaged in risky behavior, something that happens with no other crime. We don't blame the millions of Americans who experienced credit card hacking in 2014 and 2015 for sliding their Visa cards at Target and Home Depot, and we shouldn't blame rape victims either.

That said, there are some promising new prevention programs for women. For example, Senn and colleagues conducted an experiment in which they randomly assigned nine hundred first-year college women to receive either a rape-resistance training program or rape-prevention pamphlets.[22] Women receiving the training experienced rape in the first-year at a rate *half* of that of the women in the control group. Additionally, the researchers estimated that for every twenty-two women trained there would be one fewer rape in the following year. Imagine what kind of reduction in rape could be achieved on a campus with two thousand first-year women! So, why wouldn't all campuses want to start training women in rape resistance? Most likely because this type of in-person, multisession training requires many more staff hours and is therefore far more expensive than the online or "one-shot" mass prevention programs that most colleges and universities use. Given the impact of rape on the individual victims as well as the collective costs to campuses, we would argue that this would be money well spent.

Beginning in the early 2000s, activists were agitating that the real focus of prevention needed to be on the potential perpetrators, and the focus broadened to include prevention programs for men as well. Groups like "Men Stopping Rape" and the Mentors in Violence Prevention (MVP) program developed by anti-violence activist Jackson Katz focused on teaching men not to rape. These programs seem to have some success in that men who participate in them are more educated about gender-based violence, they are better allies to women who are raped, and they are stronger activists in the anti-violence movement. That said, the rates of rape have not dropped. At all. The most likely explanation, clearly, is that the programs are not reaching the potential perpetrators, and most of the participants had a low risk for perpetrating rape to begin with. And/or it is likely that the programs themselves are too limited and too late to have any real impact on influencing the attitudes that lead men to rape. We can't start teaching men not to rape when they arrive on a college campus and expect any real change in their behavior. This type of socialization must begin with boys, and girls, as soon as they are able to understand basic ideas like sharing and consent.

## Consider a Multilevel Approach

From the field of public health comes perhaps the most promising model, the social-ecological model. This model requires a comprehensive, multilevel, long-range approach focusing on individual actors but also communities and institutions. This model approaches a public health problem, like smoking or sexual violence, based on the assumption that individual actors make decisions based on their individual attitudes, their opportunities, and what others think, or social norms. This model has been successful with other public health concerns, including alcohol and drug use, cigarette smoking, and diet and exercise. For example, if we want to reduce a particular behavior, we need to provide accurate and appropriate information about the negative consequences of the behavior to children, as soon as they are old enough to understand basic concepts, we need to shift attitudes in the community, and we need to restrict access to the behavior we want to reduce and increase access to the behavior we want to encourage.

Imagine a socio-ecological approach to ending gender-based violence. It would begin with providing education to children at a very young age that would continue to be delivered in increasingly complex ways as children advance through school. The Netherlands now requires a comprehensive sex education program that appears to be having a positive impact in reducing both teen pregnancy and sexual and intimate partner violence among teens. A socio-ecological approach would also focus on shifting attitudes in communities through public service announcements, like the White House's "1 is 2 Many" campaign against intimate-partner violence, as well as creating television shows and movies that celebrate healthy relationships and alternative fashion magazines that show women of all sizes, shapes, and colors as beautiful. It would also include an intervention approach that holds perpetrators accountable—through incarceration if appropriate—and provides them with intensive, research-based interventions designed to reduce reoffending. In other words, reducing sexual violence on college campuses begins long before students arrive on campus.

Colleges and universities do not have the power to implement this kind of socio-ecological approach. However, they do have the power to implement this kind of approach on their own campuses. For example, what good are prevention programs for men and women if the campus climate continues to be one in which women are regularly denigrated and treated as if their only useful function is as sex objects? What good is any programming if perpetrators aren't held accountable?

## Change the Campus Climate

Administrators and fraternities are resistant to suggestions for how to change the campus climate because they don't think they have the power to implement them; they are afraid of losing traditions; and they are afraid, understandably, of losing their power. And fraternities are a powerful lobby on Capitol Hill. According to Fraternity Advisor,[23] fraternity and sorority members account for 75 percent of the donations that colleges and universities receive. Perhaps there exists a conflict of interest? Are college and university presidents inhibited from holding fraternity brothers accountable and requiring changes to fraternity policies, for example, prohibiting them from serving alcohol, because they are afraid of losing future donations? But, we ask, is allowing fraternities to continue to contribute to a climate where rape is epidemic worth the cost?

The financial costs to fraternities, both chapters and nationals, simply to have adequate liability insurance is tremendous, yet neither the nationals nor individual campuses are willing to address the alcohol policies that are both the primary reason for these expensive liability policies and contributing factors to rape on college campuses. As we argued earlier, when control of the party scene and alcohol in particular is held so tightly by only one group, they have tremendous power, and women are incredibly vulnerable: to drug and alcohol facilitated rape, to being in houses they aren't familiar with in communities off-campus, reliant on the pledges to shuttle them back and forth. In contrast, fraternities that seek to be inclusive for women change their party structures, by inviting more women, by lowering the music volume and raising the lights to encourage conversation, and by limiting access to private rooms. These are all campus climate issues that could be addressed by colleges and universities as well as fraternities if they really wanted to reduce rape on their campuses.

### Improve Campus Conduct Hearings

Colleges and universities are, above all else, focused on education. Under this mission, as noted previously, conduct boards look for teachable moments when dealing with student misconduct. But, as Cantalupo articulates, rape is not a "teachable" moment. Conduct boards do play an educational role in training students about their rights and responsibilities under Title IX, however. Cantalupo points out that "when minimal sanctions are levied after the institution finds that a student has perpetrated violence against another student, this teaches all the students involved, most critically the responsible student, that such violence is not serious or prohibited by the institution because there are little to no consequences for engaging in that violence."[24]

The criminal justice system and the student misconduct system are based on different principles, and a conduct board hearing has no criminal implications. The criminal justice system is concerned primarily with public safety, and incarceration is the primary tool used to ensure that goal. Because it is a travesty of the justice system to unlawfully take away a person's rights, the system must be designed to ensure no false positives, that no innocent people go to prison. Thus, the system is designed to ensure the rights of the defendant. We see this, for example, in the Fifth Amendment, which protects defendants from having to testify in ways that compromise their rights.

In contrast, Title IX, which regulates the handling of sexual assault, has as its goal the protection of everyone's *civil rights*, and it does not have the power to use incarceration as a tool. Rather, though rarely used, the worst punishment that can be enforced under Title IX is the expulsion of a student found guilty of sexual misconduct. This system is more like a civil court, which may award monetary damages but cannot impose incarceration on someone found responsible of a crime. Certainly the person found responsible in either situation—in a conduct hearing or in civil court—experiences negative consequences, but in neither case are their *rights* infringed upon.

And herein lies perhaps the most significant problem with campus rape. Civil court cases and Title IX claims *not having to do with sexual assault* use the "preponderance of evidence" standard, in contrast to the standard of "beyond a reasonable doubt" that is used in criminal proceedings. Yet many college and university conduct boards apply the "beyond a reasonable doubt" standard in *sexual misconduct hearings*. Rape myths and rape culture have invaded the conduct process, which imposes the "beyond a reasonable doubt" standard in the one type of case, sexual violence, in which people are more likely than not to believe that women will lie despite the *fact* that false rape allegations are extremely rare and almost never happen.

Colleges and universities have a vested interest in handling sexual assault cases appropriately in order to avoid Title IX investigations as well as lawsuits. Colleges and universities will never be able to eradicate sexual violence, but conduct processes could be reformed to achieve better outcomes for victims and perpetrators. Conduct boards need to be trained appropriately, police, both campus and community police, need to be *trained and required* to use trauma-informed interviewing techniques, and standards of evidence need to be shifted from "beyond a reasonable doubt" to the "preponderance of evidence standard," which has a lower bar. "Preponderance of evidence" requires the conduct board must only be convinced that the case argued by the victim is more likely than not (greater than 50 percent) as compared to the counter argument made by the accused. We argue that colleges and universities *have an obligation* to handle sexual and intimate partner violence appropriately when it does happen so that the victims can continue as productively as possible in pursuit of their educational goals and aspirations.

## Encourage Reporting

One of the primary complaints in Title IX claims is that victims do not feel supported when they report a sexual assault to a college or university official, typically the police or the dean of students. Rape victims may or may not desire a disclosure that engages an investigation, but they should be encouraged to report so that they can be directed to all of the services to which they are entitled and so that colleges and universities have more accurate data on the crimes being committed on their campuses. Victims should have options after a disclosure as well. Currently federal law requires that any disclosure of sexual assault by a student to any faculty or staff member, with the exception of confidential sources, which are generally limited only to certified counselors, sexual assault services, and religious advisors, must be reported to the university, including the student's name and any other information that the student has disclosed. And, though we agree that reporting is important, in many cases students disclose to a faculty or staff member simply to get support and not necessarily with the intent of engaging an investigation. As faculty who teach about sexual and intimate partner violence we find ourselves in this conundrum often, typically several times a semester. We may be having a discussion of sexual violence in class and a student, who has come to feel comfortable in the class, simply raises their hand and tells their story. Students often disclose their experiences in papers and journals they submit as part of the course requirements, and they often make appointments to visit during office hours to share an experience and seek advice and support. And, legally, we are required to report these disclosures to campus officials.

We advocate for giving the victim as much choice as possible to disclose safely and comfortably, to get support, and to pursue an investigation when and if they choose to. In order to ensure all of these options, we suggest that federal law be modified to require faculty and staff to report disclosures, but allow these disclosures to be anonymous, the victim's name not being revealed but the statistic gathered nonetheless.

When it comes to reporting, we are particularly optimistic about a change in policy known as "medical amnesty." Medical amnesty policies provide amnesty for a student who is underage and who is reporting a rape that occurred while they were willingly and knowingly using alcohol or drugs. One of the primary reasons victims on college campuses give for not reporting is that they had been drinking and they are afraid they will face sanctions for violating the college or university's alcohol or drug policy. Medical amnesty is still relatively new and so much remains to be seen, but we are hopeful that it will be successful in contributing to a climate where victims feel safe reporting rape.

## Use Sexual Misconduct and Assault Response Teams (SMARTs)

When a sexual assault is reported in the community, typically by dialing 911 or making an appointment at the local police department or sheriff's office, a Sexual Assault Response Team or SART responds. SARTs include not only law enforcement agents, but also rape crisis advocates and specially trained forensic nurses. Research has documented that when these kinds of teams are engaged in responding to sexual violence, as well as training judges, prosecutors, and defense attorneys, the processes and outcomes for rape victims *and for perpetrators* are perceived to be more fair.[25] Colleges and universities should follow the lead of local law enforcement and create multidisciplinary teams *that include victim services professionals* to respond to each and every report of sexual and/ or intimate partner violence. We anticipate that if they were to do this, colleges and universities would find that both victims and those accused would report perceiving the process as more fair, both would be able to complete their education there or elsewhere successfully, and the number of Title IX complaints would drop dramatically.

## FINAL THOUGHTS

Rape on college campuses is not a new issue, though it has received renewed attention. Rape on college campuses is nothing less than epidemic. Rape on college campuses is expensive. And, and as discouraging as this chapter is to read and was to write, as individuals who inhabit college campuses, we are optimistic that rape on campuses can be reduced if and when administrators are ready to implement effective prevention programming, work to change the climate on their campuses, require changes in fraternity practices, and install conduct processes that are effective. We call on all administrators to have the courage to make difficult decisions and stand up for the one hundred ten thousand women who are raped under their watch each and every year.

# 4

# THE MILITARY

A woman who signs up to protect her country is more likely to be raped by a fellow soldier than killed by enemy fire.

—Rep. Jane Harman[1]

The United States military is the largest and most expensive in the entire world. At the height of the Iraq War, the United States accounted for 50 percent of all military spending worldwide. This figure dropped slightly to 37 percent in 2015, a figure that is still extraordinary. Military spending in the United States in 2015 equaled the *combined total* of the next seven leading countries, including China, Saudi Arabia, Russia, the United Kingdom, India, France, and Japan.

The military is one of the largest institutions in the United States and one of its biggest employers. The Department of Defense estimates for 2017 that 1.6 million people are active in one of the four branches of the US military, with another 760,000 active in one of the reserve branches. The Department of Defense employs another 696,000 civilians in the United States, and another half a million people are employed by the five largest defense contractors (Lockheed Martin, Boeing, General Dynamics, Raytheon, and Northrup Grumman). All told, nearly 3 million Americans are employed in the business of the military. Although our discussion in this chapter will focus primarily on the members of the military themselves, we know that those who exit the military often end up working as civilians for the Department of Defense or the defense industry, and

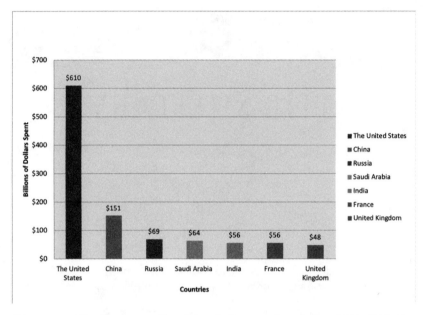

Figure 4.1.   US military spending. Peter G. Peterson Foundation. 2018. "U.S. Defense Spending Compared to Other Countries," May 7. https://www.pgpf.org/chart-archive/0053_defense-comparison  Recreated from: https://www.nationalpriorities.org/campaigns/us-military-spending-vs-world/.

therefore understanding the sheer size and range of the military's reach is critical to our analysis.

Beginning in 2011 or so, a great deal of attention began to be focused on sexual assault in the military, partly as a result of the hard work of two United States senators, Claire McCaskill (Democrat from Missouri) and Kirsten Gillibrand (Democrat from New York), but other forces were at work as well. There were several relatively high-profile sexual assault cases in the news, more and more women were returning from serving in Iraq and Afghanistan and reporting that they had been raped by their fellow service members, and the documentary *The Invisible War* was released in early 2012. It is in this context that we began to focus our attention on gender-based violence (GBV) in the military. Recent attention aside, the military has had a sexual assault "problem" for decades, both internally (service person to service person) and abroad when military men fighting wars or working in conflict zones rape local women and girls. In this chapter, we explore the structures of the military that produce such high rates of sexual assault by those whose job it is to protect our freedom and keep the world safe.

The reality is that women serving in the United States military are more likely to be raped by a fellow soldier than killed by enemy fire in Iraq or Afghanistan. Rape in the military is not an isolated event; rather, it is part of a well-defined pattern that escalates for women when they are deployed overseas. Tens of thousands of female soldiers have served in foreign posts such as Iraq and Afghanistan, and some have seen combat duty. Their personal safety and indeed their lives have been systematically put *at more risk* by rape than by IEDs or any other form of "enemy" engagement.

Resenting their presence, perhaps because they are viewed as the weak link, the boundaries of their service are policed by rape; tragically, some women serving our country, protecting our freedom, have died because of the very real fear of rape. Scott Kirsch and Colin Flint write,

> In 2006, Janis Karpinski, the former commander of Abu Ghraib prison, testified before the *International Commission of Inquiry for Crimes Against Humanity*, investigating the Bush Administration. Karpinski stated that the true cause of death for some female soldiers who served in Iraq had been covered up. She testified that the women had indeed died of dehydration, as the military had reported. However, she charged that the military failed to disclose that women were dying of dehydration because they would not drink liquids late in the day. They avoided liquids due to their fear of being assaulted when they used outdoor bathrooms in the middle of the night.[2]

They argue, and we agree, "It seems evident that a state has failed to protect its citizens when simple acts, such as urinating during convoy or going to the latrine, become markers of bravery."[3] No soldier deserves to be raped, and no soldier should put her or himself at risk for severe illness and even death because of the fear of rape. Nothing is more tragic than lives lost, but that is to be expected in a war zone. What is not expected is for lives to be lost because of the threat of sexual violence by one's comrades.

## THE MILITARY AS A TOTAL INSTITUTION

Among all of the institutions that we are analyzing in this book, the military is second only to prisons when it comes to being structured as a total institution. Nearly every aspect of the day-to-day life of members of the military is dictated to them. If a military member has dependents (spouse and/or children), they have the option to live "off base." But for members without any dependents, regardless of their age or experience, unless given permission, they are required to live in a barracks on base. Even among those with dependents who can live off base, it is common, especially among enlisted members, to live in base housing because it is more affordable and more convenient to work and other amenities such as on-base stores, schools, and child care. When living in the barracks, at the service academies, or deployed abroad, service members have to get up at a certain time, and they eat their meals together in a mess hall. Uniforms are required to be worn at all times when on duty. The uniform is more than just a pair of pants, a shirt, and a pair boots, the uniform also refers to standards for hair, piercings, and other outward manifestations of dress. Members of the military are restricted in what they wear, what they eat, and where they live.

Another feature that illustrates the total institutional nature of the United States military are the regulations that restrict behavior. The military touts itself as an institution that demands and develops discipline. Thus, there are all kinds of regulations governing everyday activities, such as the way a bunk must be made and the condition in which the barracks must be kept, as well as the way in which an individual is "kept," including standards for haircuts and facial hair. Among other things, one outcome of this kind of hyper-regulation is a lack of autonomy and decision-making, not only on the part of the soldier but also on the part of the supervisor, who has very little discretion in the face of even minor violations. The supervisor is simply following procedures, as laid out in the Operations and Procedures Manual, or OPM. When sexual or intimate partner violence is reported to a supervisor, they can consult the OPM in order to determine the appropriate and sanctioned course of action. Military leaders have made it very clear that because of the discipline that the institution engenders and the strict policies for dealing with behavioral violations, they are overwhelmingly confident that the military can and does deal with sexual assault effectively. The data we include in this chapter tell a much different story.

## Socialization into the Total Institution via Basic Training

As we wrote this chapter, Smith reflected back on his experience fifty years ago when he served a tour of duty in the United States Air Force during the Vietnam War. In hindsight he can apply the lens of years of training as a sociologist to his own experience. Like millions of other Americans, he entered and was a part of a nearly total institution, unlike any other institution he had ever experienced. Upon entering the military in 1964, it became immensely clear to Smith that the experience that takes place first, before anything else, is the stripping away of the individual's personal identity. Sociologists call this process "socialization." Symbolically, this happens for recruits directly after enlistment and during basic training, usually in the first week, and often the first "marker" of the new status is the haircut, which is always very dramatic for men but may also be for women, who are required to wear their hair in short styles as well.

Drill sergeants are those charged with this indoctrination. There are several critical lessons that are imparted during this initiation period. First and foremost is the fact that military service is dangerous. Military service is about protecting Americans from those who wish to harm us. In this world of danger and uncertainty into which the recruit is entering, absolute obedience is required. Failing to follow an order can lead to casualties, including one's own death. The recruit is trained to understand that there are two key elements to obedience: (1) hierarchy and (2) discipline. Absolute obedience can only be achieved when the service member understands authority. Orders are not to be questioned; they are to be followed. And the chain of command, the ultimate hierarchy, is a necessary element to ensuring this obedience. Service members are taught early on not only to *not* question the authority of their commander, but also to understand that the commander is enforcing the orders of his or her commander, and so on up the chain. Second, discipline is central to the following of orders. If one cannot make one's bed or keep one's barracks clean or wear the uniform properly, then one cannot be trusted with the protection of 350 million Americans. This sense of discipline—which many recruits say is what drew them to the military to begin with—is developed by controlling and policing the most mundane of activities, from dress to the maintenance of one's quarters, to the shining of one's boots. And any infraction of even the most mundane activity is subjected to the Uniform Code of Military Justice (UCMJ). Nonjudgmental punishment, meaning punishment that is not based on a disciplinary hearing, is left entirely up to the discretion of the commander who is given extraordinarily wide berth in determining and executing punishment. Infractions may be punished by oral or written reprimands, extra duties such as kitchen patrol (KP), garnishing of wages, reduction of rank, and even discharge. This same nonjudgmental punishment is often used as a strategy for commanders to retaliate against victims who report sexual assaults. The lessons are crystal clear: The commander requires absolute obedience. If I violate any of the commands, including taking care of my personal space and body, there will be sanctions. We wonder how, then, in this context, can a military service member refuse when someone of higher rank demands a sexual act? An order is an order is an order. How can a victim report her commander for sexual violence when the hierarchy prohibits going to a higher authority?

# THE FRATERNITY OF THE MILITARY

Basic training is also the time during which new recruits are socialized into the "fraternity" of the military. *Semper fidelis*, or *Semper fi*, the official motto of the Marine Corps, is Latin for "Always Loyal." Marines are fond of saying, "God, Country, Corps." These mottos and sayings impart on the new recruit, in any branch of the military, that the institution is more important than the individual. Again, many new recruits note that this is one of the main reasons they joined the military, so that they could be part of something larger than themselves. In many ways, basic training, or boot camp, resembles the pledging and initiation process we see in fraternities, with a focus on the brotherhood as well as the importance of having one another's back. In films depicting the military, we see examples of cases in which stronger recruits help out recruits who are struggling, an act of the brotherhood but also one that engenders reciprocity. It is no surprise, then, that service members cover for each other's mistakes and retaliate if one of their members is accused of rape.

Even though women and men endure boot camp together, when things go badly, women suddenly find themselves "iced out." When victims report a sexual assault, they regularly experience retaliation from both their commander and their peers. Just imagine how rape victims feel when the person who violated them is a "brother" in their own unit.

## Sex Segregation in the Military

Women have participated in the military and in war since the beginning of time and across many cultures. In the United States, until very recently, women in the military were prohibited from serving in any combat capacity, and thus the majority of women serving in the military, especially during wartime, served in support roles to men, primarily as aides and nurses. It is also interesting to point out that as far back in the United States' military history as the Revolutionary War there are accounts of women cross-dressing and hiding their gender so that they could fight alongside men. During the first two-thirds of the twentieth century, women's participation in the United States military was restricted to special units for women, and it was not until the mid-1970s that the first women were admitted to the service academies and the Department of Defense prohibited inequities in benefits and other treatment of women. For example, prior to the 1970s, military women with dependents were denied housing for their families, and their dependents were denied other benefits, such as access to the commissary, benefits that men who were service members with dependent family had enjoyed for decades.

Historically, women were denied combat positions in any of the branches of services. The wars in Iraq and Afghanistan required significant changes in the ways in which war is fought. Gone are the trenches of World War I, the foxholes of World War II, and the jungles of Vietnam. Fighting in Iraq and Afghanistan pushed the envelope in terms of the traditional definition of "combat." Service women began arguing that driving a Humvee through the streets of Baghdad and facing the possibility of injury or death from an IED was the new "combat," as was clearing houses in rural and urban Afghanistan. As of 2015, all positions in the military branches are open to women, including special forces units like the Navy Seals and Green Berets. As of the spring of 2018, no woman had yet qualified for a special forces unit, but one woman, Megan Brogden, is the first woman officer to have command of a battalion in a special forces group.

Despite all of the gains and all of the opportunities open to women, they are still vastly underrepresented in all branches of the military and they comprise only a tiny fraction of the upper leadership. Considering the culture of the various branches and the skills associated with the work of each branch, it is not surprising that the Marines, the most elite of the branches, has by far the smallest percentage of women. Even in 2018, the Marine Corps segregates women and men in basic training. Women live separately, access separate facilities, including on-base commissaries, and all of their training is conducted in a segregated manner.

In addition, even as more and more women are integrated into the military, particular settings may remain highly segregated by gender. As we were working on this book, we had a woman student in our classes, Michelle, who had served in the Navy. We invited Michelle and her close friend from the Navy, Sabrina, to talk with us about their particular experiences as women in the Navy. Both Michelle and Sabrina described long periods of deployment in which their experiences were nearly entirely gender segregated. Michelle was one of only a small handful of women on an aircraft carrier when she was deployed to the Middle East, and Sabrina was the *only woman* during her assignment to Guantanamo Bay, or "Gitmo." To make matters worse, women are nearly completely absent from the leadership of the military. Not only does this mean that there are no women setting the tone for the rank and file, but there are no women in the room when decisions are made about policies, including those concerning sexual harassment and sexual assault.

## SEXUAL HARASSMENT IN THE MILITARY

It didn't take long after the official integration of the military for sexual harassment scandals to break, the most famous of which is undoubtedly Tailhook. Tailhook remains important because of the sheer volume of victims and perpetrators, as well as because it catapulted sexual harassment in the military into public view; the military had to address Tailhook and couldn't simply brush it under the rug.

At the 1991 Tailhook Convention, more than four thousand active, reserve, and retired personnel met to debrief the Naval and Marine Corps aviation contributions during Operation Desert Storm. Apparently, things got very rowdy, and the president at the time, Captain Rick Ludwig, met with senior staff on the USS *Midway* to debrief the events, including fistfights by the pool and in the hallways. According to the Department of Defense, eighty-three women and seven men reported that they had been raped and many indicated that flag officials were aware of the rapes and didn't do anything.

Among the allegations was that hundreds of naval officers lined the hallway of an upper floor of the hotel where the convention was being held and forced the few women who tried to seek passage to their rooms to walk the gauntlet while hundreds of men's hands groped their bodies. Some women reported being manually raped as they simply sought the safety of their rooms. The gauntlet allowed men to engage in unwanted sexual touching that they could seemingly mask as accidental. That is, because women are pushed into a man by the gauntlet, the harasser feels justified in "accidentally" finding his hands underneath her shirt, touching her breasts or underneath her skirt, manually raping her. This kind of community sexual assault, much like a gang rape, allows the men to justify their behavior to themselves and to each other, and allows them to excuse it by blaming the victim for walking down the hallway and putting herself at risk. This collective diffusion of responsibility creates an opportunity for men who would not normally engage in sexually harassing or abusive behavior the permission, from their brothers, to do so.

The misogynistic culture of the military was on full display in the Tailhook scandal, and it was reinforced by the comments made by Rear Admiral Williams, who was chosen by the Navy to conduct the investigation. Williams said that he believed that "a lot of female navy pilots are go-go dancers, topless dancers or hookers."[4] One wonders about the impact of this kind of belief on women who are simply trying to pursue a career in the military. If the top brass in the military believe that the women serving in their commands are "go-go dancers, topless dancers or hookers" then not only are they not skilled enough for the jobs they are occupying, but they also are not "rapeable"; in other words, their sexuality is free for the taking.

## Resisting Integration: The Citadel as a Case Study

Despite court rulings and Department of Defense decrees that forced the branches of the military to integrate, women continue to experience resistance to their presence. One particularly chilling account comes from the first women who attempted to integrate the Citadel. Founded in 1842 in South Carolina, the Citadel was one of the last of the military institutions to allow women to enroll, and cadets resisted their presence fiercely. In 1993, Shannon Faulkner was the first woman allowed to enroll in the Citadel. She only lasted four hours before she chose to leave, citing physical and emotional abuse and exhaustion. In 1996, four women enrolled in the Citadel. Two left at the end of the first semester and filed claims that they had been hazed and sexually harassed. Jeanie Mentavlos and Kim Messer, who were eighteen years old at the time, described horrific abuse that began almost as soon as they arrived on the campus.[5] Just as was the case when Shannon Faulkner dropped out, cadets at the Citadel celebrated when Mentavlos and Messer withdrew.

Cynthia Fuchs Epstein, former president of the American Sociological Association and leading feminist scholar, provides a framework for understanding this type of resistance to integration. According to Epstein, in integrated settings, the group in power will find ways to enforce the boundary between them and the group(s) without power. Often this boundary enforcement takes the form of violence. For example, intimate partner violence can be understood, in part, as a form of boundary maintenance in households where men and women share intimate space. If boundaries are not policed in intimate spaces, it is feared that it will be possible for the marginalized person to wrestle some power away from the person with power when he is distracted by the intimacy of the situation. Epstein is not referring here necessarily to sexual intimacy, but rather to the bonding and sense of security that comes with intimate relationships. We have made the same argument with regard to race in the Jim Crow South. Jim Crow segregation is an example of this sort of boundary maintenance writ large in the Southern region of the United States where blacks and whites interacted in remarkably intimate ways, for example black women served as housekeepers and even wet nurses to white children. The film *The Help* and the book that was its source include many poignant examples of this kind of boundary policing.

So, what does any of this have to do with the Citadel? We argue that the Citadel is one of the most protected of the all-male institutions. Men attending the Citadel are choosing to attend an all-men's, sex-segregated institution for precisely this reason. The absence of women for the first one hundred fifty years of its history certainly produced a hypermasculine culture that simultaneously glorified men and devalued women. And, like all military institutions, the focus is on men's physical superiority to women. This issue comes up over and over again as women challenged and continue to challenge gender restrictions in the various military branches. In this context, it is easy to understand how members and alumni of the Citadel would resent any attempts by women to integrate this glorified male space. Much like a fraternity, one of the hallmarks of the Citadel was the sacredness of an intimate, all-male space. Women's attempts to integrate the Citadel threatened men's conceptualization of gender, what traits are assigned to men and what traits are assigned to women, and the intimate relations that men have in this space. We speculate, based on cases like the Citadel and the physical and sexual abuse of women in the military, that the more women attempt to integrate, and even rise through the ranks, the more the gender boundary will be policed with physical and sexual violence. Thanks to the tenacity, commitment, and sheer will of the early integrators, the Citadel graduated its first woman, Nancy Mace, in 1999. And, though the Citadel continues to enroll women and even offers seven women's athletic teams, women only make up 7 percent of the cadets even today.

## HYPERMASCULINE CULTURE OF THE MILITARY

All of the institutions we are analyzing in this book can be characterized as being hypermasculine. Hypermasculine culture is characterized as glorifying those traits we generally associate with men, including aggression, strength, power, competence, wealth, professional success, and sexual prowess, while simultaneously holding all the traits associated with women, including weakness, incompetence, lack of power, and being sexually discriminating, in disdain. Sexual violence is a tool that is often employed by men to reinforce hypermasculine culture. Women are raped in order to punish them for being weak and specifically for being more purposeful with their sexuality. And, men who express themselves in any way that can be interpreted as less than hypermasculine may be targeted for rape; their expressions being policed by the masculinity police.

Women enter the military with men already believing that they are inferior. The women we interviewed said that men resented their very presence. The men they served with embraced the ideology they were socialized into during boot camp that the military is only as strong as its weakest link and that women, as a collective, are a significant weak link that is a constant threat to the dominance of the United States military. The women we interviewed reported that the harassment they received from men was more or less constant. Sabrina, who served in Guantanamo Bay, or "Gitmo," said that after six years in the Navy she was so accustomed to being around men using derogatory language about women that she became desensitized to it and barely even noticed it anymore.

When we asked Michelle and Sabrina and many other women we have met over the years about the impact of this constant culture of sexual harassment, they both thought about it carefully before answering. Being one of very few women in a hypermasculine environment filled with sexist behavior took a toll in many different ways. Among other things, they became desensitized. And the more desensitized they became, the more the men amped up the sexism in the environment. Similar to the grooming that child molesters employ, the low-level sexual harassment had a similar effect. As the women grew desensitized, the line that men shouldn't cross kept moving so that, before they knew, it they were tolerating physical sexual harassment such as unwanted touching. Because the harassment escalated gradually, it became difficult to identify the line, what was OK and what was not OK.

Rape in the military can only be understood in the larger context of a culture of hypermasculinity and sexual harassment that has a normalizing effect. As unwanted physical touching turns to groping in a closet or office, sexual penetration of any kind may be minimized as just one more level of the constant harassment women deal with.

## STATISTICS ON RAPE IN THE MILITARY

As with all of the institutions we analyze in this book, getting accurate statistics on rape in the military is complicated. What is consistent across all of the institutions analyzed in this book is the significant underreporting. The Department of Defense is mandated by the White House to report annually on sexual assaults in the military and involving military members. The most recent report available is based on data collected for the entire year of 2017. The Department of Defense report includes data that is generated from several sources, including the Sexual Assault Response Coordinator, who submits data on rapes that are officially reported and the Rand Military Workplace Survey, which gathers data on sexual assault by surveying all military service members. The data reported by the United States military are also complex in that the military provides two different ways to report: restricted and unrestricted. Restricted reporting allows victims to access medical and support services but does not trigger an investigation. Unrestricted reporting provides a report to command and/or law enforcement and triggers an investigation. Before we get to the actual statistics, it is important to drill down and consider the differences between restricted and unrestricted reporting.

### Restricted and Unrestricted Reporting

There are of course pros and cons to having multiple avenues for reporting. In many ways, restricted and unrestricted reporting mirrors the process on college campuses whereby students have the option to report a sexual assault to campus authorities, which triggers an internal investigation, or to local law enforcement, which of course triggers a legal investigation.

There is value in providing an internal reporting mechanism for victims who do not want to go through the legal system but want some resolution for the person who raped them. Restricted reporting serves an important function for rape victims in the military because it provides access to much-needed resources, and it puts on record, even if it is a restricted record, who the rapist is. As college professors, we see the advantage both in campus conduct systems and the military, of having a record of how many people have been raped and who is perpetrating rape. Of course, just as is the case in our legal system, a restricted report should not be used as evidence in other cases, either restricted or unrestricted. That said, if a commander or a dean of students continues to hear the same names repeated over and over again, it might be best to encourage a victim who chooses restricted reporting to consider making an unrestricted report. It is also important to note the particular language associated with unrestricted reporting: The report will be shared with the commander *and/or law enforcement*. Yet, rarely is a report of sexual assault shared with law enforcement. Similar to every other institution we analyze in this book, the military prefers to handle sexual assault cases through an internal system rather than via the court system. And rape victims rarely get any justice when their reports are handled internally.

### TRENDS IN REPORTING

According to the Department of Defense report, 6,769 rapes were reported in 2017, which is a 10 percent increase compared to the number of reports in 2016.[6] Similar to the data in 2016, in 2017, the majority of reports, 5,110, were unrestricted and only a quarter, 1,659 were restricted. The Department of Defense is, of course, pleased that most victims feel supported in making an unrestricted report, and officials interpret this decision as reflecting confidence on the part of the victim that they will receive justice by making the report unrestricted. All of that said, the vast majority of victims do not report in any official way. The data from the Rand Military Workplace Survey document nearly fifteen thousand military service men and women reported "unwanted sexual contact" in 2016; only 30 percent of victims made any official report, while 70 percent did not make a report, restricted or unrestricted. As noted in the Department of Defense report, reporting has increased from 10 percent in 2013 to 30 percent in 2016, which is a significant increase in reporting. Obviously, the increase in reporting is positive, but we are curious what led to this dramatic rise. Was it an anomaly, or is it part of a longer trend? We will be among many who will continue to read the updated Department of Defense reports over the next few years so that we can better understand what these data mean. We also want to caution the reader that just because reporting is up does not necessarily mean that victims are receiving justice.

We are certainly not alone in our concern that the reporting rate is still so significantly suppressed. We are concerned for many reasons, among them the fact that data from the criminal justice system as well as studies on college campuses reveal that the typical rapists (or child molester) had multiple victims. And, as a result, low reporting likely contributes to higher rates of rape, rapes perpetrated by serial rapists. And, this is of concern in all of the institutions we are analyzing in this book. We have an additional concern when it comes to the military, and that is access to medical and support services. On a college campus, for example, a rape victim can access support, including advocacy and confidential counseling, for free and without reporting the rape. But accessing services in the military requires at least a restricted report, thus we are concerned that the 70 percent of victims who don't report are not accessing the services they need.

When it comes to victims, the Rand Military Workplace Study found that 4.3 percent of women and 0.6 percent of men reported unwanted sexual contact in the previous year. Given the gender composition of the military, slightly more than half of all military members reporting unwanted sexual contact are men, though *women's probability of experiencing unwanted sexual contact is more than four times higher*. When examining the *reports* of unwanted sexual contact, 88 percent were women. These data suggest that not only does the military need to be concerned with men who are victims, who are often overlooked, but also must pay special attention to men who are victims because they are extremely unlikely to report. This is problematic for many reasons, notably what it suggests about the climate, but also the fact that these victims are not able to access the medical attention and services they need and deserve to have.

Additionally, analysis from the Rand Military Workplace Study found statistically significant differences in the risk for rape. Those serving in the Air Force have the lowest risk and those serving in the Marine Corps have the highest risk, nearly three times the risk in the Air Force. These data provide some support for our argument that sexual assault is a form of policing the gender boundary, the branches with the lowest percentage of women have the highest risk of rape. Also, though data are difficult to find on the location of sexual assault, most estimates are that women are two to four times more likely to be raped on a deployment than when serving stateside.

## Why Victims Don't Report

Victims of sexual assault in the military don't report for all of the same reasons that victims in all other parts of life don't report: Because they are embarrassed, they feel shame, they think they will be judged, they think they will be blamed, they don't want anyone to know. Also, they may not want to admit other circumstances of the assault, for example getting drunk, especially if they are not legally of age, or agreeing to go to the perpetrator's house. In other cases, they may simply want to forget whatever happened to them and move on. Rape victims actually have every reason to believe that their fears about reporting are valid. Rape victims are blamed every day of the week.

In a recent study of girls between the ages of three and seventeen who had been referred to Child Protective Services because there were suspicions that they had been sexually abused, Hlavka found that the young women experienced forms of sexual violence in their everyday lives including: objectification, sexual harassment, and abuse. Often times they rationalized these incidents as normal.

> During one interview, referring to boys at school, a 13-year-old girl states: "They grab you, touch your butt and try to, like, touch you in the front, and run away, but it's okay, I mean . . . I never think it's a big thing because they do it to everyone."[7]

Hlavka's findings, though based on interviews with young adults, can be applied to describe the situation in many of the other institutions we analyze in this book, including on college campuses, at fraternity parties, in settings with athletes, politicians, and movie moguls, and in the military. Why? Because sexual abuse is a strategy for policing women's bodies and policing gender boundaries, and because one feature of patriarchal culture is the sense of entitlement that men and boys feel to touch women's bodies. Just as the boys in Hlavka's study behave, so do men in fraternities, men in Hollywood and politics, men who play sports, and men in the military. Furthermore, these boys and girls grow up to be the men and women who inhabit the institutions we are analyzing in this book. And, though not all men will grow up to continue engaging in the kinds of sexual harassment they might have perpetrated in middle school and high school, most women retain the lessons about the boundaries of their bodies as they transition to adulthood. Just as they put up with unwanted touching on the school bus in the ninth grade, they put up with unwanted touching on the metro every morning on their way to work as detailed in Holly Kearl's 2010 book *Stopping Street Harassment: Making Public Spaces Safe and Welcoming for Women*, at fraternity parties or clubs, and in their offices or workplaces.[8]

In addition to these barriers, which all women face, sexual assault victims in the military face an additional set of barriers to reporting, some of which are gendered and many of which are not. Let's begin with those barriers that affect both men and women.

## Barriers to Reporting Sexual Assault in the Military

Journalistic accounts as well as stories featured in the documentary *The Invisible War* reveal that quite often the rapist is someone with structural power over the victim. He is a supervisor, a drill sergeant, or in the case of the service academies, he is a more advanced student. The military is one of the most hierarchical institutions, a feature that is reinforced over and over again during basic training. When a victim is raped by their supervisor, to whom do they report the rape? Going up the chain of command and bypassing the supervisor can create complications for the victim, who is already afraid of not being believed.

### Fear of Disciplinary Action

As is the case for many rape victims on college campuses, a significant barrier to reporting is the fear of facing disciplinary sanctions for other behaviors related to the circumstances in which the rape took place. For example, if the victim is under twenty-one and was drinking, the victim may fear that reporting will result in disciplinary action for violating other portions of the Uniform Code of Military Justice. The military is unique in that even consensual sex among non-married partners, if it is considered to be fraternization, is a violation of the

Uniform Code of Military Justice. Many women who are raped in the service academies are told when they report that if they move forward with their cases they will be disciplined just for having had sexual contact, consensual or not.

Furthermore, there are unique features of the Uniform Code of Military Conduct that also impede reporting. Several victims whose stories are told in the documentary *The Invisible War* who were raped by their superiors were told when they reported that if they went through the process, they would likely be charged with adultery—even though they were not married—*because the man who raped them was married*. Having little experience with the military, we consulted the Uniform Code of Military Justice to confirm that this was in fact a possibility.

> Article 134 of the Uniform Code of Military Justice makes criminal the act of adultery when certain legal criteria, known as "elements," have all been met. There are three distinct elements to the crime of adultery under the UCMJ: first, a Soldier must have had sexual intercourse with someone; second, the Soldier or their sexual partner was married to someone else at the time; and third, that under the circumstances, the conduct of the Soldier was to the prejudice of good order and discipline in the armed forces or was of a nature to bring discredit upon the armed forces.

As many of the women in *The Invisible War* reported, they chose not to report out of the fear of being accused of adultery and of losing their entire career. It is quite clear that the culture of the military makes it extraordinarily difficult for victims not only to report but also to seek justice. It is no wonder that reporting rates are so low when victims are counseled out of reporting by their superiors who threaten them with disciplinary actions.

### Fear of Retaliation

There are so many aspects of rape in the military that are disturbing. Perhaps one of the most perplexing aspects of rape in the military is the retaliation that victims regularly experience when they report. The Human Rights Watch report on retaliation found that 62 percent of victims who reported a sexual assault experienced retaliation. In other words, victims who report a sexual assault are twelve times more likely to experience retaliation than the offender is to be punished. In addition, "Survivors have little recourse if they experience retaliation and few of those who retaliate are held accountable. Human Rights Watch was unable to uncover more than two examples of even minor disciplinary action being taken against persons who retaliated against a survivor."[9]

Victims who were interviewed as part of the Human Rights Watch Report noted that they experienced several different kinds of retaliation, including bullying and interpersonal abuse, professional repercussions, and other disciplinary actions, which might include, as noted earlier, being disciplined for underage drinking.

Victims reported a wide range of bullying and interpersonal abuse, which ranged from the mild (not being invited to parties) to the extreme. Some victims reported experiencing verbal harassment and threats of violence that occurred nearly every day. One victim reported that she was besieged by phone calls after the members of her unit put Post-it notes on all the cars parked on base with the message, "For a good time, call . . ." One victim reported checking herself into the hospital because men in her unit told her "better sleep light" and disabled her car. Many victims reported that they were physically attacked by the man who raped them or by his friends after reporting the sexual assault.

Victims also reported a wide range of professional repercussions, including suddenly receiving negative performance evaluations after many years of very positive evaluations, as well as suddenly having their duties changed or being reassigned. Many victims reported that even after being prepped by their commanders for a promotion, if they reported a sexual assault, they suddenly found the pathway to promotion blocked.

A high-achieving sergeant in the Air National Guard told Human Rights Watch that she was up for promotion when she reported a sexual assault that had occurred earlier in her career. Afterwards, a colleague told her a wing commander said, "Over my dead body will she get promoted now." She lost her responsibility for training people and was demoted twice. "Despite all those awards, I got nothing," she said.[10]

Victims also reported that they were denied access to the kinds of experiences that were necessary for advancement, such as deployments. Michelle, whom we interviewed, reported that as a result of stalking by her ex-husband, she was forced to return stateside seven months early from a deployment, which delayed her advancement in rank and pay and made her commander reluctant to deploy her again. Additionally, men in her unit resented her because they believed she was getting a benefit from getting to return home early that they were not receiving. Never mind the toll that the stalking took on her emotional and physical health, something none of her colleagues could apparently understand.

Other victims reported that they were removed from their positions and assigned to less desirable work. One woman noted that before she reported the sexual assault, she was doing high-level intelligence work, and after she reported the sexual assault she found herself reassigned to garbage detail. Another victim with high-level computer training found herself reassigned for four months to working in a locked cage with five men handing out weapons.

All of the victims whose stories are recounted in the Human Rights Watch report and featured in *The Invisible War* talked about the impact of reporting on their professional aspirations. All of them said they went into the military because they wanted to serve their country and because they wanted to pursue a career that the military offered. They took their training and profession seriously, and they were understandably devastated when they reported a crime and found that they were the ones paying the price, not the men who raped them. Women in many non-military professions tell of a similar phenomenon if they report a sexual harassment. Women who report sexual harassment in both the military or in civilian professions often find that they are labeled as "difficult to work with" or "unable to handle personnel matters." The critical difference for women in the military is that it is a quasi-total institution. Unlike in civilian professions, they cannot just quit the military and find another job. Because the military is a nearly total institution, the retaliation often literally follows them home, especially if they live on base or are deployed. The nature of a total institution also means that it is difficult for those who may want to support the victim to do so without experiencing similar retaliation. A colleague in the military cannot simply tell the boss off without also risking demotion. Thus, even when victims have allies, even men who are allies, the hierarchical and quasi-total institutional nature of the military makes this nearly impossible for them to get the support they need, first to heal and second to pursue justice. Lastly, the quasi-total institutional nature of the military means that retaliation can also take the form of other types of disciplinary actions.

One of the dominant features of the military is that commanders are given relatively broad discretion in using punishment in order to achieve discipline. For example, commanders may order non-judicial, but nevertheless severe disciplinary actions such as notations in the personnel file, reductions in rations, confinement, forfeiture of pay, and even reduction of rank. Many victims found that after they reported a sexual assault they received these types of nonjudgmental disciplinary actions that were unusual and more severe than they had typically experienced or observed. For example, victims reported getting written reprimands for wearing the wrong socks or leaving dirty dishes in the sink, infractions that would normally warrant only a verbal warning.

This is yet another example of the ways in which the hierarchical and quasi-total institutional quality of the military is different from the civilian world. Victims who report sexual harassment in the workplace will not find their boss giving them a poor performance evaluation for something they do at home, like leaving dirty dishes in the sink. Furthermore, in civilian workplaces, the boss or supervisor does not have the same kind of total discretion that military commanders do. Moreover, in the military, the victim of this kind of retaliation does not have any recourse; they cannot go to the human resources (HR) office, for example, and make a complaint. This unfettered power bestowed on commanders creates an environment in which it is very difficult for a victim to have a report taken seriously, and they have no guarantee of personal safety or professional protections after a report is made. *When commanders themselves can engage in retaliation, a rape culture is truly enforced.*

Perhaps not surprisingly, many victims reported that the retaliation was far worse than the rape itself. Kearl quotes Ashley Parker, a former Army specialist: "Sexual assault is not what messes you up. It is the reprisals, the hazing. I could recover from the assault, but nothing is done for the retaliation."[11]

One can only imagine what it's like to have to continue to serve in this environment in which the victim is subjected to retaliation, much of which is sanctioned by her commander, and her rapist is allowed to go about his business. We must also ask the question: What is the impact of this on the rapist, his colleagues, and future victims? We don't believe that it's overly speculative to conclude that the rapist feels empowered in this context. Not only is he not held accountable for rape, but he is allowed to continue abusing the victim by retaliating against her, and he can all but be assured that if his friends retaliate, they will not be held accountable either. The other men in the unit are sent a very clear message that rape is tolerated, and so is retaliation for reporting. The other future victims, both men and women, in the unit are sent an even clearer message that not only will they not be believed if they report, but they risk serious retaliation that, as many victims said, is worse than the rape itself, if they do report. It is quite clear, then, that if the military is serious about increasing reporting and providing a safe environment for victims, commanders need to sanction any retaliation severely. Sadly, it is also not surprising that many victims said in the Human Rights Report that they intended to leave the military once their commitment ended.

The structure of the military also creates barriers to reporting that are experienced differently by men and women.

## Fear of Being Labeled

In all parts of society, we know that reporting by men and boys who are victims of sexual violence is even more suppressed than among girls and women.

The explanation for this is that because most perpetrators of rape against boys and men are also men, boys and men may fear that reporting sexual contact with another man, even if it is nonconsensual, will result in them being labeled as gay.

Not only is the military a hypermasculine culture in which anything remotely effeminate is despised and policed, until very recently the military *prohibited* LGBTQ individuals to serve openly in the military. The century-long prohibition was followed by two decades of "Don't Ask, Don't Tell" (1994–2011), which allowed LGBTQ individuals to serve, as long as they did not serve openly. Not until 2011, when President Obama repealed "Don't Ask, Don't Tell," were gay and lesbian individuals allowed to serve openly in the military. So, for male victims, reporting a sexual act with another man, consensual or not, could result in his being discharged for the mere perception that he is gay, even if he is not. It is no wonder why men seldom report.

For women, the additional barrier they face in reporting has to do with the highly sex-segregated nature of the military. We asked Michelle and Sabrina about why they thought women wouldn't report being raped. They were quite clear that one significant barrier to reporting was the sex-segregation of many units. For example, Michelle was deployed twice on aircraft carriers in the Middle East. Michelle reported that often there were only a small handful of women on the aircraft carrier at any given time. The Uniform Code of Military Justice requires that a crime report be issued every week. Imagine, Michelle said, if a woman was raped and reported it. When the crime report was released the following week, each of the thousands of service members on the ship would read that "a Hispanic woman on the aircraft carrier had reported being raped." If there is only one Hispanic woman on the aircraft carrier, everyone will know who made the report. We do agree that it is important for crimes to be reported to the community, just as is required on college campuses, but it is imperative that these reports take every precaution to protect the identity of the victim and the accused; the report should only be made public if and when an accused is found guilty. Additionally, as is the case on college campuses, we wonder if there is an alternative reporting mechanism that could be designed that would eliminate this concern. Removing this kind of barrier would likely result in increased reporting.

Taken all of these barriers into consideration, it is no surprise that victims of rape, men and women, significantly underreport. Similar to every other institution we are analyzing in this book, if the military really wanted to increase reporting, they would remove the barriers to doing so.

## RAPE INVESTIGATIONS IN THE MILITARY

One of the biggest criticisms of the military as an institution focuses on what happens after a rape is reported. When an unrestricted report of sexual assault is made, the commander is required to launch an investigation. If the commander, in consultation with legal counsel, concludes that there is enough evidence to bring a case, then there are several routes that can be taken, a court martial can be convened or alternative sanctions may be administered, such as reassigning the accused, or dismissing the accused from the military. Mandated by the White House, the Department of Justice is required to review the cases that are reported. The most recent review is based on the data and cases from 2014. Of the 4,501 unrestricted reports in 2014, approximately 10 percent were judged to be baseless or false, which we note is similar to the rate of false reporting in national-level data. Only 359, or 8 percent, were convicted of any charge at trial, which is only slightly higher than the rate of conviction in criminal court when rape victims report to the civilian police. Of those convicted of at least one crime in a court martial, most received more than one form of punishment. The most common punishment was some kind of confinement (71 percent) which could mean as little as barracks restrictions. Even fewer, only 57 percent, were punitively discharged or dismissed. The vast majority, 81 percent had their rank reduced and 61 percent were fined.

Assessing the outcomes of these cases, we are struck by several things. First, that the internal system of justice convicts only slightly more of those accused than the criminal justice system. Yet victims are persuaded that they will get more justice or that that the process will be easier for them if they do not report the crime to the police and instead seek justice inside of the institution in which they are also—or so they are told—an equal member with the person they are accusing. Thus, much like the cases of rape on college campuses, which also have extremely low disciplinary rates, we wonder about the veracity of this advice. Second, the types of discipline that are invoked in these convictions also seem eerily similar to those utilized by college and university conduct boards. Although the military confines 71 percent of those convicted, something universities are not able to do, and dismisses more than half of those convicted, something colleges and universities refuse to do, we wonder about the 61 percent of those convicted who are fined. This seems a bit like college and university conduct boards that require students held responsible for sexual misconduct to write research papers on rape. Perhaps victims would get better results by pursuing criminal charges. It is probably not surprising that the primary focus of those seeking to reform the system of justice in the military point to removing the adjudication of rape cases from the military and handling them exclusively in the civilian criminal justice process.

The military has a serious problem with sexual assault, with nearly fifteen thousand service members each year indicating that they were sexually assaulted. The number of men and women reporting sexual assault is pretty much even, but given the underrepresentation of women in the military, women are five times more likely than men to be raped. Stunningly, women in the military are two to three times more likely to be assaulted than civilian women. Although part of this difference is explained by age, women in the military are younger than the overall population and younger women are at higher risk for sexual assault in general, it is deeply concerning that women who are serving our country are subjected to violent sexual assaults by others wearing the same uniform.

## WHAT CAN BE DONE?

We identify five areas that the military needs to address in order to reduce sexual assault in the military: (1) prevention and education strategies, (2) barriers to reporting, (3) retaliation, (4) adjudication of cases, and (5) women in leadership.

### More Effective Prevention and Education Strategies

As is the case with any significant social problem, prevention is a much more efficient and effective strategy than intervention. Teaching men not to rape is far more efficient than dealing with the costs of a rape, which include the human resources required if a report is made, even a restricted report; the services that the victim will need; the loss in productivity as the victim recovers; the likelihood that they will leave the military and have to be replaced; and so on. There is also the cost of embarrassment at having to admit that fifteen thousand service members are raped every year, that women are more at risk for rape by their colleagues than violence by the "enemy" when they serve in combat zones, and that women are dying of dehydration because a walk to the latrine after dark is too dangerous. Finally, even the requirement to assess sexual assault in the military, producing the annual Department of Defense report, costs $5 million.

The military has, unfortunately, employed several approaches to prevention that fail to get at the root causes of sexual assault—power and control—and portray rape using old stereotypes that rape is nothing more than a misunderstanding induced by alcohol. For example, in 2012 the military released a poster campaign "Ask Her When She's Sober." Beginning in 2010 and in a second edition launched in 2013, the military used a video game Team Bound to train service members about the importance of bystander intervention and the impact of sexual assault on the victim, with the obvious intent to reduce sexual assaults. Team Bound is a video game that offers the player opportunities for decisions at various points in the game. If the player chooses passive options and fails to interrupt a problematic interaction between two soldiers in a bar, the woman is taken back to the man's barracks by an aggressive male service member and raped. In the video game she reports the assault and ultimately leaves the military, with the conclusion being "A life damaged, a career ended, a unit falling apart. But it didn't have to be this way. All you had to do was stand up and be strong."[12]

There are many critiques of this approach to rape education, among them the fact that it fails to acknowledge what the data show, which is that most victims report being raped by someone of a higher rank. The game also misrepresents what the data tell us about reporting, that the vast majority of victims don't report. As we noted, Team Bound reinforces the stereotype that rape is really about having too much to drink, in which context a misunderstanding can arise between the perpetrator and the offender.

We raise several other concerns. First, video games and violent video games in particular are extremely popular among young men. They spend hour upon hour playing games that involve rape and torture. We wonder if this game is viewed as any different from Call of Duty or Grand Theft Auto or, rather if Team Bound is just another game that is construed to be fantasy. Second, we wonder if, as in games like Grand Theft Auto or Call of Duty, there are some players who actually enjoy seeing the woman raped and intentionally make passive decisions so that the game ends that way.

We praise the military for thinking of creative ways to engage young men in rape prevention. Research of all kinds indicates that meeting people where they are is a more effective strategy for any kind of prevention. That said, the content must also be appropriate and accurate. And we, like many others, would argue that with the kind of problem the military has with sexual assault, much more work needs to be put into identifying effective prevention strategies. As we noted in our discussion of rape on college campuses, the research is clear that effective prevention strategies are longer-term, multiple-interaction programs and not one-time, short-term approaches.

## Address Barriers to Reporting

As we have noted, not only do rape victims in the military face the same sorts of barriers that all victims face—shame, embarrassment, and just wanting to move on—there are particular barriers that victims in the military face. Similar to victims on college campuses, many of whom are afraid to report because they have been drinking underage, we urge the military to take a page out of the playbook from college campuses and provide amnesty from prosecution of underage drinking or drug use when reporting a sexual assault. Second, unlike any other institution we have analyzed in this book, rape victims in the military are often threatened with being prosecuted for violating adultery provisions in the Uniform Code of Military Justice. This practice is absolutely ridiculous. *Nonconsensual sexual contact cannot, by definition, constitute adultery.* Victims who report rape or sexual abuse must be ensured that they will never face disciplinary action associated with the adultery provisions. Third, we understand that need for sharing crime statistics in contained communities, the same is true on college campuses and is, in fact, required by the Clery Act. That said, the military must find a way to protect the identity of victims who are easily identifiable in small communities, for example, the often very small number of women on an aircraft carrier. This should never be a barrier to reporting. Lastly, the military must be honest and accept what the data show, that often victims are raped by their direct supervisors. Thus, requiring a victim to report through the chain of command is nothing short of a requirement to report to the rapist. This is simply absurd. Identifying and appropriately training designated people to receive reports seems like a simple, straightforward, and efficient solution that would likely result, as all of these measures would, in increased reporting.

## Address Concerns Regarding Retaliation

Like many learning of this for the first time, we were quite simply stunned at the rates and types of retaliation, both official and unofficial, that victims reported experiencing. Though no system is perfect, Human Resource (HR) offices, and the Office of Civil Rights, *explicitly prohibit retaliation for individuals reporting any type of harassment*, including sexual harassment, racial harassment, or any other kind harassment. The Department of Defense has an *obligation* to protect victims from retaliation. We are quite certain that military leaders would argue vehemently that the ability of commanders to use a variety of nonjudgmental disciplinary actions is fundamental to the maintenance of a disciplined unit and that this is especially necessary for commanders of units with a high percentage of young men who often engage in behavior that is not disciplined. That said, we urge the military to identify appropriate strategies for ensuring that victims who are reporting a serious, violent crime *are never retaliated against* by anyone, but especially their supervisor. Perhaps any action taken against a victim who has reported a rape must be reviewed and "signed off" on by a second supervisor or, ideally, the person designated to receive sexual assault reports.

## More Effective Adjudication of Cases

The data in the Department of Defense report reveal just what Senator Kirsten Gillibrand has been arguing: that the military is not adequately adjudicating the relatively small percentage of sexual assault cases that are reported. As we noted, fewer than 7 percent resulted in any disciplinary action, and among those that did, very few guilty soldiers were confined for any length of time or discharged. The majority were given sanctions that included fines, reduction in rank, and reassignment of duties. Fines and reduction in rank are not an appropriate sanction for any felony, including a sexual assault. As is the case with sexual assault on college campuses, we can be persuaded that some internal system of adjudicating cases may be appropriate but only when it is clearly in the best interest of the victim, when it is what the victims want, and when it is conducted appropriately and yields satisfactory results. Given the fact that many victims in the military report that they were raped by someone of higher rank, often someone who supervised them, we are more skeptical than in the case of college campuses that there is any internal system of justice that would be effective. We urge military leaders to consider both internal and external reporting, and we stand with Senator Gillibrand, that unless otherwise requested by the victim, cases should be reported and handled by the local law enforcement agency.

## Empower More Women in Leadership Roles

As is the case with the Catholic Church, the absence of women in leadership capacities in the military contributes to the approach the military takes to preventing and responding to sexual violence. We would never argue that all women understand the dynamics of sexual assault or that no men do or can, but there is evidence that including women in sexual assault prevention yields more effective programming. More than simply being a voice at the table to develop sexual assault prevention and response strategies, having more women in all ranks of leadership is absolutely necessary to transform the hypermasculine culture that provides the incubator for rape. We are well aware that members of the military who are reading this are cringing because the hypermasculine culture of the military is believed to be absolutely central to the qualities of a successful military that is required to engage in the physical and psychological challenges of war. We agree wholeheartedly that people who are going to trek through Afghanistan or Iraq need to be highly trained, strong physically and psychologically, and able to endure severe challenges. However, there is no evidence that an ideology that devalues anything feminine and resents the presence of women, even when they demonstrate their capabilities, is necessary for an effective military. In fact, we would argue quite the opposite, that there is evidence that in the new landscape of war, not only are women not a liability, in many cases they can be an asset, especially because of their ability to work with women in the very Middle Eastern countries in which we are currently at war, to empower them to help themselves and influence the men around them to stop engaging in violence. Much research has documented that terrorism breeds in spaces where gender inequality is high, women's literacy is low, and poverty is high. There is also evidence that empowering women, especially through education, reduces poverty and ultimately terroristic activities. Now, more than ever, we would argue that *women are essential to the military*.

But, perhaps more so than that, if we have demonstrated anything in this chapter, it is that a hypermasculine culture that devalues women and resents their presence is actually quite damaging to the military. Everything from sexually demeaning comments to rape create a culture in which women cannot be free to do their jobs or function at their maximum capacity. When women and men are not able to do their jobs at maximum capacity, when they fear their supervisors, and when they feel threatened on a daily basis, this is nothing short of a tremendous cost to the military. As *The Invisible War* reveals, many highly qualified members of the military leave the service after they are raped and are retaliated against. Others are physically injured to the point that they are disabled and discharged. The military must continue to pay them disability pay and benefits for decades. None of these are costs the military, and by extension the taxpayer, can afford. And the case of the women dying of dehydration because they were afraid to go to the latrine is perhaps the best illustration of functioning under capacity and paying the ultimate price.

## FINAL THOUGHTS

The advantage to the structure of the military hierarchy and the requirement of ultimate obedience is that when the military decides to end rape among its ranks it will end. Women who enter the military shouldn't have to fear for their lives or die of dehydration because they fear being raped by their colleagues. It would be tragic but understandable if men or women died of dehydration because they were afraid to go to the latrine out of fear of an IED being exploded, but it is *unthinkable* that anyone should die of dehydration because they fear being raped by their brother when they go to the latrine. If service members can be trained to make their beds and clean their barracks and dress to particular standards, why can't they be trained not to rape? If soldiers can be ordered to sweep a neighborhood in Iraq or guard detainees in Abu Ghraib or "Gitmo," why can't they be ordered not to rape? We believe they can be. The truth is that if commanders ordered those in their command not to rape, rape would become a rare thing in the military. We challenge the Department of Defense to take rape as seriously as they take clean barracks, shined shoes, and hospital corners on beds.

**\*\*YOU HAVE EARNED\*\***
**0 POINTS**

WEEKLY MAX REACHED

mylibraryrewards.com

Account No: XXXXXXXXX6306
Total Points This Week: 100

Read-Reward-Redeem®

# 5

# PRISONS

We should not be tolerating rape in prison. And we should not be making jokes about it in our popular culture. That's no joke. These things are unacceptable.

—President Barack Obama, 2015[1]

This chapter will depart somewhat from the others in the book because one cannot adequately analyze GBV or child sexual abuse inside the United States prison system without understanding the wider context of violence and abuse inside of the prison. Somewhat unique compared to the other institutions we are analyzing in this book is that in the United States prison system there are other forms of GBV in addition to rape and intimate partner violence. GBV in prisons includes the rape of men, the sexual abuse of boys, discrimination against trans inmates, and transwomen in particular, and the abuse of women's reproductive lives, including shackling women during childbirth. All of these issues will be explored in this chapter. But, we begin with a brief history and overview of the prison system in the United States.

## BRIEF HISTORY OF PRISONS IN THE UNITED STATES

Until about 1970 prisons in the United States were geared toward rehabilitation. They were set up to provide opportunities for individuals to modify their behavior so that when they left the institutions they would have replaced the behaviors that landed them in prison with alternative behaviors that would allow them to succeed in the legitimate economy. Education programs, GED courses, technical skills programs, art, music, and vocational skills such as plumbing and masonry were all part of rehabilitation programs.

Beginning around 1980, fueled in large part by the Reagan administration's War on Drugs, prisons grew exponentially, and the focus turned toward sheer punishment rather than rehabilitation. The carceral state that characterizes the United States of the late twentieth and early twenty-first centuries is a system designed to remove poor people, and people of color in particular, from mainstream society, cordoning them off in human warehouses for years, even decades at a time.

## What Do the Numbers Tell Us?

According the Bureau of Justice Statistics, 2.25 million American adults are incarcerated. Nearly twice as many Americans, 4.7 million, are on probation or parole. A total of 6.8 million American adults or 2.8 percent of the population of the United States are in some way "policed" by the criminal justice system, a system fed by a pipeline: 54,000 juveniles are also currently incarcerated.

Two well-known news reporters, Adam Gopnik and Chris Hayes, have both noted that the incarceration rate in the United States is *higher* than that under Stalin's Gulag. Chris Hayes writes: "Americans under penal supervision, some have argued, even rivals the number of Russians in the gulag under Stalin."[2] The United States makes up 5 percent of the world population and 25 percent of the incarcerated population. And this doesn't even count the number people on parole or probation. There is no better way to put it than to say that the United States is addicted to incarceration.

So, how did this happen? It was not by accident. Instead, a very deliberate set of racialized policies and practices that target low-income people, Black men in particular, are the cause. If we focus only on the state of mass incarceration, we miss the critically important story of the process, the fact that official federal and state policies and practices specifically target Black bodies. Today, roughly one-third of all Black men will be incarcerated in their lifetime, and nearly three-quarters (70 percent) of Black men without a high school diploma will be locked up. Many people argue that more Black men are in prison because they commit more crimes. This is a myth. No system applied equally to all people could result in the system of mass incarceration that exists in the United States today, a system in which *nearly one of every two* inmates is a Black man. To put this number in context, there are approximately sixteen to seventeen million

Black men living in the United States, and on any given day, one million of them are in prison.

## Juvenile Detention Facilities

According to the US Department of Justice, in 2013 there were more than fifty-three thousand juveniles in detention centers, youth facilities, and adult prisons in the United States. Fourteen percent of incarcerated juveniles are girls. Black youth are the most likely to be incarcerated, followed by Native Americans and Hispanics, with Whites and Asians having the lowest rate of juvenile incarceration. Black youth are five times more likely to be incarcerated than their White counterparts. Sixteen- and seventeen-year-olds are the vast majority of incarcerated youth, but it is important to note that youth as young as twelve years old are incarcerated, making up 1 percent of all youth in jail or prison. *The majority of juveniles are incarcerated for property crimes including arson, vandalism, and burglary. A very small number of juveniles are incarcerated for violent offenses like rape and murder.*[3]

Deeply troubling is the fact that while the vast majority of these Black young men and women are being incarcerated for what amount to minor, nonviolent property crimes, they are at tremendous risk for physical and sexual abuse.

## PRISONS AS TOTAL INSTITUTIONS

Of all of the institutions we are examining in this book, prisons meet every requirement of Goffman's definition of a total institution. Nearly every aspect of an inmate's daily routine is controlled, although there is some variation depending on the custody level of the inmate. For example, in solitary confinement, inmates are locked down twenty-three hours per day, with virtually no human contact, while inmates who work on farms like the Mississippi State Penitentiary at Parchman are outside eight to ten hours per day and sleep in dormitory-style facilities. All inmates are required to wear prison uniforms and eat what is served when it is served. They may have restrictions on when they can shower and how often they get a shower. They may have limits on when, if, and how long they can have access to exercise facilities. Their phone calls, mail, and in-person visits are limited and highly controlled. Thus, when we are considering rape and other forms of sexualized victimization in the prison context, it is paramount to understand the fact that inmates have very little control over their lives. We can imagine that the loss of control that victims of rape experience is heightened by the lack of control inmates have in nearly every other part of their lives. On the other hand, inmates who are raped may feel less of a loss of control because they have become used to not having control. Unlike the other institutions in this book, prisons are total institutions that are run by a set of hierarchical rules that govern their entire being. One major indicator of this total control is that when people are released from these institutions they often have difficulty functioning in a free society where they must make most of their decisions about daily life. The case of Brooks, the long-timer in the movie *The Shawshank Redemption* is a moving illustration of what it's like when men and women, having become institutionalized after years in prison, cannot make the adjustment necessary to live in the "free world."[4]

The power structure in prisons is among the most extreme of any of the institutions that we are analyzing. Guards are charged with implementing the total institution. It is their job to ensure that inmates comply with all of the regulations from dress to food to showering and exercise. Failure to comply with regulations can result in punishments that range from missing a shower or exercise time to being confined to the "hole," or solitary confinement. Guards can also influence other aspects of the inmate's experience, such as passing on medical requests to the infirmary (or not), requesting changes in "cellie" or roommate assignments (or not), and searching the inmate's person and/or personal belongings before and after a visit (or not). As a result, it can be extremely difficult for inmates to refuse the sexual demands of guards who control literally every aspect of their lives.

Although each of the institutions we are analyzing in this book have an internal system of justice, prisons have by far the greatest ability to remain removed from the larger criminal justice system. Sometimes there seem to be almost no rules for dealing with incarcerated populations. For example, the now infamous Joe Arpaio, former sheriff of Maricopa County (Phoenix), Arizona, ran the jail system under his direction in what would normally be considered in violation of basic human rights, forcing inmates to sleep in tents while the summer temperatures soared above 110 degrees Fahrenheit. In the spring of 2017, the Milwaukee County jail came under scrutiny when inmates died from dehydration after being denied water for nearly a week while they served time in solitary confinement.

When inmates commit what would normally be considered crimes in the "free world"—including assaults and rapes, but even murder—they are almost always handled by an internal hearing board. There is no right to a trial, and based on guidelines, more time is typically added to an inmate's sentence. For "lifers" there is little concern about holding a hearing because there is no greater sentence that can be imposed. Thus, in this context, when rapes occur, they are not reported externally but managed internally, whether the perpetrator is another inmate or a guard.

While writing this chapter we had an experience that reinforced the total institutional nature of prisons. We wanted to share one of our books with an inmate who is currently housed in Attica. We followed all of the rules about sending books according to the New York State Corrections website. Specifically, the book had to be ordered and sent from a retailer and the package had to come with a receipt. So, where did we purchase the book? Amazon of course. Two days after purchasing the book on Amazon, a text message confirmed that the book had been delivered and signed for by "David." A few weeks later, a letter arrived from the inmate. The opening line of the letter read, "I know the book arrived, but they wouldn't let me have it." In a total institution, even the privilege of having a book is controlled. The story continued as we called Amazon to track down the book. The customer service representative confirmed that the book had been delivered. He admitted that this was not the first time he had heard that an inmate had been denied a shipment. As we lamented that all we wanted was to give the poor guy a book to read to ease the boredom of being locked up 23 hours a day, the customer service representative revealed that he understood. He had been in prison. After contacting Amazon, we called Attica and talked to the "counselor" assigned to the inmate. After learning who we were sending the book to, he responded that this inmate "ain't getting no book." We cannot emphasize enough the impact of a total institution on one's daily life.

When it comes to prisons, the United States seems to be out of step with the rest of the world, at least those postindustrial economies to which we regularly compare ourselves. Inmates constantly complain about the quality of the water and the food. At Parchman, a processed meat is served that seems to come alive when it is heated up in the microwave. They call it "wolf booty." Inmates also claim they can taste and feel the sand left on the unrinsed greens that are harvested from the Parchman farms. Because of inmate allergies and dietary restrictions, there are almost no spices available for use in prison kitchens.

In contrast, most European countries take an approach to incarceration that seeks to limit the experience inside of a prison to the removal of freedom of movement while retaining all other human rights, including access to health care, nutritious food, and a variety of opportunities to develop skills that can be applied to work and home life once the inmate is released back into society. A model for humane incarceration is the system in Norway. What does Norway get for leading the world in human rights–centered approaches to incarceration? One of the lowest recidivism rates in the world.

The comparison between the system of incarceration in the United States and in Norway is often cast as a debate about the purpose of prison. Is it punitive or rehabilitative? Rather than enter that debate, we pose a different question: Would the same conditions exist in prisons in the United States if the population of inmates were of a different complexion? Locking people in literal cages, often in solitary confinement, even for decades, and providing nonpotable water and inadequate nutrition are forms of abuse. These are bodies that have no value, for which there is no rehabilitative hope, that require cordoning off from mainstream society, not so much for what they have done, *but for who they are.*

## THE FRATERNITY OF CORRECTIONAL OFFICERS

Although the socialization or initiation processes of the institutions we interrogate in this book vary, a common, central process is one that builds in-group bonds and loyalty. For example, in chapter 7, we scrutinize the seminary as the site for socializing incoming Catholic priests. This is where they bond. This is where they learn the rules of "priesthood." It is also where members become well versed in the doctrines and protocols that facilitate the moving of child molesters from one parish to another. Out of sight and out of mind. In chapter 4, we examined the "all for one; one for all" concept that has a deep meaning for members of the military. Their identities are inextricably linked, both symbolically and emotionally.

Corrections officers often have a background in the military. Many of the corrections officers we interviewed described the role of prison guard as a kind of natural transition after a career in the military. Both jobs are very hierarchical, both involve discipline and weapons training. What makes the job of prison guard potentially more attractive is that it does not require deployments and can be done in one's home community. Obviously not every military member's hometown has a prison, but the communities where military recruiting is high are often the same kinds of communities where prisons are built—rural and economically depressed.

Regardless of previous experience, the same sort of fraternal bonds that are built among members of the military are built among correctional officers. Most of these bonds, however, are developed on the job rather than in training, which in some states may last for no more than a month. Correctional officers identify strongly with the larger team in the prison in which they work, and they build especially strong bonds with the other officers on the same post. For example, we interviewed correctional officers who worked in solitary confinement units in a state prison system, and one of the most common things they talked about were their relationships with each other. Because the work they do is so unique and so stressful, they often spoke about how they couldn't share what they do at work with their families, and this made their work relationships that much more important. Prisons are difficult places to work, and it's not an exaggeration to say that correctional officers share more emotionally with their colleagues than with their families. When we heard officers talk about Prison Rape Elimination Act (PREA) accusations, something officers especially do not want to talk about with their families, it was clear that they banded together, that they believed their peers over the inmates.

Two officers we interviewed in two different prisons described an even more deliberate strategy: "fixing" their stories so that the official report of events was consistent in cases where inmates might protest their rights. For example, an inmate refused to put his handcuffs out through the door on the cell, the wicket, to be removed after an officer returned him from his shower. The officer called for backup and several other officers responded and proceeded to pull the inmate nearly out of his cell, through the wicket, in order to restrain him. The inmate suffered injuries as a result. Later, when we were talking with one of the sergeants about what he likes about his job, he said, "The paper work." When we remarked, "Wow, that's interesting, no one seems to like paper work," he responded, "I write up all of the reports for the COs; . . . that way we have the record straight and they just have to sign it." When we observed that they must appreciate that, he said, "Yep, they do. . . . If they type up their own paper work, they miss things. I have to fix it anyway." And he added, pointing to the lieutenant's office, "There's a lot they don't know."

A CO offered a similar response: "It would never be the case that COs would 'dime out' a guy they didn't like . . . never go to management to complain. Even if someone makes a bad call, I'm going to go with it all the way."

The process of socialization had accomplished exactly what it was designed to do, build fraternal bonds so that even when an officer violates protocol or an inmate's civil rights, his teammates cover up for him.


## SEX SEGREGATION IN PRISONS

Of all of the institutions we analyze in this book, prisons are the most rigidly sex segregated. To begin with, women make up a disproportionately small percentage of all incarcerated people, approximately 10 percent. The majority of jails house both men and women inmates, primarily because it's not efficient to build women-only jails to incarcerate such a relatively small number of people. That said, the housing units are strictly organized by gender. In a county jail this often means that one floor of ten will be dedicated to housing female inmates. But most prisons are entirely sex segregated and are built to house inmates of only one gender. Because women are such a small percentage of all inmates, there is often only one women's prison in each state, and all inmates in that state are housed together. The numbers are even smaller in the federal prison system, where women make up only 7 percent of all inmates. In fact, there are no federal prisons for women in the Western region of the United States, and as a result, many women in federal prison will be incarcerated hundreds if not thousands of miles from their homes.[5]

Though jails and prisons are sex segregated in terms of the incarcerated populations, both male and female units employ corrections officers or guards of varying genders. Having a mixed-gender guard staff is controversial for all of the reasons one might expect, including the presumption that the solicitation of sex acts for favors will be higher in mixed-gender settings. There is also the concern that strip searches, a common practice in prisons, by guards whose gender is different from the inmate, will violate the constitutional right to privacy or even PREA. In this regard, there is a greater concern about placing men guards in women's prisons than vice versa.

## RAPE IN PRISON

Rape has been rampant in prisons for decades, though there is some public debate about how much of prison rape is real and how much is myth. In 2003 the Prison Rape Elimination Act (PREA) was passed. PREA requires that the federal government, implemented by the Bureau of Justice Statistics, must conduct an annual survey of all correctional institutions and measure the incidence of rape and its impact. One of the most interesting things about the institutions we examine in this book is the difference between the "official" reporting of rape and the rape statistics that come from surveys conducted with the individuals themselves.

In the official survey of prisons and jails required by the PREA, for the most recent year for which data were available, 2012, there were eight thousand three hundred rapes reported by all correctional institutions in the United States.[6] In contrast, in the most recent survey of inmates, 4.0 percent of prison inmates and 3.2 percent of jail inmates, or nearly ninety thousand individuals, reported being sexually victimized *in the previous twelve months*.[7] The reports were nearly evenly split between the two types of rape that are measured: inmate rape of other inmates (51 percent) and correctional staff rape of inmates (49 percent). It's interesting that just like college campus statistics and statistics in the military, rape is systematically underreported by about 90 percent. We will continue to explore issues of underreporting in the final chapter.

As demonstrated in figure 5.1, women in jails and in prison report significantly higher rates of sexual victimization by other inmates compared to their male counterparts. However, when we look at rape by guards, men and women report remarkably similar rates by gender and across institutions. Interestingly, men report being raped at remarkably similar rates across both the type of perpetrator (inmate or guard) and the kind of institution (jail or prison). Women, on the other hand, experience significant differences, depending on the type of institution and the type of perpetrator. In short, women are at much greater risk for rape in prisons and by other inmates, and they are at least risk for rape by guards in jail. Lesbian, gay, bisexual, and trans inmates report rates of rape that are twelve times higher for inmate-on-inmate rape and twice as high in cases of guards raping inmates. Rates are higher for other groups as well, including inmates who are significantly over- or underweight, those with more education, and those who are serving longer sentences.[8]

Many of the findings from this report seem to make sense on the surface, but others do not. Though it is true a far greater number of men are victims of rape in prison than women, because men outnumber women by nine times, women's

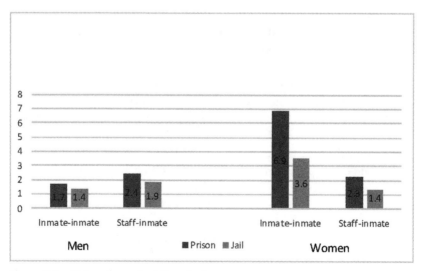

Figure 5.1.   Rates of rape by jail and prison.

risk for some forms of rape is significantly higher than men's. Most discussions in the popular media and, sadly, most prison rape jokes, however, are in reference to male victims. Lost in the discussion is the fact that women in prison face a risk for rape that is significantly higher than women in the "free world."

Second, when we do talk about women being raped in prison, the focus is on rape by guards. Although this is very concerning, especially because of the power the guards have and the limited ability inmates of any gender may feel they have to resist any form of sexual solicitation by guards, the data indicate that the greatest threat of rape for women is other inmates. This is a particularly challenging finding to explain, given everything we know about rape as a gendered crime.

In their review of the report by Beck et al. in the *New York Review of Books*, David Kaiser and Lovisa Stannow attempt to explain this very finding:

> In our experience, many people do not take sexual abuse committed by women as seriously as abuse committed by men. That includes many corrections officers. We have often heard staff members in women's facilities refer dismissively to "cat fights" among the inmates and to the tendency of female inmates to replicate "family structures" inside prison. (In one such structure, for example, a woman assumes the role of "protective husband" in return for sexual favors.) But if such family structures involve sexual abuse, then this is a serious human rights issue. Rape by women is just as much of a violation as rape by men, and corrections authorities must start treating it accordingly.[9]

Fluctuating definitions of rape are common, for example, many women who are raped by their husbands or intimate partners rarely label these actions as rape; rather, they understand these events as part of their wifely duty. Perhaps, as Kaiser and Stannow suggest, rape among female inmates is understood by the victims as rape but labeled by the perpetrators as transactions: sex for protection. This concept of women trading sex for something, usually economic gain, but also protection, is not new. In our research on battered women and men who batter, we interviewed women who accepted abuse from their husbands and boyfriends in exchange for the protection they provided from the abuse they would otherwise experience in the streets. Candy is one of more than fifty women we interviewed who were living with violence, and though she is not incarcerated, her story illustrates the dilemma that many women face, both in the "free world" and in slightly different ways in prison: They fear harassment and violence in the public sphere—sexual harassment at work, men cat-calling them on the streets, men trying to pick them up in bars—and in some cases they accept oppression and abuse in the private sphere in order to avoid it in public. Candy explained,

> When things were good, they were so good. Like I said, I was always secure with him. *He might try to hit me and he might try to kill me, but nobody else was going to do it.* Nobody else was going to talk bad to me or hurt me or talk bad about me. That just wasn't going to happen. I was secure in that sense with him. He was going to protect me from everybody else.

In prison, perhaps the women who are serving as protectors "in exchange" for sex define this behavior as consensual, whereas the victims in these situations may not. Rape of any kind is a violation of one's human rights. It must be addressed appropriately, but in order to address it, we must be able to identify it when it occurs and name it.

A common theme throughout this book is that GBV is rooted in patriarchy, and as a result women's bodies are far more likely to be raped. As noted feminist and legal scholar Catharine MacKinnon argues, *rape is the condition that defines women as women.* That said, a more complex analysis of patriarchal ideologies focuses on the elevation and preferencing of normative masculine qualities over those that are normatively feminine. In short, women are raped because they are defined, by men and by our culture, as less valuable. And rape is among the most common tools men employ to remind women of their status as lesser beings. Thus, the rape of women in prison is not really that different from women's experiences in all other parts of life, not only in the institutions we interrogate here, but in their homes, at work, in the streets, and on dates. Prison is just one more place where women's bodies are sexually abused as a demonstration of power.

Why do so many incarcerated men report being raped? For many of the same reasons that ten thousand men each year who are serving in the military report being raped: because rape is about power. Rape is also a tool for enforcing norms and expectations for behavior. Though not always, often when men rape men, it is because the men being raped exhibit feminine qualities, which if they are devalued in women are held in disdain when they are exhibited by men. It is not surprising, then, that nonheterosexual inmates report the highest rate of rape. Just as in the "free world," gay men or men who have effeminate qualities face significantly higher rates of rape than heterosexual men. According to the Centers for Disease Control (CDC) 40 percent of gay men indicate that they have been sexually assaulted, compared to one in thirty-three heterosexual men.[10]

Prison is an environment based entirely on power. Men in prison rape other men in order to demonstrate power and dominance. Those with the power, especially the guards, set the rules and control access to privileges and even to basic human rights. Rape is just one tool used to control another person's behavior. Guards rape inmates just as they withhold privileges, such as access to a phone call, or writing up inmates for minor infractions. These are both forms of discipline and ways to reinforce power. Inmates use rape as a tool, along with fighting, to establish one's position in the hierarchy. As a result, prison rape is generally extremely violent.

Overall, activists concerned with prison rape have been calling for efforts to address it. Until the passage of the Prison Rape Elimination Act, prison officials denied the existence of rape in prison, and the studies done by the Bureau of Justice Statistics finally provided the data that can be used to identify that the problem is real. The next step, of course, is to identify the factors that lead to prison rape and then propose strategies for reducing it. We do believe that acknowledging that sexual contact is taking place among inmates and between guards and inmates is a good first step in eliminating prison rape, but much more will need to be done.

## RAPE IN JUVENILE DETENTION CENTERS

On any given day there are more than fifty-four thousand individuals under the age of eighteen incarcerated in juvenile detention facilities, and several thousand more, having been tried and convicted as adults, are serving time in adult prisons. In fact, the United States is the only country in the world that allows for juveniles to be sentenced to *life without the possibility of parole*. There are more than two thousand five hundred people serving these life sentences.

As is the case in adult jails and prisons, PREA requires that data on rape in juvenile facilities also be collated annually. Data from the Bureau of Justice Statistics' most recent report on juvenile rape reveal that in the previous twelve months, 10 percent of boys and 8 percent of girls reported being raped by either another inmate or by a guard.

Because this measure is restricted to rapes that occurred in the previous 12 months, similar to rape in the military or on college campuses, the rate of boys and girls who have been raped *at any time during their incarceration will be much higher*. And, as noted, as a direct result of significant underreporting, these numbers are a gross underrepresentation of the actual percentage of boys and girls who are sexually victimized.[11] By the time they are released, we esti-

# Reported Rapes in Juvenile Detention

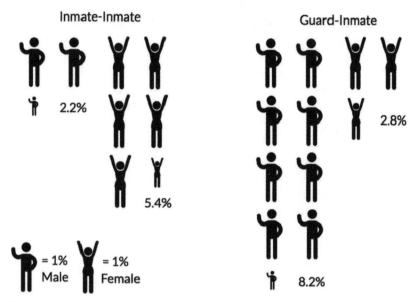

Figure 5.2. Reported rapes in juvenile detention.

mate that as many as 40–50 percent of all boys and girls who are detained in juvenile facilities will have been raped by another inmate or a guard.

Overall, boys report significantly higher rates of sexual abuse than girls, which is the opposite of what we find in the "free world," where one in five women report being raped in their lifetimes compared to one in seven boys and one in thirty-three adult men. This pattern of rape in juvenile facilities does mimic what we see in adult prisons; incarcerated men have a significantly higher rate of rape than incarcerated women. Also similar to adult facilities, girls are more likely to be sexually abused by another inmate, whereas boys are more likely to be raped by a guard.

It is especially important to note that these statistics are only based on children locked up in juvenile facilities. A disturbing number of young men are incarcerated in adult prisons, including those serving life without the possibility of parole, and their experiences are not captured in this data. Based on conversations we have had with staff at Parchman Prison in Mississippi, we can speculate confidently that the rates of rape are significantly higher for boys incarcerated alongside adult men, including convicted child molesters.

Boys report that they are more likely to be sexually abused by a guard than by another inmate. Despite the fact that women make up only 44 percent of the guard staff, an overwhelming majority, 89 percent, of boys reported that the person who sexually abused them was a woman guard. Even more disturbing, 85 percent of the boys who reported sexual victimization by a guard indicated that they had been victimized more than once in the previous year and 20 percent reported *more than eleven incidents in the previous twelve months.*

When asked about the process by which the sexual contact was initiated, boys described two themes that are common in other settings where women sexually abuse boys, particularly middle and high schools: grooming and "relationship." Among the boys who were incarcerated, they reported that grooming behavior included providing "favors" and gifts in "exchange" for sex. Boys also reported that the women guards who abused them presented the abuse as if it were a "relationship." They wrote the boys letters, sent them pictures, talked inappropriately to them about other aspects of their lives, and even contacted them when they were transferred to other facilities.

A case from Woodland Hills, a juvenile detention center in Tennessee, provides an interesting and unfortunately common illustration:

> A Tennessean investigation found suspicious indications of female staff abuse of male students at Woodland Hills [a juvenile detention center in Tennessee], including a female kitchen employee who transmitted chlamydia to a 17-year-old youth through a sexual encounter, and later lived with another male she had a relationship with at the facility.[12]

Among the many negative outcomes of this kind of sexual abuse is that it often leaves the victim believing they were in some way responsible for the abuse because they accepted gifts or because they were made to believe that the abuse was part of a consensual relationship. Sexual molestation of children by adults is a crime. Even if the child is led to believe that they "want" the relationship, sexual contact by adults with children always constitutes abuse precisely because it is based in a power relationship that muddles the ability of the child to give consent freely. In the case of the rape of juveniles by guards, consent is impossible *precisely because of the power the guard has to impact the victim's daily life,* withholding food or restricting access to privileges from recreation time to telephone calls or visits, or even locking them in solitary confinement.

The boys and girls who are confined in juvenile detention centers are there almost exclusively as the result of being convicted of committing *nonviolent* crimes, and they are subjected at very high rates to sexual abuse while they are confined. Nearly *10 percent of juveniles reported experiencing a sexual assault in the previous twelve months,*[13] which means that our young people are at significantly greater risk for rape while in a detention facility than they are in the "free world." Given all of the negative outcomes for rape victims more generally, we can be sure that unless their experiences with sexual violence are addressed, boys and girls who have been raped while incarcerated will face significant obstacles in reentering society and ultimately living healthy, productive lives. Juvenile offenders have a great enough set of challenges without the additional burdens of being a rape survivor.

## CRIMINALIZATION OF PREGNANCY

GBV in the context of incarceration takes a variety of forms. One of the more recent developments in this area is what we term the "criminalization of pregnancy." The criminalization of pregnancy is a movement in state legislatures and the criminal justice system whereby pregnant women who engage in behaviors that "harm" the fetus they are carrying are increasingly being charged with crimes. The most common of these situations involves pregnant women who use drugs or abuse alcohol being charged with child endangerment or fetal homicide if the fetus is born dead.

In her influential book, *Killing the Black Body*, Dorothy Roberts devotes an entire chapter to a discussion of the criminalization of pregnancy in which she details not only the cases but the laws that are used to prosecute and ultimately to imprison women for their behavior while pregnant. She argues, and we agree, that criminalizing pregnancy is a form of GBV.

According to Roberts, the first cases of prosecuting women for endangering their babies through their behavior while pregnant took place in the early 1990s. The focus of these prosecutions were poor Black women who give birth to "crack babies." Roberts argues persuasively that this movement began as an attempt to deal with what many in the public perceived as an "explosion of crack babies" (p. 153).[14]

These laws, called "fetal harm laws," are controversial but also compelling for those who believe that criminalizing women's behavior is a solution to drug problems. Instead, what Roberts and others note is that these laws end up forcing women to make difficult choices about their reproductive lives. Women can choose to continue with their pregnancies and risk going to prison—often for very long sentences—or they can "choose" to have an abortion, which will limit their prosecution to drug possession rather than child endangerment. We wonder what kind of a choice this is.

Additionally, the criminalization of pregnancy, because of its focus on drug laws was justified as part of the larger war on drugs, a justification much needed in a society where a special place is otherwise reserved for pregnant women. The "crack epidemic" is critical to the ushering in of an era of criminalizing behaviors during pregnancy. We agree that crack is a highly problematic drug; it is highly addictive and because it is smoked, it produces an instantaneous high. Because it is cheap, it was confined primarily to inner-city, Black communities that were already highly policed and resource poor. Crack became an easy target for President Reagan's War on Drugs. And, low-income Black women became the "poster children," providing a powerful and visual rationale for the program. Chief among the women's major offenses was delivering babies addicted to crack. Crack babies quickly became a primary concern of policy makers, not necessarily because they were addicted to crack per se, but because of the perceived burden they would place on society. A burden that could have been avoided, it was argued, had their mothers simply behaved responsibly.

The solution to the crack epidemic was clear: prevent poor Black women from becoming pregnant. And one strategy for achieving this goal, in addition to forced contraception, a subject that Roberts takes on persuasively in her book, was the criminalizing of drug use during pregnancy, with the hope that doing so would provide a deterrent effect.

Today, the focus has shifted away from crack babies and toward white women who are pregnant and addicted to opioids. Perhaps, as we argue elsewhere, because the majority of these women are white, their pregnant bodies are not being criminalized. These moms and their unborn or newborn babies are provided appropriate drug interventions, and by all accounts this approach has proved to be much more effective. But, as we know from experience, for many white women who are also poor, their pregnant, drug-addicted bodies are also often criminalized. Regardless of the drug—crack or meth or opioids—taken together, the criminalization of pregnancy and the control of women's sexuality is itself a form of GBV.

## SHACKLING DURING CHILDBIRTH

Approximately 6 percent of women entering state prison each year are pregnant at the time of their admission to a correctional facility. The majority of these pregnant women are sentenced to longer terms than the remainder of their pregnancy and thus the correctional institution must have a policy and set of practices for handling prenatal care, labor, and delivery as well as postnatal care. As with many other policies and practices inside correctional institutions, there are few federal regulations, and as a result, there is wide variance across states and even within institutions under the same department of corrections. However, the majority of research, journalistic reports, and our own interviews confirm that the policies and practices for inmate movement are based on standard protocols that require that inmates be shackled with handcuffs, leg irons, and belly chains every time they are moved in and out of the jail or prison, including into court rooms and hospitals, and funerals of their loved ones if they are lucky enough to be granted permission to attend. This practice of shackling is applied across the board to all incarcerated people moving in and out of any setting, including laboring women on their way to giving birth in the local hospital.

### Kezia: A Case Study of Being Shackled During Childbirth

As part of another project, we interviewed Kezia, a thirty-something African American woman, about a year after she had been released from prison after serving a five-year sentence for possession of crack cocaine. She was pregnant with her youngest child at the time she was first admitted to prison and she finished her pregnancy and delivered her child while incarcerated. Her story illustrates the typical experience for pregnant inmates.

Kezia was a mother at sixteen. When she entered prison in her mid-twenties, she had four children and was six months pregnant with her fifth. To save the father of her children from a life sentence imposed under the "Three Strikes You're Out," or habitual felon law, she took the "rap" for him during a drug raid on their apartment and was sent to a women's prison in Raleigh, North Carolina. As is standard practice while transporting an inmate—laboring or not—Kezia was shackled for the trip to the hospital to deliver her baby. Her handcuffs were attached to a belly chain and her feet were put into leg irons that were then shackled together, forcing her to endure the "inmate shuffle" while simultaneously tolerating contractions. Once in the hospital bed, Kezia's wrists and ankles were shackled to the rails. The only "support" Kezia was allowed in her room during labor and delivery were guards stationed with pump shot guns, to make sure she didn't attempt to escape.

The logic behind this practice is that any foray into the "free world" by inmates presents an opportunity to escape. Thus, inmates are always shackled and guarded during any and all transport and during their stay in the "free world."

The reader might recall seeing inmates transported this way in airports, on buses, or in hospitals or courtroom settings.

We understand the logic behind this practice, for at stake is the public safety of our society. An inmate's comfort must always be weighed against the likelihood that they pose an escape risk and the probability that if they were to escape, this would threaten public safety. We wonder, though, about the practice of shackling pregnant women as they labor and deliver their babies. We are certain that any specialist in obstetrics and gynecology would argue that this practice puts both the mother and the infant at risk for medical complications, especially the practice of shackling through the delivery. And any woman who has had a baby, and perhaps any person, regardless of gender, who has witnessed a birth, would conclude that this practice constitutes cruel and unusual punishment and violates even those few human rights retained by inmates. Once a shackled mother in leg irons delivers her infant into the world and the medical staff have certified that mother and baby are "doing well," the baby is taken to the nursery and as soon as she is stable, often less than twenty-four hours after giving birth, the inmate mother is returned to the same corrections facility she left just hours before. Postnatal care, whatever that entails, is now in the hands of the prison medical staff. The baby is in the temporary custody of the state, and the mother has but twenty-four hours to make arrangements for a designated relative or friend to take custody of the child from the neonatal unit. As was the case with the criminalization of pregnancy, shackling during childbirth focuses on an aspect of women's sexuality, violates their basic human rights, and is a form of GBV in the prison context.

## TRANSGENDER ISSUES IN PRISON

Before we dig down into the experiences of transgender inmates, we want to ensure that everyone is on the same page with regard to language. Gender identity refers to how individuals identify in terms of their gender. Transgender is the identity of individuals whose sex assigned at birth—based on genitalia—is different from the gender they believe themselves to be. Transgender individuals may choose a variety of ways in which to achieve congruence or gender affirmation. Some choose to adopt the traditional dress and mannerisms of the gender with which they identify; some have body modification procedures (for example, breast augmentation or mastectomy); and some have gender congruence surgery, including procedures to reconfigure their genitals. The term *cisgender* refers to individuals whose sex assigned at birth is congruent with their gender identity. Finally, terms like *queer*, *gender-queer*, *gender-nonconforming*, and *gender-fluid* refer to individuals who don't identify with either identity in the binary—male or female—but rather view their gender identity as more fluid. Individuals who identify as gender queer or gender fluid may prefer pronouns like *they*, *their*, and *them*, as opposed to *he* or *she* or *him* or *her*.

There have been transgender inmates incarcerated in US prisons since at least the early parts of the twentieth century. In our many visits to Parchman Farm—the Mississippi State Penitentiary—we have seen the booking photographs of an inmate who was incarcerated first as a man and many years later, on an unrelated conviction, as a woman. The increase in the number of individuals who identify on the trans spectrum has created many challenges for prisons, and as we demonstrate here, they are the targets of GBV in the free world, but also in prisons.

We focus our attention on transwomen because they are far more likely to experience rape and other forms of GBV overall, but specifically in prison, than are transmen. Though it is difficult to get data on the sexual assault of trans individuals, the best data we have come from *The Report of the U.S. Transgender Survey 2015* which reports that 47 percent of people who identify as transgender have been sexually assaulted, a rate that is significantly higher than either cisgender women or men.[15] Furthermore, given the gendered patterns of rape coupled with the rape of gay men perpetrated by men who identify as straight, we can speculate with confidence that transwomen will be more likely to experience sexual assault and that given the sex segregated nature of prisons their risk will be particularly high when they are incarcerated.

Based on self-report data, 21 percent of transwomen, compared to 1.2 percent of women, report being incarcerated in their lifetimes.[16] And the risks for transwomen begin when they are taken into custody and assigned to a cell. Although there are many different factors taken into consideration when an inmate is assigned to a cell, because of the completely sex-segregated nature of jails and prisons, the most important and first factor that is considered is the inmate's gender. Assignment by gender is quite simply "gender assigned at birth," or, put more plainly, the genital test. If an inmate has a penis, that inmate, regardless of how the inmate identifies or of any other physical or psychological qualities the inmate may have, will be assigned to and incarcerated in a men's housing block or prison.

There is no question that housing trans women in men's prisons is dangerous and highly problematic for a variety of reasons. According to one of the leading researchers on the rape of trans people in prison, 59 percent of trans women incarcerated in men's prisons report being raped.[17] This is an extraordinary rate of rape, more than 10 times greater than the rate for cisgender inmates in men's prisons.

Prison officials argue that there are very few options for housing trans inmates safely in a sex-segregated prison system. Though there is absolutely no evidence of this, opponents of housing inmates by their self-identified gender identity argue that doing so puts cisgender women in danger of being sexually assaulted by trans women with penises. This is not a new concern, as it is the same fear expressed in debates about bathroom use or housing trans students in residence halls on college campuses. In some of the largest prison systems, such as New York and California, some jails and prisons have managed the housing of trans inmates by designating LGBTQ blocks, where any inmate who identifies in the LGBTQ community and who feels unsafe in sex-segregated units may apply to be placed. This may be, for now, the safest and most appropriate strategy. However, there are very few jails and prisons with the space to set up these kinds of blocks, and thus they are extremely uncommon.

Another strategy that prison officials utilize to ensure the safety of trans inmates and trans women housed in men's prisons in particular is administrative segregation, more commonly known as solitary confinement. There are, of course, many problems with solitary confinement as well, including the fact that long-term solitary confinement has been identified as "cruel and unusual punishment" by the United Nations. Solitary confinement is deemed cruel and unusual primarily because it significantly restricts an inmate's human contact and because it imposes additional burdens on those in solitary confinement. The whole notion behind solitary confinement is isolation, and thus, inmates are allowed only minimal, if any, contact with other inmates. For example, at the Mississippi State Penitentiary at Parchman, inmates in solitary confinement are brought outside and put into cages—that look like large dog kennels—for their exercise time. Occasionally there may be more than one inmate in a set of these "kennels," who can holler back and forth to each other, but that is the limit of their contact with other inmates. Furthermore, because solitary confinement requires a one-to-one ratio of inmates to guards and typically a one-to-two ratio anytime an inmate is moved—to the shower, to the exercise space—understaffing can result in inmates housed in solitary confinement having fewer opportunities than inmates in the general population to take showers and get exercise time. Finally, solitary confinement does not ensure that an inmate will not be harassed or raped. According to research by the Bureau of Justice Statistics, nearly 40 percent of trans women, including many housed in solitary confinement in men's prisons, reported that they were sexually harassed or assaulted by guards.[18]

## CeCe: A Case Study of Being Transgendered in Solitary Confinement

CeCe is a transgender woman who was twenty-three years old at the time of her violent, racist attack one summer night in Minneapolis, while walking at night to get groceries with her roommates. She and her friends preferred to shop at night because under the cover of darkness they were less likely to be subjected to stares, catcalls, and harassment. While walking past a bar, CeCe saw a "handful of cigarette-smoking white people" including "47-year-old Dean Schmitz, in a white button-down and thick silver chain, and his 40-year-old ex-girlfriend Molly Flaherty, clad in black, drink in hand." Suddenly CeCe found herself the recipient of hateful and racist insults: "Look at that boy dressed as a girl, tucking his dick in!" "You niggers need to go back to Africa!"[19]

Although CeCe says she and her friends asked to be left alone and tried to move along the sidewalk past the bar, Molly Flaherty continued to hurl more insults and threw a glass tumbler that hit CeCe in the face. A fight broke out between CeCe and Molly that left both bleeding. Once CeCe realized she was OK, she ran, not realizing that Schmitz was behind her. Terribly afraid, CeCe grabbed a pair of fabric scissors from her purse that she carried regularly because she used them in her fashion classes. Though accounts differ as to whether CeCe stabbed Schmitz in self-defense or not, Schmitz's chest was impaled by the scissors. He died of his wounds.

What CeCe did not know about Schmitz is that he was a self-declared racist with a swastika tattooed on his stomach. Much of Schmitz's behavior, including the racist tattoo and his prior arrests for assault, were inadmissible in court, and CeCe was convicted by a *mostly white jury* and sentenced to forty-one months in prison. She was released after nineteen months for good behavior and because she had served nearly a year's time between her arrest and her conviction. But because the Minnesota prison system does not have an LGBTQ block, CeCe served her entire sentence in solitary confinement.

## Transgender Health Care in Prison

In addition to their safety, trans inmates face additional challenges during periods of incarceration. According to research conducted by the Prison Policy Initiative,[20] only twenty-one state prison systems have any policy on transgender health care. Although there is some variation by state and institution, in the majority of jails and prisons the most common approach to providing ongoing health care for trans inmates is the "freeze-frame" approach. The freeze-frame approach dictates that the inmate is provided the exact same medical care that they were receiving before being incarcerated. For example, if a trans woman had been receiving a certain amount of estrogen and androgen blockers before being incarcerated, she would continue to receive that same amount during the period of incarceration. There are several problems associated with the freeze-frame approach. For example, for an inmate who desires to transition but has not been receiving hormone therapy under medical care prior to being incarcerated, there will be no treatment available under the freeze-frame approach. And, because the freeze-frame approach is predicated on existing medical records, this can present an additional problem for low-income trans inmates. Because hormone therapy is very expensive, many lower-income trans people obtain hormones in the illegitimate economy and therefore do not have prescriptions and are not officially "under medical care"; thus, when they are admitted to prison they will not receive any hormone therapy. This will have disastrous effects in that it will put the trans inmate into an immediate reversal of their transition; trans women who have been growing breasts will see their breast shrink and trans men who have been growing facial hair will experience this reversing.

Additionally, the freeze-frame approach assumes that a constant level of hormone is medically appropriate. Transitioning, like many other hormone-related medical treatments, such as thyroid replacement or medication to control diabetes, typically varies based on a variety of factors, including the time between diagnosis and when treatment first begins, age, stress, diet, and so on. Similarly, the amount of hormone necessary to maintain a trans person's physical changes may vary. Lastly, the freeze-frame approach does not allow for the transition to continue. According to the World Transgender Health Standards of Care, transitioning at the desired and medically supervised pace is the most appropriate treatment protocol, and to slow or stop the transition when this is not medically recommended or the desire of the trans individual can cause emotional and psychological stress.

Of course, the freeze-frame approach is currently the "best-case scenario," and unfortunately the vast majority of jails and prisons have no trans health policy whatsoever. Absent any health policy, most jails and prisons simply discontinue hormone therapy upon the trans inmate's admission. This practice is in clear violation of the World Transgender Health Standards of Care. But even without the protocols laid out by knowledgable medical professionals, it is only common sense that immediate withdrawal from hormone therapy has significant negative physical and psychological outcomes. For a trans woman, an immediate withdraw from hormones is exactly like medically induced menopause, the type that occurs when a woman has a hysterectomy, and it is much more problematic than the slower transition that occurs during a naturally occurring menopausal process.

## CONCLUSIONS

Taken all together, the data suggest that the risk of being raped in prison or jail is significantly higher than for people who are not incarcerated. A woman living in the "free world" has a 1 percent chance of having been raped in the past year, but a woman in jail has a 3.6 percent chance of being raped and a woman in prison has nearly a 7 percent chance of being raped. Men and juveniles also have higher rates of being raped in prison than they do in the "free world."

Total institutions are designed such that those with power control nearly every aspect of the institutionalized person's life, and rape is a powerful tool in the arsenal of the guards as well as inmates who hold more power in the internal system of stratification. Prisons are not only sex segregated from the inmate perspective, they also have extreme power differentials, and they tend to be characterized as hypermasculine; even in women's prisons, it is women with more masculine identities who are more likely to hold the power. As noted, the power they hold to provide protection of others can be used to extract a price for that protection, and that price is often sexual victimization.

Juvenile facilities are perhaps the most perplexing, not only because the sexual abuse that is perpetrated is upon children, but also because of the inverted nature of an otherwise gendered crime. Though there are cases of women sexually molesting and raping boys and young men in the "free world," the majority of boys and young men who are raped are raped by men—older brothers, cousins, uncles and men in positions of power, including scout leaders, coaches, and Catholic priests. We argue that the best way to understand this gender inversion in juvenile facilities is to consider the outcome when a highly sex-segregated space is coupled with the enormous power differential between guards and inmates. The result? Women adopt the same gendered practices that men do: using sexual violence as a tool of power and control.

As we have noted throughout this chapter and the entire book, the sex-segregated nature of institutions creates an environment ripe for sexual violence which is then coupled with an internal system of justice that allows it to be perpetuated. Trans inmates and trans women in particular pose a particular threat to the sex-segregated structure of prisons because they don't fit neatly into the gender binary on which the entire prison system is built. It is not surprising, then, that they face the highest rate of rape of all inmates, especially when they are incarcerated in male prisons, but also when they are in solitary confinement; a strategy reportedly utilized to keep them safe from other inmates leaves them vulnerable to guards.

## WHAT CAN BE DONE?

Prisons are a difficult institution to reform. and because prisons are hidden from public view, only the most committed activists and family members of the incarcerated pay any attention to the sexual violence that is taking place inside the walls. Nevertheless, we believe that there are several reasons to be optimistic, and several areas of low-hanging fruit, where minimal changes would result in significantly reduced rates of violence.

### Reduce Prison Population

As we have argued in many different places, including in our most recent book, *Policing Black Bodies: How Black Lives Are Surveilled and How to Work for Change*, which was published in 2018, the first issue that needs to be addressed when it comes to prisons is that the United States is addicted to incarceration. We incarcerate a significantly higher percentage of our citizens than any other nation in the world. The Rockefeller Drug Laws, which reclassified the possession of many substances such as marijuana from misdemeanors to felonies, and imposed the "Three Strikes You're Out" law, which mandated a life sentence for anyone convicted of a third felony, resulted in hundreds of thousands of people being incarcerated, some for life, for what is essentially a drug addiction. The first step in addressing prison rape is reducing the prison population to be more in line with other postindustrial nations.

### Find Alternatives to Incarceration for Children

The vast majority of children who are incarcerated were convicted of nonviolent offenses like drug possession and breaking and entering. Some incarcerated children were convicted of behavior that adults engage in all the time, like hanging out in a park after midnight, which is illegal for children. The majority of incarcerated children were the victims of physical and sexual abuse prior to their incarceration. In fact, the crimes they are convicted of are often related to attempts to escape the abuse or to self-medicate. Many children need interventions, but few need incarceration. As the "greatest country on Earth" we can and should do better than this. By investing in intervention and diversionary programs to support children we could reduce the juvenile population significantly and thus reduce the incidence of rape these children experience while they are under our watch.

## WORK TO ELIMINATE PRISON RAPE

As specified in the Prison Rape Elimination Act, we need to continue to get accurate measures of prison rape and the factors that produce it. We need to acknowledge that both consensual and nonconsensual sex are taking place inside prisons and provide appropriate prevention and intervention mechanisms; for example, condoms should be provided to reduce the spread of HIV.

The elimination of prison rape requires us to acknowledge that freedom from sexual violence is a basic human right as defined by the United Nations Declaration of Human Rights, and the fifth principle of the Basic Principles for the Treatment of Prisoners: "Except for those limitations that are demonstrably necessitated by the fact of incarceration, all prisoners shall retain the human rights and fundamental freedoms set out in the Universal Declaration of Human Rights."[21]

### Stop Shackling Women in Labor and Delivery

We have been inside many prisons and watched inmates be moved from one location to another handcuffed and shackled, often with a dog leash attached to their belly chain just in case they get out of line. We understand the need to keep people safe and to prevent inmate escapes. That being said, the way that we treat women who are in labor and delivery is absurd. Women who are in the throes of childbirth do not pose a flight risk. They and their newborns pay a price. This practice and the criminalization of pregnancy need to be stopped immediately. Mothers who are addicted, regardless of their race or income or the substance they abuse, need treatment. We know anecdotally from communities that have an epidemic of opioid abuse and that have bravely tried rehabilitation rather than incarceration that the results are better not only for mothers but, most importantly, also for their babies.

### Provide Safe and Appropriate Housing for Trans Inmates

This may be a more difficult "fix," given all of the concerns, totally unfounded, we note, that trans people, and trans women in particular, pose a threat to cisgender women and children. Unseating transphobia will take a great deal of time and intensive training. But, ideally, jail and prison officials will come to learn that it is safe and appropriate to incarcerate people based on their gender identity, not necessarily their anatomy. In the meantime, while this social transformation is taking place, more and more trans inmates are being incarcerated, and jails and prisons need to invest in appropriately caring for their needs. If entire LGBTQ units cannot be created, as would be true in very small jails, then perhaps, at a minimum, trans and LGBTQ inmates can be housed together in "safe" cells.

At the end of the day, prison officials have an obligation to provide a safe environment for everyone that is free from the threat of sexual violence by staff as well as other inmates.

## FINAL THOUGHTS

Sadly, many in the public believe that people who have committed crimes deserve what they get. We hope that at the conclusion of this chapter, the reader will disagree. People in prison deserve to have their basic human and civil rights respected. This is especially important for the thousands of children, nonviolent offenders and often victims, themselves, of abuse, who are incarcerated every day in the United States.

# 6

# SPORTSWORLD

The young man locked eyes with Jerry Sandusky in a packed courtroom Tuesday and stared him down. He'd waited a long time for this moment. "You were the person in my life who was supposed to be a role model," he seethed angrily at the man convicted of sexually violating him and nine other boys. "I can't begin to express how this has screwed up my life. Because of you, I trust no one and I will not allow my own child out of my sight for fear of what might happen to him."[1]

When the first *Indy Star* article came out, my life changed. I put the pieces together and realized I was molested by Larry Nassar. I thought back to my appointments with him and could still feel what my 9- and 12-year-old self felt then, alone, scared and in pain. You took advantage of my innocence and trust. You were my doctor and I trusted you and you took complete advantage of that. Why? I used to ask myself that question all the time, especially when I was laying in bed crying myself to sleep. What you did to me was so twisted. You manipulated me and my entire family. How dare you.

—Jessica Thomashow[2]

On any given crisp fall Saturday afternoon or evening, in almost every geographical region of the country, millions of fans pour into the stadiums of colleges and universities for "football Saturday." And both the teams and their fans immerse themselves into these contests as if they were the Super Bowl.

On football Saturdays at Pennsylvania State University, for example, the college town of State College, Pennsylvania, balloons from its 41,757 year-round residents, to approximately 150,000 people, most of whom (over 100,000) are temporarily occupying Beaver Stadium. Folks in State College say that on football Saturdays this sleepy town grows to be the third-largest community in Pennsylvania, second only to Philadelphia and Pittsburgh.[3]

This craze is repeated at Ohio State, Michigan, Notre Dame, Alabama, Texas at Austin, and Wisconsin, as well as countless other universities, even at those colleges competing in Divisions 2 and 3. The point of this discussion is that football—more than any other college sport—reigns king among the students who attend the institutions and among faculty, alumni, and local citizens, many of whom are rabid football fans. If there are any doubters reading this, just look in on an Ole' Miss tailgating party, where fine linens and chandeliers adorn the tailgate tents along with the BBQ, bourbon, and beer, drunk out of red Solo cups, as required by state law. In football towns, support for sports is widespread and deeply systematic.

In the first edition of his book *Race, Sport and the American Dream*, one of the authors, Smith, coined the term "SportsWorld" to refer to the complexity of the institution of sports. Sports, he argues, is much more than the games that are played on fields or courts. SportsWorld encompasses the personnel—players, coaches, managers, owners, league commissioners—as well as properties, including stadiums and arenas, the television broadcast rights that carry enormous financial incentives, as well as all of the ancillary functions such as travel, hotels, tickets, and of course fandom. SportsWorld is a global institution, although most Americans focus on the somewhat narrow range of sports that we consume in the United States: baseball, football, men's basketball, hockey, and NASCAR. Globally, however, soccer (or futbol), cricket, tennis, and many other sports produce billions of dollars in revenue and are consumed by a billion fans. Our focus in this analysis will be limited to the United States context, but having an awareness of the global reach of SportsWorld is critical to understanding the power of the institution. It is impossible to estimate the total value of SportsWorld, but it is safe to say that it is in the hundreds of billions of dollars. Thus, including a discussion of this influential institution in a book such as this is critical. Finally, sports are a mirror of society. This means that all of the norms and values that are present in society also takes place in SportsWorld.

Nevertheless, the institution of sports is like no other, evolving from the "toy department of life," to a major American institution embedded in our schools and colleges and in the professional ranks as major corporate entities. From the outside, SportsWorld looks like one thing, but inside it is something else: It is, to be sure, a quasi-total institution. Yet SportsWorld embodies a space of its own quite different from the military or the Catholic Church.

We interrogate, as we do with each institution, the structures that contribute to high rates of GBV in SportsWorld, including its fraternal nature, its status as a quasi-total institution, its sex-segregated nature, the culture of hypermasculinity, and its reliance on internal systems of justice for dealing with accusations that are brought against athletes and coaches. This chapter is also different from all of the other chapters in this book because in SportsWorld, both violence against women and violence against children coexist. Investigating them both results in a somewhat longer chapter, but rather than break these discussions apart, we consider them together because the mechanisms that facilitate both are the same, namely, power and the ability to effectively cover up allegations.

## SPORTSWORLD AS A QUASI-TOTAL INSTITUTION

SportsWorld can best be described as a quasi-total institution, somewhere on the continuum between the military and fraternities. The degree to which participants in SportsWorld are subjected to its control is largely dependent upon their location inside of SportsWorld. For example, coaches and owners set the terms of the institution, and as a result, their lives are not particularly constrained by the institution, at least no more than most of us who work as supervisors or owners. For example, coaches must adhere to the schedule for play, they do not get to determine on which days or times their contests will be set, but this is no different from college professors, who can't adjust the term of the semester or the days and times that classes are offered.

Athletes, on the other hand, though this varies by age, the sport played, and the level of play (little league, college, professional), are far more constrained in their daily lives by the institution of SportsWorld. In addition to having to play contests on a given day and time and under the current conditions—including football games played when the windchill is below zero or soccer matches played in Amazonian heat and humidity—athletes, certainly those playing in college or competing as professionals, are also required to attend practice, travel with the team, and attend team meetings. Similar to the military and prisons, athletes are also required to wear only official uniforms and gear, at least when they are acting in their athletic role, practicing, traveling, and competing. Because of lucrative "shoe contracts," which in reality extend well beyond the shoe itself to encompass the entire uniform, including undergear and socks, athletes are prohibited from wearing anything personal and most notably anything that visually represents another athletic company. College and professional football and basketball teams are beholden to their sponsors; they are "Nike teams" or "Addidas Teams" or "UnderArmour Teams." Period. And, many athletes, including Michael Jordan's son, have been fined for wearing the competition's gear. Jordan's son played for an "Addidas" team but preferred to wear his father's brand: Nike.

Athletes are also subjected to curfews and bed checks, especially when traveling, and their food is highly regulated through a regimen often referred to as the "training table." Of course, athletes can choose what to eat from the options presented on the training table, but the options are selected based on the advice of nutritionists and the budget for the team. As college professors, we have had the privilege of teaching many athletes over our careers. On one occasion, Hattery, who was teaching at a Division 1 university, had a class that included a men's basketball player, a women's basketball player, a women's soccer player, and a men's cross-country runner. One day, the class discussion turned to the subject of the pregame meal. The men's basketball player revealed that their pregame meal was held at the top local steak house, and they were able to order whatever they chose from the menu. The women's basketball player described a pregame meal that was catered by the campus dining contractor. The women's soccer player noted that they didn't have a pregame meal, but the postgame meal involved the coach giving each player $5 to spend at Wendy's, the fast-food restaurant. As for the men's cross-country team, this athlete shared that postrace they were given $4 to spend on anything they liked in a 7-Eleven. We could certainly have a lengthy debate about the nutritional needs of each athlete and the class system revealed by the pre- and postgame meal options, but the point here is to note that the athlete's meal is more or less determined for them, just as it is for inmates in prison or service members living in barracks or deployed abroad.

Again, though there is variation by gender, sport played, and the division and conference in which the athlete is competing, many other aspects of a student athlete's life may be tightly controlled as well. For example, athletes are often restricted to pursuing certain majors and taking certain types of classes. Athletic department compliance officers rationalize this practice based on the fact that the National Collegiate Athletic Association, or NCAA, the governing body that oversees all of college athletics, requires athletes to maintain a minimum GPA of 2.0 in order to be eligible to compete. They believe that the only way they can keep student athletes eligible is by restricting them to "gut majors," keeping them away from any curricula that requires additional time in the lab, such as the natural sciences or statistics, in order to ensure that athletes can attend practice and travel to compete. Not to overstate the obvious, but the typical college student chooses majors, minors, and course schedules based on their interests and goals, and over many decades of college teaching, many student athletes have revealed to us privately that they were forced to pursue majors and courses that did not align with their interests and goals. As another part of academic compliance, student athletes are typically required to attend study sessions and receive tutoring, especially during their freshman year, even if they don't need it. Compliance staff make the rounds of campus classrooms to ensure that student athletes are attending their classes, a phenomenon we have witnessed thousands of times. Clearly, then, from the perspective of athletes, and particularly college and professional athletes, SportsWorld functions as a quasi-total institution.

## SEX SEGREGATION IN SPORTSWORLD

Obviously boys and girls and men and women can compete on athletic fields of play, as individuals and as members of teams. As sociologists invested in gender equity, we find nothing more delightful that watching four- and five-year-old boys and girls playing soccer or T-ball on gender-integrated teams. Soon after, and certainly not later than middle school, however, boys and girls are forced to compete, with very few exceptions, on gender-segregated teams. Perhaps not surprisingly, the rationale behind this is the idea that men and women are so fundamentally different physically that in integrated settings women would have no chance at competing successfully.

Though there is some variation, men who play college or professional football or basketball live in a world that is highly gender segregated. Male athletes spend the vast majority of their time each day almost exclusively with other men. Their teammates, coaches, athletic trainers, and virtually everyone else associated with the team is male. Though there are many men coaching high-profile women's basketball teams, for example, at both the college level and in the Women's National Basketball Associate (WNBA), there are no women coaching men's basketball at either level. Period. And, much like fraternities, the only roles that are available for women to play in SportsWorld are as sex objects: cheerleaders and groupies. In this context, in which athletes have almost no contact with women in any other capacity—not as leaders, experts, or even peers—it becomes much easier to reduce women exclusively to their function as sexual beings, and thus define their interactions with women as primarily for sexual satisfaction. Additionally, for men playing college football or basketball in a Division 1 program, women may also have additional functions: as servants. The majority of people charged with keeping college athletes academically eligible, from compliance officers to tutors, are women. At the prestigious University of North Carolina, the scandal that erupted in 2013 and launched a multi-year NCAA investigation, revealed that *women were in fact doing almost all of the academic work of football and men's basketball players, including writing all of their papers.* Women often serve in the capacity of student trainer as well, a role that has them wiping the sweat off of men's brows and squirting water in their mouths, always poised, as any good servant is, directly behind the player so as not to disturb him but to be 100 percent available when he has sweat trickling down his face or needs a drink of water. Anecdotally we know that many young women serving in the capacities of tutor or trainer are often viewed by the athletes as servants off the field as well, making requests that they wash their clothing, bring them food, and service them sexually. The environment of male athletics, then, becomes one in which women's total function is to serve men's needs, and when women refuse, there are consequences to be paid, including rape and assault.

## FRATERNAL RITUALS WITHIN SPORTSWORLD

In our discussion of fraternities, we include a lengthy description of pledging and initiation rituals. We have no source of documentation of this sort when it comes to athletic teams. Unlike national fraternities that dictate rituals at local chapters, it is simply not the case that there is a specific ritual required of all hockey players or on all soccer teams. What we do know is that initiation rituals, many of them focused on the tenets of hypermasculinity, occur on many teams, at the high school, college, and professional levels.

Many of these rituals are harmless and are rationalized as team bonding that is necessary to the success of the team. Much like the socialization processes we document in the military, fraternities, and the Catholic Church, male athletes, especially in football and basketball—and probably soccer players outside of the United States context—are socialized as members of a fraternity: a group of men whose individual interests are replaced with and superseded by the interests of the team. This is reinforced by some athletic teams that focus on "team" before "individual," (there is no "I" in "Team") and refuse to put individual player names on the backs of jerseys. New members are socialized into the sports fraternity as a measure of ensuring that they will take the side of their "brother" above all else, especially when their "brother" is facing an accusation of wrongdoing. When there are allegations of sexual assault, intimate partner violence or child sexual abuse, athletes close ranks and stand together, defending the accused even when they have been witness to the violence.

Other rituals are specifically designed to reinforce the hierarchy of SportsWorld, with seating on buses and airplanes and even on the bench dictated by status, for example. Or by requiring rookies to perform services for the more experienced players, such as carrying their bags or, in the professional ranks, buying rounds of drinks or picking up the tab for dinner, often to the tune of $10,000.

Many initiation rituals, however, go far beyond the innocuous we have described above and resemble those we described in the fraternity initiation ceremonies. Anecdotally, we have been told about a "ball wash" ritual in which upper-class football players stand naked with their legs spread widely while rookies are forced to crawl, faceup, between the players legs.

## HYPERMASCULINE CULTURE OF SPORTSWORLD

SportsWorld is among the most hypermasculine of all mainstream institutions in the United States, and certainly as hypermasculine as any of the other institutions we are analyzing in this book. That said, it is important to distinguish among various sports inside of SportsWorld. In our extensive research on gender-based violence (GBV) in SportsWorld,[4] the overwhelming majority of rape and intimate partner violence is perpetrated by men who play the most hypermasculinized games: football, men's basketball, hockey, and boxing. Thus, unless otherwise warranted, our discussion is focused on these five sports.

SportsWorld combines some of the elements we see in fraternity culture and in the military together in ways that makes it not only unique, but a culture that encourages GBV. Similar to fraternities, there is a strong culture in SportsWorld that values and rewards alcohol and drug consumption and hypersexuality. Many athletes' careers are harmed by drug and alcohol addiction, and although some avoid alcohol and drugs as part of a healthy lifestyle they believe contributes to a competitive advantage, many, as with fraternity brothers, drink excessively, even openly when they are minors. It is not surprising, then, that many of the sexual assaults that athletes perpetrate take place after a night of drinking in the local college town bar or in the VIP section of the hottest clubs. Hypersexuality is another mainstay of the hypermasculine culture evident in both fraternities and in SportsWorld. Athletes seek to have as much sex as possible with as many different women as possible. And, this focus on hypersexuality is not hidden from view. Hall-of-fame basketball players Magic Johnson (who contracted HIV in the early 1990s) and Wilt Chamberlain both boasted of having sex with *thousands* of women.

College and professional sports provide a source of images of strength and power. For example, when LeBron James dunks over his competitors and runs down the court pumping his chest or Cam Newtown mimics Superman after he throws a touchdown pass, these images become part of highlight reels that are broadcast to hundreds of millions of viewers, consumed by millions of young men. All of these images transmit the ideology that real men, masculine men, are powerful, strong, dominating, and rich. Consider the advertisements that run, especially during sporting events. The ad time is filled with ads for trucks "built Ford tough" and "home makeovers" that feature cases of Bud Light. The Marines are looking for "the few, the proud." Either central to the ads or in the background there are always beautiful women who admire the men for their strength, success, and beer-guzzling ability.

## Racial Differences in Masculinity: The Cool Pose

Unique to our discussion of SportsWorld is an analysis of racial differences as they relate to masculinity but also to rates of GBV. SportsWorld is unique when compared to the other institutions we have analyzed because of the overrepresentation of Black men involved as players—though not as coaches or managers or owners—but also because of the disproportionate percentage of cases of GBV that are perpetrated by Black male athletes.

SportsWorld is unique racially both in terms of who plays football and men's basketball—most of the other mainstream sports, and thus the vast majority of professional athletes, we point out, are disproportionately white—but also in terms of who is accused of perpetrating GBV. In order to understand the nuances of this racial difference, it is important to understand the uniqueness of the construction of Black masculinity.

Majors and Bilson provide us with the framework of the "cool pose" in order to analyze Black masculinity. According to their research, cool pose is an attempt to make Black men more visible. Cool pose is a way to counteract the requirements in the dominant construction of masculinity that many Black men will never achieve, such as high-paying jobs, owning their own home, and driving a luxury car, and replace them with other qualities that describe a different type of masculinity, one that more Black men are able to achieve.

Cool pose is a ritualized form of masculinity that entails behaviors, scripts, physical posturing, impression management, and carefully crafted performances that deliver a single, critical message: pride, strength, and control. It eases the worry and pain of blocked opportunities. Being cool is an ego booster for black men comparable to the kind white men more easily find through attending good schools, landing prestigious jobs, and bringing home decent wages.[5]

Majors and Bilson conclude that Black men construct their masculinity behind masks, worn to survive not only their second-class status but also their environment, and as a result of striving for the cool pose, they make choices that leave them, as a group, with the lowest high school graduation rates, the highest rates of unemployment and incarceration, and very few opportunities to access the American Dream, except in an institution that values the cool pose: SportsWorld.

## A PERVASIVE CULTURE FROM THE TOP DOWN

Sports teams, especially high-profile sports, including football and men's basketball, at both the college (NCAA) level and the professional level, are extremely tightly controlled. Not only is SportsWorld a quasi-total institution for the athletes, and to a lesser extent the coaches, SportsWorld functions in total isolation from the public view. High-profile sports teams and their athletes, even at public colleges and universities, are highly protected from scrutiny in virtually every way, but especially when it comes to athlete misbehavior.

All of this begins at the top. To the surprise of many people not steeped in the intricacies of the world of higher education, in most if not all Division 1 NCAA athletic departments, the head football coach, and often the head men's basketball coach as well, report directly to the president of the university, not to the athletic director, whose function is primarily to oversee all of the other sports offered at the university. In nearly every Division 1 college football and men's basketball program the head coaches earn substantially more than the college president, often five or six times more. In fact, in many states, the head football coach at the flagship university—for example, Nick Saban at the University of Alabama or Dabo Swinney at Clemson—are the *highest paid public employees in the state*, earning more than senators, governors, hospital administrators, and the like. This simple fact alone is critical in understanding the incredible power the head coach has not only to create a culture in his locker room, but to protect this culture and this locker room from the scrutiny of the leader of the institution, the college president. This ability to keep virtually every aspect of their organization private and away from public scrutiny plays a significant role in a coach's ability to create, maintain, and tolerate a culture that perpetuates violence against women. When we look closely at certain football teams, and to a lesser degree men's basketball programs, specifically at the Division 1 level in the NCAA, we see patterns that emerge.

Though we could include examples from many universities, from the University of Montana, about which Jon Krakauer wrote in *Missoula*, to Notre Dame to Florida State University, the most recent example comes from Baylor University.

## BAYLOR UNIVERSITY

Just when we thought we would never see a sexual abuse scandal that would rival that involving the football team and the entire community of Missoula, Montana, which in 2010 was dubbed "the rape capital," in 2015 news began to trickle out that something was amiss at Baylor University in Waco, Texas. By 2016, the scandal broke wide open, sports outlets began investigating, and ultimately those at the top would lose their jobs. Though there is disagreement about the numbers, no one denies that the Baylor football team was involved in sexual and intimate partner violence at levels not seen or at least not reported before and that the football program was totally out of control. John Clune, a Colorado lawyer who specializes in cases of campus assault and has settled several cases on behalf of victims at Baylor, argues that between 2011 and 2014, thirty-one Baylor football players raped fifty-two victims. Baylor officials argue that this is an overestimate, but their numbers, though smaller, are nonetheless disturbing. These same officials claim that there were seventeen rapes perpetrated by nineteen football players, including four gang rapes, in the same three-year period. Regardless, what is clear is that Baylor has a rape problem, and it runs deeper than a few bad apples in the football barrel. As of the summer of 2018, two Baylor football players have been convicted of sexual assault and are incarcerated, several others have been indicted, and based on the findings of an independent investigation conducted by the consulting firm Pepper Hamilton, Baylor fired head football coach, Art Briles, university president Ken Starr, and accepted the resignation of athletic director Ian McCaw. According to the report by Pepper Hamilton, the mishandling of sexual assault went all the way to the top tier of the university, much as it did at Penn State University during the decades that Jerry Sandusky molested at least fifty young men. The report documents that the sex abuse scandal at Baylor was covered up and mishandled in all of the ways that we outline in the book, including a failure to hold perpetrators accountable, football staff suppressing reporting by victims, and the athletic department operating an internal system of justice.[6]

The choices made by football staff and athletics leadership, in some instances, posed a risk to campus safety and the integrity of the university. In certain instances, including reports of a sexual assault by multiple football players, athletics and football personnel affirmatively chose not to report sexual violence and dating violence to an appropriate administrator outside of athletics. In those instances, football coaches or staff met directly with a complainant and/or a parent of a complainant and did not report the misconduct. As a result, no action was taken to support complainants, fairly and impartially evaluate the conduct under Title IX, address identified cultural concerns within the football program, or protect campus safety once aware of a potential pattern of sexual violence by multiple football players. Football staff conducted their own untrained internal inquiries, outside of policy, which improperly discredited complainants and denied them the right to a fair, impartial, and informed investigation; interim measures; or processes promised under university policy.

To complicate matters, Baylor is a university not only founded on Christian principles, but one that requires adherence to Baptist principles by faculty, staff, and students. Revised as of May 15, 2015, Baylor's policy on sexual conduct—not sexual assault—reads: "Baylor will be guided by the biblical understanding that human sexuality is a gift from God and that physical sexual intimacy is to be expressed in the context of *marital fidelity*. Thus, it is expected that Baylor students, faculty and staff will engage in behaviors consistent with this understanding of human sexuality."

In other words, not only does sexual assault violate the student code of conduct, but sexual behavior outside the context of marriage is a clear violation of Baylor's sexual misconduct policy. It's quite clear, then, that the Baylor University football program failed to hold its athletes to the same standard of student conduct that guides the behavior of all other Baylor students. If the women victimized by football players were unsuccessful in making rape allegations stick, why didn't the university at least pursue the sexual contact as a violation of the student conduct policy? Perhaps because they threatened victims that if they pursued this route it would put them in violation of the student code of conduct and they, the victims, would be subjected to university disciplinary action. Sounds just like the threats of retaliation many victims of military sexual violence report: they, not the perpetrator, will be charged with adultery if they report the rape.

# VIOLENCE AGAINST WOMEN IN SPORTSWORLD

SportsWorld is unique in our discussion of GBV for two reasons: first because it is the only institution we're analyzing in this book where both sexual assault and intimate partner violence are prevalent, and second because it is the only institution in which both GBV and child sexual abuse take place on a systematic basis.

## Sexual Assault in SportsWorld

As we have argued throughout this book, rape is a vastly underreported crime. We have no reason to believe that cases involving athletes are any more likely to be reported. Additionally, systematic and extensive systems of cover-up result in few players ever being formally arrested or charged, and thus the allegations never make it into the public record or the media where we would have access to them. That said, journalists such as Jeff Benedict and others have compiled lists of cases that *do* make it into the news, and what we know from examining these lists is that if these cases represent 5 or 10 percent reporting rates, which is what we would expect, then there are hundreds of athletes involved in sexual assault every year. Moreover, as a direct result of the culture of SportsWorld, cases tend to cluster on certain campuses, like Baylor.

In the summer of 2015, Paula Lavigne, an investigative journalist working for ESPN's program *Outside the Lines* published the findings of her yearlong examination of rape by college athletes.[7] Lavigne's report was prompted by the case of Jameis Winston at Florida State University. Winston's case was characterized by many of the same issues that came to light a few years later at Baylor, but what contributed to the high level of publicity in Winston's case was the fact that the police investigation was intentionally stalled by the Florida State athletic department until *after* Winston won the coveted Heisman Trophy and led his team to a National Championship. Winston and his accuser later settled the case out of court. Lavigne's investigation sought to determine if the case of Jameis Winston was terribly unique or part of a larger pattern, especially in "college towns."

Lavigne's investigation uncovered a series of systematic practices that impacted the impartial investigation of high-profile athletes accused of a crime, and of sexual assault and intimate partner violence in particular. She argues that these practices explain the statistically significant finding that athletes are far less likely than college age-men in the same communities to be arrested and charged when they are accused. For example, in Tallahassee, Florida, the college town that embraces Florida State University, 70 percent of athletes accused of a crime had those charges dropped or were never charged at all, compared to 50 percent of college men at Florida State University who are not athletes. She identified several deeply disturbing patterns that, in any other situation, would be examples of prosecutable obstruction of justice.

In many college towns, athletic department officials inserted themselves into investigations often and in many different ways. Some tried to control when and where police talked with athletes; others insisted on being present during player interviews, alerted defense attorneys, and conducted their own investigations before contacting police. In one case, they even handled potential crime-scene evidence. Some police officials were torn about proper procedure—unsure when to seek a coach's or athletic director's assistance when investigating crimes.

Some athletic programs have, in effect, a team lawyer who showed up at a crime scene or jail or police department—sometimes even before an athlete requested legal counsel. The lawyers, sometimes called by athletic department officials, were often successful in giving athletes an edge in evading prosecution—from minor offenses to major crimes.

In communities like Tallahassee, Florida, but also Madison, Wisconsin, the high profiles of both the athletic programs and the athletes had a chilling effect on whether cases were even brought to police and how they were investigated. Numerous cases never resulted in charges because accusers and witnesses were afraid to detail wrongdoing, feared harassment from fans and the media, or were pressured to drop charges in the interest of the sports programs.

Systematic special treatment like this does not take place in a bubble, but rather is part of a deeply embedded culture that is designed to protect athletes from any external scrutiny.

## Intimate Partner Violence in SportsWorld

There is much debate about the rates of violence against women that is perpetrated by athletes. Those who argue that athletes don't perpetrate any more violence against women than non-athletes point out that it is simply that we are more aware of these cases because of athletes' celebrity status and the newsworthiness of their bad behaviors. Others note that it is difficult to measure rates of GBV perpetrated by athletes as compared to non-athlete men because crime statistics are not recorded in such a way as to identify athlete status—or any other profession, for that matter. Finally, others note that the relationship between high rates of GBV reportedly perpetrated by athletes may be a spurious one, that in fact the real relationship is one of age, that men in their teens, twenties, and early thirties are the most likely to perpetrate GBV, which just happens to be the age range that most college and professional athletes fall into.

In 2014, amid the Ray Rice case that rocked the NFL, Benjamin Morris, a statistician for the online publication *FiveThirtyEight*, conducted a sophisticated statistical analysis that involved extrapolating from the data reported in the Bureau of Justice Statistics annual crime report combined with a database compiled by *USA Today* that included all arrests of NFL players beginning in 2000.[8] Morris's sophisticated analysis revealed that although NFL arrest rates for intimate partner violence were lower than the average for men of the same age group, nevertheless, 55 percent of the arrests of NFL players were for intimate partner violence and an additional 38 percent of arrests were for sexual violence. Morris further compared the data by social class, one of the key predictors for perpetrating and experiencing intimate partner violence. In the general population, only 20 percent of women in the upper-income bracket report an incident of intimate partner violence, yet among NFL players, who are members of the upper class, 55 percent of their arrests are for intimate partner violence. In other words, given their income level, it appears that NLF players are being arrested at twice the rate of men in their same age and social class for intimate partner violence.

Additionally, based on research we conducted for another project, we found that when the police were called, high-profile athletes, especially those playing football, basketball, and baseball were *less likely to be arrested* than less well-known athletes playing the same sports. Extending Morris's analysis, then, assuming that *arrest rates* for NFL players are actually lower than the *arrest rates* for non-athletes, *the actual incident rates are significantly higher than the arrests reflect*. For us, the take-away message that Morris persuasively demonstrates is that at least in the NFL, there is a significant problem with GBV, both intimate partner violence and sexual assault.

Violence against women has always existed and been tolerated, if not encouraged, in SportsWorld, but it has not always been identified for what it is. Violent athletes are often described as having domestic problems. Often the focus in the media is on the outcome they experience—arrest, jail time, even suicide—and less on naming the events for what they really are: violence against women. Even rarer is sports analysts' examination of the patterns in these cases. Instead, they tend to treat each incident as isolated and unique, which denies and often prevents the consumer of this news from identifying the patterns as well. What this ultimately means is that an opportunity to address violence against women in SportsWorld is lost each and every time another athlete perpetrates violence against a woman.

## WHY VIOLENCE IS SO PREVALENT IN SPORTSWORLD

Images that transmit beliefs about masculinity and the rigid construction of gender roles are extremely narrow, and as a result a limited set of traits have come to signify manhood in contemporary America, including physical strength, aggression, financial success, and sexual prowess. In our own research with men who batter and as observers of cases of athletes who perpetrate intimate partner violence that receive media attention, with remarkable consistency, the key issues that both the batterers and the battered women identified as the "triggers" to violence are threats to this narrow construction of masculinity.

In 2012, Jovan Belcher, a former NFL player with the Kansas City Chiefs, killed his fiancé, Kassandra Perkins, in front of their three-month old daughter and Belcher's mother, who was there helping to care for the newborn. He then turned the gun on himself and committed suicide in front of his coach, Romeo Crennel, in the parking lot of the Kansas City Chiefs' Arrowhead Stadium. The "trigger" that led to this tragedy was Belcher's concern that his fiancé was flirting with another man. Jealousy is one of the most common triggers for intimate partner violence and, along with the threat of ending the relationship, is the most common precursor to intimate partner violence. After his death, an examination of Belcher's brain revealed that he also suffered from chronic traumatic encephalopathy (CTE), which may have left him predisposed to violence. That being said, when we look at the high rates of sexual and intimate partner violence among college and professional football players, it is clear that CTE is not the only factor predisposing them to engage in violence against wives and girlfriends.

Additionally hypermasculine behaviors may be difficult to compartmentalize. So, for example, an athlete who is trained and rewarded to win at all costs, to "take out" an opponent, to deliver an injuring blow, may not be able to leave these conditioned responses on the field of play. Just as he responds to conflict on the field through violence, he may respond to conflict or threats in his personal life using the same skill set. If we do not build other toolkits for conflict resolution in athletes, we shouldn't be surprised when their violence erupts into their personal lives. In fact, we should be surprised when it doesn't.

Increasingly, as Harry Edwards, renowned sport sociologist and scholar has pointed out to us, athletes, especially in football and basketball, come into college and professional sports with gang experience and affiliations or having grown up witnessing violence. This has been offered as an explanation for the high rates of gun violations in professional sports, including homicides committed by athletes. In 2013, then twenty-three-year-old New England Patriot tight end Aaron Hernandez murdered Odin Lloyd. Sadly, Hernandez was sentenced to life in prison and died in his cell in 2016. The cause, suicide or homicide, remains questionable. Like Jevon Belcher, research on Hernandez's brain revealed that he, too, suffered from CTE.

Only in SportsWorld can men who have committed so much crime continue to work, and demand salaries that often reach into the tens of millions of dollars. We can think of few other occupations in which a convicted felon, like Michael Vick or Mike Tyson, or someone convicted of vehicular manslaughter (Donte Stallworth) or someone with multiple drug and alcohol violations, like Adam "Pacman" Jones and Chris Henry, would be allowed to continue with their employment and continue to demand top salaries for doing so. It's quite clear that if a team believes that the contributions by the player on the field are critical or even important to the team's success, then as long as he's not currently in jail he will be allowed to participate. This, we argue, contributes to the overall context in which athletes engage in violence against women—because it is tolerated and because there are no consequences when they do.

## THE ROLE RACE PLAYS

One of the critiques of discussions like ours, as well as the media portrayals of athletes who engage in violence against women, is that the conversation is always focused on Black men. We will not simply dismiss that critique. We are, like other scholars and activists of racial equality, deeply concerned about the images of Black men that populate our media. In the spring of 2015, when the riots raged in Baltimore, there was much critique of politicians and journalists who referred to the rioters as "thugs." Even a cursory review of the images of Black men on TV, in the movies, and in social media reveals quickly that Black men are relegated to just a few roles: as athletes, entertainers, and criminals. We were very concerned in the wake of the now infamous security footage that showed Ray Rice punching his then fiancée, Janay Palmer, unconscious, as more and more media attention focused on athletes who perpetrated violence against women, that all of the images we saw were of Black men.

Therefore, we address the issue with transparency and logic. First and foremost, as concerned as we are about the impact that these images may have on shaping Americans', especially White Americans', attitudes toward race, we are more deeply disturbed by the possibility of *not* showing these images, which would ultimately *erase* the experiences of women who are experiencing tremendous violence at the hands of men. This need to expose GBV supersedes our concerns about the images themselves. However, we implore the media, rather than simply bombarding us with the faces of Black men, one after the other, to engage in thoughtful analysis that helps us to understand why so many of the images we see are of Black men. That need for complex analysis was one of the most important reasons we wrote this book. We offer four explanations, based on the evidence.

First, it's simply a numbers game. If we limit our discussion for the moment to college and professional football, which is reasonable given that the vast majority of the cases involve football players, Black players are significantly over-represented in both leagues (see figure 6.1). Therefore, we would expect that the majority of the cases in the NFL and at least half of the cases coming from college athletics would involve Black men.

Second, when we dig deeper into the cases that are reported in the media, versus those we cataloged by researching newspaper reports, in fact, there are plenty of white male athletes who are engaging in GBV as well, raping women and abusing their partners, including Josh Brown, kicker for the New York Giants, who was suspended in September 2017 after both images and a journal documenting his abuse surfaced. As we have documented in our other work, however, Black players are disproportionately identified as "star" players, and thus their behavior garners more national attention than that of the bench-warmer. As such, when the media is selecting which stories to feature and tell,

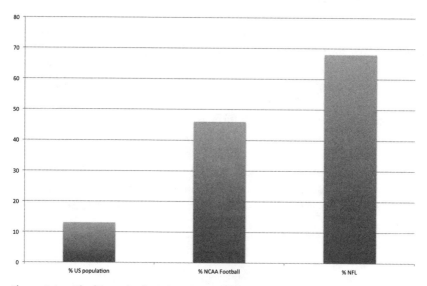

**Figure 6.1. Black men in the US, NCAA, and NFL.**

they are more likely to select stories associated with athletes that have national name recognition—those who are "stars"—than those who are well-known only locally. This practice not only results in a disproportionate number of Black faces in the news stories about violence against women but also demonstrates the critical role that local media outlets can play in painting a more accurate picture of athletes engaged in GBV.

Third, of equal importance is the white privilege that cloaks white athletes who perpetrate sexual and intimate partner violence. As we discuss extensively in our book *Policing Black Bodies: How Black Lives Are Surveilled and How to Work for Change*, at every point in the criminal justice system, Black defendants are treated more harshly than white defendants, from racial profiling to sentencing to successful reentry. And, SportsWorld is no different. When Black athletes are accused of violence, especially sexual violence, this reinforces the deeply rooted stereotypes about Black men as sexual predators, and they are sometimes treated more harshly by the criminal justice system, the media, and the organizations for which they play.

Fourth, there may be some intricacies of race that matter. For example, as Harry Edwards suggests, Black male athletes may be disproportionately more likely to have grown up in situations in which they were exposed to violence, either in their homes or in their communities. And, the research is absolutely clear that exposure to violence increases the risk that one will grow up to perpetrate violence. Boys raised in homes where they witness intimate partner violence, typically perpetrated by their father or stepfather or mother's boyfriend against their mother, are *three times more likely* to engage in intimate partner violence against their own intimate partners. In addition, exposure to violence in one's community, for example, living in a neighborhood with high levels of gang violence, also predisposes men to engage in violence as they grow up. All of this may be compounded by the "cool pose" masculinity that many Black men feel constrained by, which often leads them to express and establish their masculinity through violence. Therefore, if we are honest about the reasons why more Black male athletes are accused of violence against women, we must interrogate the role that race plays, not only in their overrepresentation in SportsWorld but in their overexposure to violence. Quite simply, ignoring race or dismissing a discussion of it because it could be perceived as racist does more harm than good.

## SYSTEMATIC AND SYSTEMIC COVER-UPS WITHIN SPORTSWORLD

SportsWorld is an institution that is deeply embedded in every social institution, including education, religion, and municipal governments—which approve stadium building projects—as well as with local law enforcement. No other entity has these interconnections so deeply embedded in college towns that, among other things, protect athletes who run afoul of the law.

### Internal Systems of Justice

SportsWorld is yet one more example of an institution that would prefer to handle all kinds of scandals and allegations of misbehavior internally. And, we would argue that from their vantage point, and for many decades, they have been very successful at doing so. What is unique about SportsWorld, compared to the other institutions we analyze in this book, is that SportsWorld operates on college campuses as private entities, able to take advantage of the power they have in both sectors, to uniquely police, or not, the misbehavior of their athletes.

Professional athletes are employees in private organizations. As such, their employers, the owners, managers, and coaches, handle problems internally, and if all goes well, outside of the purview of the criminal justice system. Similar to any private organization, there are disciplinary actions that can be taken when an employee is accused or convicted of a crime, and we see this play out in dozens of cases each year in the NFL and the NBA. For example, in cases of drug or alcohol violations, driving while intoxicated, and especially in cases of violence against women, if the organization comes to the conclusion that the player is responsible for the behavior, if they admit to it, or if they are charged or (rarely) convicted, typically players are sanctioned through suspension and fines.

Beginning in the late 1990s, with player misbehavior in the news nearly every day, both the NFL and the NBA commissioners enacted explicit expectations for player conduct. And, it is under these player conduct policies that sanctions can be enacted by the league itself. For example, a football player who violates the substance abuse policy faces an automatic two-game suspension for the first DUI conviction and an eight-game suspension for the second offense. And players who have are judged to be "repeat" offenders can be permanently banned from the league.

## Special Treatment for Student Athletes

Student athletes, according to the standards of the college or university they attend, are subjected to the same code of student conduct as every other student. And, just as we articulated in our discussion of fraternities, in this context student athletes are no more or less likely to be held accountable for their crimes than are other men enrolled as students. Yet, as the case of Baylor University and the research of Paula Lavigne demonstrate clearly, college athletic departments are in the business of ensuring that athlete misbehavior and even violent crime is handled internally to the athletic program and that athletes accused of crimes never see the inside of a college conduct hearing room, let alone an interrogation room at the local police department. In our own experience on college campuses, we know anecdotally, and this is confirmed by Lavigne's report, that student athletes who come from impoverished backgrounds and are prohibited by NCAA rules from either working or accepting gifts, show up at campus police departments with the highest-paid lawyer in the college town. How can these things happen on a college campus? For all intents and purposes, the athletic team functions as a total institution, and one headed by the most powerful, most highly paid leader on campus, and perhaps in the entire state. Coaches restrict athlete's accessibility every day by not allowing them to enroll in classes that meet after a certain hour in the afternoon so that they can attend practice. They also strong-arm the university into excusing athletes from class so that they can travel to compete in games, often leaving days ahead of the actual competition. In this context, it's not hard to understand that when an athlete is accused of a crime of any kind, but especially violence against women, the coach takes total control of the situation, the athlete complies with the coach, and there is not much anyone else in the university can do to stop the intervention and special protection.

## Special Treatment for Professional Athletes

If college athletes receive special treatment, then it is not hard to imagine what happens when high-profile professional athletes find themselves on the wrong side of the law. High-profile athletes are paid tens of millions of dollars per year and are worth vastly more than that to the teams for which they compete, as they generate hundreds of millions of dollars per year in ticket and merchandise sales, and most notably from lucrative television contracts.

Though there are a number of high-profile cases in which athletes were charged with serious violent crimes, including Kobe Bryant and O. J. Simpson, much of the controversy that has fueled debate about GBV in SportsWorld was ignited by the Ray Rice case, which rose to national attention for several reasons, including Rice's celebrity, the viral nature of the video in which the whole world could see the violence, and also because of the way in which it was handled by NFL commissioner Roger Goodell.

The case of Ray Rice illustrates several important points, including how athletes receive special treatment within the criminal justice system and the problems with internal systems of justice. First, upon his arrest, Rice was allowed to enter a pretrial intervention program, something only 1 percent of those facing similar charges are allowed to do. Second, Roger Goodell—like many coaches, athletic directors, and owners throughout SportsWorld—did not take Ray Rice's assault on his then fiancée Janay Palmer seriously. Initially Goodell handed down only a two-game suspension to Rice, which is the same sentence mandated for a DUI conviction. After the video of Rice punching Palmer in the face surfaced and went "viral" on social media, both Rice and Goodell became the subject of journalists, bloggers, and victim's rights activists, who were understandably disturbed by both Rice's behavior and, even more so, by the minimal punishment that Goodell imposed. After all, is intimate partner violence really equivalent to a first DUI offense? Under severe pressure from the public, Goodell admitted that he "didn't get it right" and responded by increasing the league's domestic violence policy to include a mandatory six-game suspension without pay for the first offense and a lifetime ban for a second offense. Goodell then proceeded to suspend Rice for life. Rice appealed his lifetime ban based on a sort of "grandfather clause," arguing that his original infraction could only be punished under the suspension guidelines in place at the time, and that it was inappropriate for him to be suspended under new rules that came into place after his case was resolved. Rice was successful in his appeal, and he was reinstated into the NFL.

Many scholars and activists were initially enthusiastic about Goodell's apparent interest and attention to "getting it right" when it comes to the high rates of violence against women that his players perpetrate. In order to "get it right," he hired several consultants, all women, with expertise in intimate partner violence. Yet, the enthusiasm soon waned, not only in response to the final resolution of Ray Rice's case, but also in the subsequent weeks and months and years when Goodell was faced with new cases of intimate partner violence perpetrated by other NFL players. One of the most egregious cases involved Greg Hardy, who was *convicted* of intimate partner violence in Charlotte, North Carolina, in the summer of 2014. Goodell sentenced Hardy after he revised the intimate partner violence policy in the wake of the Ray Rice debacle, and

Hardy received a ten-game suspension. During June 2015, Hardy appealed his suspension and Goodell reduced it by 60 percent from ten games to four. Many critics referred to this as the "60 percent discount." A year later, in the summer of 2016, Goodell was faced with yet another troubling case, that of New York Giants kicker, Josh Brown. After being arrested for domestic violence in 2015, the Giants suspended Brown for one game. One. The game they selected for his suspension was a preseason exhibition game that was played in London. By October 2016, the NFL was faced with renewed controversy regarding Brown's treatment after his ex-wife released a diary in which she documented dozens of instances of severe violence she faced at Brown's hands. Throughout their marriage he had been charged with twenty counts of intimate partner violence. The New York Giants coaching staff had to admit they knew about Brown's extensive history with intimate partner violence but decided to keep him on the roster anyway.

In the summer of 2018, just as we were finishing this book, one of the domestic violence experts that Roger Goodell appointed wrote a *Washington Post* opinion essay titled "I'm Done Helping the NFL Players Association Pay Lip Service to Domestic Violence Prevention," saying, "I simply cannot continue to be part of a body that exists in name only."[9] We can only interpret these cases, and Deborah Epstein's resignation, as further evidence that Goodell and the NFL have no real interest in addressing the acts of GBV perpetrated by their players. Their only interest, fleeting as it was, seems to have been to appease fans and would-be consumers who witnessed, only briefly, and perhaps for the first time, a visual image of intimate partner violence. With the Ray Rice video safely out of the news and stored in the files of YouTube, Goodell and the NFL returned to business as usual.

Violence against women is not the only form of interpersonal violence that takes place and is covered up in SportsWorld. The cases of Jerry Sandusky at Penn State and Larry Nasser at USA gymnastics and Michigan State University rocked SportsWorld and provided new windows into child sex abuse scandals that have been going on for decades in a variety of youth sports.

## CHILD SEXUAL ABUSE

As the term implies, child sexual abuse, or CSA, involves all forms of sexual abuse of a child. Unlike sexual abuse of adults, children are legally unable to consent to sexual contact, and therefore any sexual act—consensual or not—with a child under the age of consent (which varies from state to state but is typically sixteen years of age) is considered sexual abuse. Sexual abuse may involve sexual intercourse, but is more likely to be sexual touching or molestation and for boys, forced oral sex. In addition, it's important to recognize that sexual abuse doesn't always involve body contact. Exposing a child to sexual situations or material is sexually abusive, whether or not touching is involved. Many years ago, Hattery, working as a rape crisis advocate, supported a survivor who, as a young teenage girl, was victimized by her father, who was taking sexually explicit pictures of her and selling them as part of a child pornography ring.

The sexual abuse of children is most likely to be perpetrated by an adult the child knows. Often, but not always, this adult is a family member, with the most likely perpetrator the child's stepfather or mother's boyfriend. However, as we have become increasingly aware due to stories in the news media, children are also at a reasonable risk for sexual abuse from adults who work with children, including Catholic priests, coaches, Boy Scout leaders, and other adult mentors. The least common type of sexual abuse but the one that receives the most attention is the abuse that typically accompanies abductions and murders of young boys and girls. Contrary to what many believe, it's not just girls who are at risk. Boys and girls are both targets of child sexual abuse. In fact, sexual abuse of boys may be even more underreported due to shame and the stigma associated with the myth that boys who are abused by adult men are gay. The shame of sexual abuse makes it very difficult for children to come forward. They may worry that others won't believe them, will be angry with them, or that it will split their family apart. Because of these difficulties, false accusations of sexual abuse are extremely common, so if a child makes an accusation or confides in someone it should be taken very seriously.

## Child Sex Abusers and Power

Not all child abusers are pedophiles. Many child sex abusers have no sexual attraction to the children they abuse, but rather, as with other forms of sexual abuse, including rape, the sexual abuse may be primarily motivated by the abuser seeking strategies to hold power over and control the child. As with other forms of sexual abuse, child sexual abuse may be used as a punishment, as a tool of humiliation and/or as a tool of control. Cases of child abuse in institutions like SportsWorld and the Catholic Church tend to fall into two categories: abuse perpetrated by pedophiles and abuse perpetrated by adults seeking power and control. Pedophilia is a relatively rare mental illness, but because is it so powerful, pedophiles typically have dozens if not hundreds of victims. Adults who engage in child sexual abuse as a tool of power are more common, but they also typically have a very small number of victims. In other words, with regard to child sexual abuse, a small number of men account for the vast majority of victims, especially in these institutional settings.

## Identifying and Grooming a Victim

How does a child come to find him or herself being sexually abused by an adult, in this case by a beloved coach?

In contrast to rape, which may be perpetrated with what feels like little warning to the victim, child sexual abuse generally involves a long grooming process. As Malcolm Gladwell summarizes the research on child sexual abuse, child molesters target their victims and engage in a series of grooming processes of the victim, of the victim's family, and of the community.[10] Although any child can be a victim of sexual abuse, child molesters target children who are vulnerable. Vulnerable children are ideal targets for several reasons, they are easier to manipulate, they have more to lose in reporting, and they are less likely to be believed when they do report.

## Easier to Manipulate

Child molesters choose vulnerable children because they are easier to manipulate. In two of the most well publicized cases, both of which we deal with in this book, the Penn State/Jerry Sandusky child sex abuse case and the child sexual abuse scandals in the Catholic Church, child molesters targeted children who were needy because they were poor, because their parents, most often a single mother, was unable to give them the attention they needed, or because they were unpopular at school. The attention and the gifts that the child molester offers the child he is grooming are welcomed; it fills a void. Once the child molester has earned the trust of the child, he has effectively prepared the child for the next stage of the process, grooming the actual abuse.

## Vulnerable Children Have More to Lose

Vulnerable children have more to lose. In many cases, child molesters are serving as surrogate father figures to the children they victimize. This was certainly true in the case of Jerry Sandusky, and it is true in many of the cases in the Catholic Church as well. In some cases, what the child has to lose is material—access to school tuition, a place on an athletic team, a PlayStation or some other gift that is meaningful for the child. Quite simply, once the sexual abuse begins, the molester makes it clear that if they child reports the abuse, the benefits of the relationship will stop. Many victims of child sexual abuse don't report because they are afraid of losing the status they may have gained through the relationship—being the priest's special boy or the favorite of the coach. They are afraid of losing the only male role model they have in their lives. Or, especially for poor victims, they are afraid of losing the material gifts, including a nice house to sleep over at and warm food on a table.

## Vulnerable Children Aren't Believed

Status carries power, and regardless of the situation, people with power are always more likely to be believed than people without power. Regardless of who the perpetrator is, an uncle, a stepfather, a coach or a priest, children are incredibly scared to tell anyone about the abuse. The abuser has been very clear that if the child reports, no one will believe them. In addition to this kind of direct message, children learn early on that they are less likely to be believed than adults, and children who are vulnerable are the least likely to be believed of all. This sense of not being believed is bolstered by the fact that children are afraid to make their parents feel upset, and often when they do start to disclose an incident of abuse, understandably, the parent may "freak out" and begin to cry or express other negative emotions. Afraid of hurting their parent, and not understanding that it is the behavior of the child molester that is actually hurting the parent not their own behavior, children will often limit their disclosure to the least offensive acts and downplay their experiences, telling them, "It really wasn't that bad," or even second-guessing themselves: "Maybe he didn't really mean to touch me like that, he just slipped in the shower."

## Grooming of Parents

Child molesters are incredibly deliberate in both their choice of victims and in the ways that they groom their victims, but they are also incredibly deliberate in grooming the parents, typically the mother, and the community. Child molesters groom the parents in two ways, by testing them and by making them co-conspirators in the abuse. In the case of Jerry Sandusky, he created tests for the mothers of his potential victims. In one case, after spending time with Sandusky, the child returned home and because he and Sandusky had showered, his hair was wet. When the mother questioned Sandusky about the boy's wet hair and the need for the shower in the football locker room and not at home, Sandusky apologized and never approached the boy again. This mother had "failed" Sandusky's test; she was suspicious, and thus he moved on to other victims whose parents were less so. This type of a test with a mother is part of the grooming strategy. He was preparing the way for mothers to believe him over their own child should the child make an accusation and complain about any unusual behavior.

Child molesters also groom parents by making them coconspirators, by constantly reminding them of the ways in which their child is benefitting from the relationship, of the experiences and things the child is getting as a result of the relationship, but also the ways in which the parent is also benefitting. Again, by targeting mostly single mothers who "have their hands full" the molester, because he takes the child with him for extended periods of time, is providing the mother with the time she needs to care for other children or just a few moments to relax. Again, this grooming is preparing the way so that if the child tells about what is happening to them, the mother will blame herself and/or be reminded of how much the molester is helping her out, and both of these sentiments will likely result in her downplaying an accusation a child makes and reducing the likelihood that she will make a formal complaint.

## Grooming of Communities

In 2012, in the wake of the Jerry Sandusky trial, Malcolm Gladwell wrote one of the clearest explanations of the ways in which child molesters also groom communities, and we are astounded at how often an abuser is successful at this practice. The child molester has already carefully selected his victims, he has groomed them and their parents, and now he must groom the community in the event that a child discloses the sexual abuse and on the off chance that his parents believe him. The child molester must ensure that the community will take his side and not believe the allegations. The most effective way to do this involves, according to Gladwell, at least two strategies: (1) I'm just a grown-up kid and (2) I'm the guy next door.

The "I'm a grown-up kid" strategy involves behaving in a variety of public settings in ways that convince the community that the child molester loves being around kids, that he loves to play with kids, and that he is generous in giving his time to kids. In retrospect, the child molester is the guy who is always playing on the playground or running the sack race at the church picnic, or horsing around in the pool or at the beach or taking kids to Disney movies while all of the other adults prefer to sit on the sidelines. This is not to say that all adults who love to play with kids or go swimming or watch endless Disney movies are child molesters; most of us do all of these things as a routine part of parenting. But the difference between the rest of us and child molesters is that we do this because we want to be engaged with our children and their friends in a meaningful way, or just because we really do love to play or watch Disney movies. In contrast, child molesters engage in these behaviors deliberately and publicly so that if a child tells his parent that the coach rubbed up against him in the swimming pool or touched his knee in the movie theater, the parent will remember how active the child molester was at picnics or in the swimming pool "horsing around" with all of the children and because the parent has seen the molester act this way with many children, the parent will be more likely to assume that the child must be mistaken. Gladwell writes about many different child molesters and their grooming of communities, but he gives specific examples from the Sandusky case. When Sandusky is accused of molesting boys in the shower, many, including Sandusky himself reacted by noting that Jerry was always horsing around, flipping towels in the shower. This grooming results in the community redefining what the child is reporting as "normal" behavior for the accused, rather than the sexual violence that it really is.

The "I'm the guy next door" strategy is the one that we see constantly in the news and in our own personal experiences. "Everyone loves Jerry" has many iterations. It is incredibly common that when an accusation of child abuse comes out, the response of community members is shock because everyone believes the accused is such a great guy. This was certainly evident in State College, Pennsylvania, among the Penn State community nationwide, and we see it in the Catholic Church child sex abuse scandal as well. Hattery grew up in a Catholic parish where one of the priests was sexually abusing boys. The Boy Scout leader in the parish-supported troop was also a child molester. He abused boys on camping trips, in the basement of the church, and in the back of his custom van. When the allegations became public, the community was in total shock and disbelief, because Mr. Boy Scout Leader was such a great guy! We all loved him. He spent a great deal of time with the boys in his troop. He seemed to love them. Knowing what we know now, that should have been our first clue that something was wrong.

Any child molester who looks like a monster would have a very difficult time convincing any child to spend time with him, let alone any parent to agree to it or any community to welcome him into their homes. Child molesters have to get people to like them, to trust them, and to believe their version of the story should an allegation be made. We are not advocating that people be immediately suspicious of anyone, especially a man who is nice. But we need to be trained to pay attention so that we recognize grooming strategies when they are happening to us, our communities, and our children. And when we see these strategies at work, we should be more cautious about allowing our children, especially our young boys, to spend too much alone time with the person. In hindsight, after child abuse allegations become public, many parents and communities realize that there were warning signs, but child molesters engage in deliberate strategies to decrease the likelihood that anyone will be suspicious of their behavior. Their ability to lure children in and convince parents to allow them to spend time with their children is predicated on this very deception.

## Grooming for Sexual Abuse

As we noted, unlike rape, which can often happen very suddenly and seem "out of the blue," from the perspective of the victim, child sexual abuse involves a significant amount of physical grooming. Child molesters must get their potential victims to trust them and to feel comfortable with physical affection. Victims of child abuse often recall that the perpetrator began by touching them in physically affectionate but not necessarily abusive ways, a touch on the arm or a hug or an invitation to sit on his lap. The typical child molester slowly expands the touching—a hug that lasts a little too long, a touch on the knee that slowly moves up the thigh. Each time that the child doesn't resist or stop the touching, a new boundary is established; this allows the child molester to slowly and systematically move the boundary from appropriate to inappropriate. When he first touches the child in an abusive way, it is often just a short distance, literally, from his last touch. This strategy is effective for several reasons. First, it gets the child used to being touched. Second, it becomes difficult for the child to figure out when the touching becomes inappropriate. Was it the touch way up the leg or when his hand finally slid into the young boy's crotch? Third, it makes it much easier to rationalize that the abusive touching is an innocent mistake. Both the child and the abuser can explain away the abusive touch in this way. The child may rationalize that the abuser didn't mean for his hand to move into his crotch, it simply slipped as he scooted on the bed or as they turned in the car. And, if the child protests, the abuser will rationalize the abusive touching in the same way, it was unintentional.

Child sexual abuse perpetrators also use other strategies for grooming their victims, including alcohol. Alcohol is important for at least three reasons. First, like any gift, it can lure a child into engaging with the child molester. A common ploy is that the abuser offers the victim alcohol or makes alcohol available to him as a way of endearing himself to the child. Second, if the victim drinks some alcohol, he may become drowsy or fumble around, which can make it easier for the child molester to get away with some of the inappropriate touching that is a precursor to the abuse. Third, too much alcohol will impair the victim's memory; he may simply not be able to remember exactly what happened. This will inhibit reporting, but it will also make it more difficult if he makes an allegation and an investigation ensues. If he can't remember exactly what happened, perhaps what he is alleging didn't actually happen. Finally, if the victim has been drinking, he may be reluctant to report at all, out of fear that he will get in trouble for drinking. Sadly, it is not uncommon for allegations of child sexual abuse to emerge as the child gets older and continues drinking and begins to get into trouble for this behavior. In Hattery's hometown, the allegations against both the priest and the Boy Scout leader emerged when one of the victims revealed the abuse while he was undergoing treatment for alcohol use. He was in the seventh grade. Again, all of these strategies are deliberate on the part of the abuser; they are engaged in for specific reasons and in systematic ways across victims and across cases.

Finally, we cannot overstate the fact that victims of child sexual abuse have generally not had any previous experiences with sexual behavior. This gives tremendous power to the child abuser who understands a great deal more about sexual behavior. A child probably does not realize, for example, that sexual encounters with a new consensual partner often begin with physical affection, so this warning sign is often missed by young children. A young boy will not likely understand that having his penis touched will cause an erection whether he has sexual desire or not or is consenting or not. Child molesters use these misunderstandings to their advantage by suggesting to a young boy that he actually desires the sexual contact, thus placing blame on the boy, which will significantly inhibit his likelihood of ever reporting the event. In the victim's mind, not only would he have to admit a sexual encounter with a coach, but he would have to admit a sexual encounter with another man. It is not uncommon for young boys who've been sexually abused by adult men to question their sexuality, and this is often a barrier to their reporting, seeking help, and pursuing healthy sexual relationships when they are old enough to do so.

## JERRY SANDUSKY: A CASE STUDY OF CHILD SEXUAL ABUSE

Child sexual abuse is a tragedy in SportsWorld. Although there are no convenient data bases that catalog child sexual abuse by institution—other than the abuses taking place in juvenile detention centers—media reports, legislation, revelations in memoirs, and anecdotal data tell us that every year, young people are sexually abused by their coaches. Thus, it should have come as no surprise when a child sex abuse case rocked SportsWorld. Yet, it did come as a surprise. As the nation struggled to deal with the horrific allegations, what emerged was an even greater tragedy—that officials deep and high in SportsWorld had known about the allegations for at least fifteen years before they came into public view. How many young boys were raped and abused by Sandusky because athletic coaches and administrators at Penn State couldn't lift a finger or ask a question?

Though there are many coaches who sexually abuse children, and there are many sports institutions that, like the Catholic Church, turned a blind when allegations were made and allowed coaches to move from one club to another, we choose the Sandusky case as our illustration for a variety of reasons. First, because it highlights the structures of SportsWorld that allowed it to occur in the first place and to go on for so long; second, because of the widespread media attention; and third, because of the Freeh Report, a comprehensive examination of the Sandusky child sex abuse scandal that was commissioned by Penn State University but conducted independently and provided data we could analyze on our own.[11]

Jerry Sandusky coached for over three decades (1969–1999) as an assistant to the legendary coach, Joe Paterno, who's career spanned fifty years, all at Penn State University. He was widely considered to be Joe's right-hand man and was the heir apparent—second only to Paterno's son Joe—to succeed the legendary coach should he retire.

Sandusky retired abruptly in 1999 and never sought another coaching job. There was speculation at the time about this decision, but it was only after his trial and conviction on forty-five counts of child sexual abuse that we know the real reason: accusations of his abuse had begun to surface in the late 1990s, forcing him to resign.

Sandusky's main targets were young boys from disadvantaged backgrounds whom he was able to "recruit" and groom through his now infamous charity, the Second Mile. As is typical of so many sex abuse cases involving coaches and other leaders (Catholic priests, Boy Scout leaders), the mothers of the boys Sandusky mentored in the Second Mile were so incredibly grateful for his attention to their sons—most of whom lacked father figures—that they overlooked the obvious warning signs of sexual abuse, including sleepovers at Sandusky's house and out-of-town trips to away games with Sandusky and the entire Penn State football program. Sandusky not only groomed the most vulnerable, but he lavished them with gifts and experiences—standing on the sidelines with him at Nittany Lions games, even traveling with him and the team when they were bowl bound—that ensured both their continued "relationship" with him and most importantly their silence.

Perhaps most grotesque, but certainly not unusual when major institutions are involved, was the cover up. On several occasions between 1999 and 2011, Joe Paterno and other Penn State leaders, including then president Graham Spanier, not only covered up the allegations but, incredibly, continued to allow Sandusky access to the Penn State football facilities, where he perpetrated much of the abuse.

After his official retirement from coaching, Sandusky was allowed to maintain an office in the Penn State football complex and access to the athletic facilities, including the locker room, where he was accused of carrying out several of the acts of abuse. In 2001 he was discovered abusing a boy in the locker room shower by then graduate assistant coach Mike McQueary, who reported the incident to coach Paterno. Paterno allegedly assured McQueary that he would handle things. And yet Sandusky retained access to Penn State and allegedly abused other boys for nearly another decade. According to the Freeh Report, even at the grand jury hearing in the late summer of 2011, coach Paterno, then President Spanier, and then athletic director Tim Curly each continued to deny knowing anything about the alleged abuse, *despite the fact that there were emails circulated among the men in which they discussed what to do about the "problem."* On June 22, 2012, after ten of his victims provided highly disturbing testimony of nearly fifty individual acts of child sexual abuse, Sandusky was convicted and sentenced to thirty to sixty years in prison, which, for a man of sixty-nine, amounts to a life sentence.

When it was all said and done, Graham Spanier and Tim Curly did face criminal charges; both were charged with child endangerment. Curly took a plea deal and Spanier was convicted at trial. This was, in many ways, a dissatisfying outcome, given the roles that these men played in facilitating Sandusky's crimes. Everyone who works with children is considered a mandatory reporter of child abuse. The silence of Joe Paterno, Graham Spanier, and Tim Curly amounted to more than child endangerment, their actions violated their responsibilities as mandatory reporters. We wonder how the landscape of child sexual abuse in SportsWorld and the Catholic Church would change if more mandatory reporters were held legally responsible for knowingly ignoring their legal mandate.

Commentators pointed to one of the most troubling aspects of this case and so many like it: Coaches and sports programs are supposed to provide safe spaces for young people to develop physically. When coaches violate this trust through sexual abuse and administrators hide the abuse rather than protect the most vulnerable, the very sanctity of youth sports has been irreparably violated.

Perhaps most revealing of all is the continued reluctance by many Penn State fans to accept the fact that their hero, Joe Paterno, who died suddenly just a few months after the allegations came to light and he was fired as head coach, knew something and didn't do anything. Initially, many fans and especially former players were angry at the young men who finally had the courage to tell the truth. Many thought the young men were lying, and most found it impossible to believe that Jerry Sandusky would perpetrate such horrible acts of abuse. Eventually, after the trial, most did come to hold Sandusky responsible, and they turned their anger on him. At the same time, many still refuse to put any responsibility on Joe Paterno, the legend of Penn State University football. Each football Saturday in State College, loyalists to Paterno erect a make-shift memorial to him and to the hundreds of victories he led the football team to. This action speaks volumes about the power of SportsWorld.

The child sex abuse scandal waged by Jerry Sandusky under the cover of Penn State University football may have been the first national exposure many people had to child sex abuse in sports. Yet, for a variety of reasons that we unpack in this chapter, child sexual abuse in sports is incredibly common.

Child sexual abuse in sports is pervasive in part because sexual predators have easy access to potential victims; they have almost unlimited opportunities to be in close, often intimate contact with children; and they have organizations that shield them from accusations and enable their abuse by moving them from one location to another, never holding them accountable, much like in the Catholic Church scandals. One case that stands out along with that of Sandusky and Penn State is the case of Dr. Larry Nassar, who served as the national team doctor for UAS Gymnastics and osteopathic physician at Michigan State University.

## LARRY NASSAR AND USA GYMNASTICS

As horrifying as the Jerry Sandusky case is, we could not have imagined the volume of abuse perpetrated by Dr. Larry Nassar. When the story of sexual abuse in USA Gymnastic broke, thanks to the painstaking investigative research of *Indianapolis Star* journalists Tim Evans, Mark Alesia, and Marisa Kwiatkowski, the role that a single individual, Larry Nassar, played was not yet clear. We quote from the original article: "At least 368 gymnasts have alleged some form of sexual abuse at the hands of their coaches, gym owners and other adults working in gymnastics. That's a rate of one every 20 days. And it's likely an undercount."[12] As a light was shined on the extensive child sexual abuse in USA gymnastics, victim after victim revealed the same name: Dr. Larry Nassar. At the time of his trial and sentencing in the spring of 2018, no fewer than 265 athletes, including 160 USA gymnasts, accused him of sexual abuse. Nasser ultimately pleaded guilty to seven counts of criminal sexual conduct, and he admitted to using his position as official team doctor to sexually assault and abuse young female gymnasts under the guise of "medical treatment." He was sentenced to 75–140 years in prison.

As one victim, Morgan McCaul, said, "Since reports of Larry Nassar's misconduct to Michigan State faculty began in 1997, two years before I was even born, I can't help but wonder how many little girls could have been spared from this life long battle if someone at the university had just done the bare minimum and listened."[13]

In 1997, two women spoke to MSU women's gymnastics coach Kathie Klages regarding concerns they had about Nassar's "treatment." They were discouraged from reporting him and made to believe they simply didn't understand medicine. Again, in 2014, a young girl and her parents went to the Meridian Township Police Department, accusing Nassar of sexual assault during a medical appointment, but the investigation never made it to prosecutors. In all, at least eleven official attempts were made by victims to bring attention to the abuse they faced at the hands of Nassar, to either law enforcement, USA Gymnastics, or Michigan State prior to his prosecution.

Amanda Thomashow filed a report in 2014 with Michigan State University's Title IX coordinator after Thomashow's first medical appointment with Nassar. Thomashow was seeking treatment for years of hip pain that were caused by cheerleading injuries. Nassar had come highly recommended by everyone she knew in SportsWorld, including her sister, who was a patient of his. Thomashow told investigators that Nassar spent nearly an hour touching her vagina and massaging her breasts, even while Thomashow repeatedly tried to stop him. No one else was in the room, as Nassar had sent a female resident outside. Afterward, Nassar refused to let her leave until a follow-up appointment was scheduled.

During the investigation, Nassar vehemently denied any wrongdoing, going as far as to describe himself as "the body whisperer" for giving treatment other physicians pass over. He touted a PowerPoint lecture he often gave, titled "Pelvic Floor: Where no man has gone before," in an attempt to win over investigators. Nassar also provided three other presentations, a research article, and ten videos of himself performing the procedures in question, without gloves. Those procedures included the "intravaginal adjustment," one he frequently performed without supervision.[14]

This first official investigation let Nassar off with a warning, and he was *admonished to wear gloves when treatment involved private areas of the body.*

Seriously? Is it any less harmful to digitally penetrate young girls vaginas while wearing gloves? The investigation report stated Nassar's actions were troubling but amounted to no more than a failure to clearly communicate treatment with Thomashow. Four of the experts involved in the case were medical doctors with close ties to Nassar and Michigan State University.

It was Nassar's prior elaborate defenses that prompted Rachael Denhollander, a lawyer, gymnast, and the first to accuse Nassar in court for sexual assault, to bring a stack of evidence with her to Michigan State officials and the media in 2016. Assistant Attorney General Angela Povilaitis stated that, over time, "he had developed a built-in defense, . . . [h]e was a doctor, and a good one, so the world thought."[15] Denhollander brought medical journal articles that disproved Nassar's claims of unique medial techniques. She didn't stop there:

> I brought with me to those reports, my medical records showing that Larry had never charted penetrative techniques. I brought medical records from a nurse practitioner documenting my graphic disclosure of abuse way back in 2004. I had my journals showing the mental anguish I had been in since the assault, a catalog of national and international medical journal articles showing what real pelvic floor treatment looks like. I brought a letter from a neighboring district attorney vouching for my character and truthfulness and urging detectives to take my case seriously.[16]

Prompted by Denhollander's police report, the FBI searched his home and discovered that Nassar possessed over three thousand seven hundred images of child pornography on his *official Michigan State University computer*, including a video of Nassar sexually molesting several young girls.

In September 2016, the *Indianapolis Star* ran a story about Denhollander and Thomashow, revealing the accusations against Nassar. Michigan State fired him a few weeks later. Then, in February 2017, three more former gymnasts gave an interview to *60 Minutes* in which they accused Nassar of sexually assaulting them. These gymnasts also accused Béla and Márta Károlyi of significant emotional abuse at the Karolyi Ranch, where the world's best gymnasts trained, and where Larry Nassar provided medical attention. During the fifteen years Nassar provided medical care to the athletes at Karolyi Ranch, he did so without a Texas medical license, a third-degree felony. What the *60 Minutes* interview with these young women revealed was a network of people willing to, at the very least, look the other way, and possibly cover up continued abuse. The cover up of decades of abuse of hundreds of girls is eerily similar to the way that Penn State coaches and administrators covered up for and hid Jerry Sandusky for decades.

More and more young women began coming forward. McKayla Maroney, an Olympic gold medalist, revealed on Twitter, using the #MeToo hashtag, that Nassar repeatedly molested her for four years. Maroney then filed a lawsuit against Nassar, Michigan State University, the USA Olympic Committee, and USA Gymnastics. She had this to say at Nassar's trial:

> People should know that sexual abuse of children is not just happening in Hollywood, in the media, or in the halls of Congress. This is happening everywhere, wherever there is a position of power, there seems to be potential for abuse. I had a dream to go to the Olympics, and the things that I had to endure to get there, were unnecessary, and disgusting. . . . Our silence has given the wrong people power for too long, and it's time to take our power back.[17]

Some of the biggest names in gymnastics began to come forward, including Aly Raisman and Simone Biles, both of whom won gold medals in the 2016 Olympics. By January of 2018, there were 150 women who had come forward to publicly accuse Nassar of sexual assault, with 332 victims on record in total.

Tiffany Thomas-Lopez was another victim who came forward. Thomas-Lopez had hoped Nassar would be able to help her with chronic back pain. During her appointment, Nassar digitally penetrated her vagina without medical gloves. Thomas-Lopez desperately tried to speak to other coaches and trainers at Michigan State University about the treatment she was receiving, only to be silenced and brushed off. Speaking at Nassar's trial, Thomas-Lopez said, "the army you chose in the late '90s to silence me, to dismiss me and my attempt at speaking the truth will not prevail over the army you created when violating us."[18]

In July 2017, Nassar pleaded guilty and was sentenced to sixty years in federal prison on child pornography charges. In January 2018, Nassar pleaded guilty in the state of Michigan to seven counts of criminal sexual conduct. Judge Rosemarie Aquilina sentenced him to 40 to 175 years in the Michigan state prison system to run sequentially with the federal term. When giving the sentence, Judge Aquilina described Nassar as "precise, calculative, manipulative, devious, despicable." The judge stated, "I just signed your death warrant."[19]

There have been several inquiries regarding how and why Nassar was allowed to continue practicing for decades, even after several accusations of sexual abuse. Local police, Michigan State University, and USA Gymnastics seemed to turn a blind eye to his activities. Multiple people in these institutions received numerous complaints from young girls over the course of twenty years, but they never removed Nassar from his position as a celebrity doctor. Even after the charges in 2016, Nassar continued to see patients for eleven more months, and disturbingly, in those eleven months, Nassar sexually abused forty additional girls. One of Nassar's victims, Larissa Boyce, stated, "I was not protected by the adults I trusted."[20]

In addition to perpetrating sexual violence on dozens of USA gymnasts, he also abused college athletes at Michigan State University when they sought treatment for sports-related injuries, including male gymnasts, softball players, rowers, and dancers. After his conviction, Michigan State University agreed to pay $500 million to his victims, their students, who were abused by the team doctor they employed. It is not yet clear how Michigan State will raise these funds, but some speculate that current and future students will pay the price through increases in tuition. We find it hard to believe that the athletic department and the department of sports medicine can't "find" funds like this and not pass on their mistakes to innocent students.

Additionally, as was the case at Penn State, top officials, who knew they would be investigated for the cover up, abruptly resigned after the trial, including Michigan State University President Lou Anna Simon, Michigan State Athletic Director Mark Hollis, and the executive director of the alumni association, Scott Westerman. And, on January 22, 2018, several USA Gymnastics board members announced their resignation. Fallout continues, as subsequent proceedings take place and further charges are brought forward against Nassar, Michigan State University, and other athletic institutions. Initially we were optimistic that there would be accountability at Michigan State. But, in August 2018, the National Collegiate Athletic Association ruled that the university broke no NCAA rules in investigating the sexual abuse rampant on the campus at least since the 1990s.[21]

That the NCAA was willing to overlook the testimony of the student athletes and other evidence in the case is a clear example of the issues exposed in this book. Institutional loyalty is stronger than the voices of hundreds of sexual abuse victims, even when loyalty means ignoring the bylaws of the organization. In this case, the bylaws of the NCAA state that it is the responsibility of member institutions to protect the welfare of their athletes.

What makes the Nassar case even more egregious, if there is such a measure, than Sandusky at Penn State is that Nassar was not only the head doctor at USA Gymnastics but also a physician and professor at Michigan State University's sports medicine practice. Because of his status in both organizations, his access to potential victims was enormous. These two institutions were well aware of the allegations against him and did nothing. Nothing, that is, except cover up for him.

According, once again, to the excellent reporting of the *Indianapolis Star*,[22] top officials at USA Gymnastics, one of the nation's most prominent Olympic organizations, *failed to alert police* to many allegations of sexual abuse that occurred on their watch and stashed complaints in files that have been kept secret. But the problem is far worse. A nine-month investigation found that predatory coaches were allowed to move from gym to gym, undetected by a lax system of oversight, or dangerously passed on by USA Gymnastics-certified gyms.

When it came to Larry Nassar, emails that were uncovered by the *Indianapolis Star* revealed that while he was undergoing an internal investigation, USA gymnastics, on two separate occasions, colluded with him to generate excuses for his absence from high-profile events, where he otherwise would have been present, including the USA national championships in 2015.

At the time of this writing, Ohio State University is also embroiled in two major scandals involving their athletic program and sexual and intimate partner violence. Similar to the case against Larry Nassar at Michigan State, at Ohio State, former members of the wrestling team have accused the late team physician doctor Richard Strauss of sexually abusing wrestlers across his twenty-year position with the team. Between 1978 and 1998 it is estimated that Strauss sexually assaulted and/or raped fifteen hundred to two thousand of these athletes.[23]

Only weeks after the sexual abuse allegations hit the news, the university was sent into a tizzy when legendary head football coach Urban Meyer was accused of failing to adequately report domestic violence on the part of his strength coach, Zach Smith. After an external review, Meyer was eventually suspended for three games because he failed to report the allegations against Smith.

Unique to the institutions we analyze in this book, SportsWorld has a problem with both GBV *and* child sexual abuse. Athletes at both the college and professional levels are engaged in rape and intimate partner violence at levels that exceed non-athletes in the same age and social class groups. Violence takes a toll not only on the women who are on the receiving end, but ultimately on the men themselves, especially when they perpetrate intimate partner violence. Intimate partner violence ultimately alienates the victim from the abuser, and she is often the only person he has standing in his corner—a scene we watched play out with Ray and Janay Rice.

Child sexual abuse is unfortunately also rampant in SportsWorld. We chose to illustrate this with two tragic cases, Jerry Sandusky at Penn State University and Larry Nasser of USA gymnastics and Michigan State University, in part because these are cases known to many readers but also because these are cases about which there is the most available information for us to build our argument. In fact, child sexual abuse is sadly too common, on local sports teams as well as in major AAU organizations like swimming and even boxing, where young men and women are regularly and repeatedly abused by their coaches and other adults whom they should be able to trust.

There are several reasons why GBV and child sexual abuse are unfortunately too common in SportsWorld, including its quasi-total institutional structure; internal systems of justice; and, perhaps most important, its highly sex-segregated nature coupled with a culture of entitlement. SportsWorld can be characterized not only as hypermasculine but also as exclusive, a combination that produces a unique culture in which rape and intimate partner violence flourish. Many women are eager to be around high-profile athletes; many even seek them out at parties or clubs. It is not surprising, then, that these are frequently the sites where rapes begin or even occur. Much like the young college women who attend fraternity parties because they live in a culture in which their value is assigned by men, many young women are attracted to high-profile athletes for the same reason. Athletes are socialized into a culture of entitlement; everything is done for them, from their class work to their laundry. Whatever problems they have are solved for them as they arise. In this toxic mixture of hypermasculinity and entitlement, athletes can come to believe that they are entitled to women's bodies and specifically their sexuality, whenever and however they desire it. And it is beyond their comprehension that any woman would ever say "no," so rape becomes an impossibility in their world. This elitism and exclusivity not only creates opportunities for would-be rapists, but it protects them when they are accused. When a woman accuses an athlete of rape she receives messages from players, coaches, and fans urging her to leave the player alone and not destroy his career. Victims have even received death threats from fans on Twitter and Facebook, as was the case for the victim who accused Florida State University Seminole Jameis Winston. Fans turned out in droves when Jerry Sandusky was initially accused as well, critical of the young men who would accuse the beloved coach at the end of his career.

The exclusive nature of SportsWorld facilitates the reliance on internal systems of justice as well. As Lavigne's report and our research document, SportsWorld is able to insulate itself from the criminal justice system perhaps better than any other institution we analyze in this book, not so much by creating rules and operating procedures, as the military, colleges, and the Catholic Church do, but by building on this sense of exclusivity and celebrity. Police officers, prosecutors, and even judges are often fans, if not alumni, of the local university, or fans of the local professional team, and they are often as enthralled by the close contact with the athlete as anyone else. In some cases, they may even receive benefits from the team, such as being included in the athletic department's luxury box at the football game. All of these relationships set up a conflict of interest when an athlete is accused of a crime and facilitate SportsWorld's strategies for maintaining an internal systems of justice.

## WHAT CAN BE DONE?

We offer a set of recommendations that we believe, if implemented, would reduce GBV and child sexual abuse from occurring in the first place, and would result in the handling of cases appropriately when they are reported.

### Demand Accountability

If an institution is invested in reducing GBV and child sexual abuse, the most efficient way to do this is to remove the perpetrators from the institution. If the reader takes nothing else away from reading this chapter than this point, our time writing will have been well spent. Athletes and coaches are never, ever, held accountable in any meaningful way in SportsWorld. Their crimes are hidden and handled internally. Sanctions are imposed and then reversed on appeal. Even on the rare occasions when their crimes are reported to law enforcement, they are still rarely held accountable. Wide-eyed police officers and prosecutors are often more interested in getting an autograph from a superstar athlete like O. J. Simpson or Ray Rice or Jameis Winston than in conducting a proper investigation. If there is any inkling of a proper investigation, those in power in SportsWorld jump in to protect the athlete by making him unavailable or by providing the absolute best legal representation. We find this to be one of the most perplexing aspects of studying athlete's violence against women. College athletes with no money, who are not allowed to work, who are not allowed to receive "improper benefits," who often come from meager if not impoverished backgrounds, suddenly have the same kinds of lawyers that Wall Street types like Bernie Madoff hire. Interesting.

When it comes to child sexual abuse, we make the same recommendation. Hold the perpetrators accountable. Believe children when they find the courage to report an incident of their abuse. Understand that pedophiles will not simply stop sexually abusing children on their own or by being reassigned to another team or banned from the locker room facilities. Pedophiles must be prosecuted, and they must receive treatment. And, unless they can demonstrate that they will never sexually abuse a child again, they need to be banned from having any contact with children. Lastly, with regard to child sexual abuse, we recommend that all coaches, from Little League to the major leagues, go through a rigorous vetting process, a set of backgrounds checks, to reduce the chances that a sexual predator has been able to slip under the radar screen and enter a new community seeking victims.

## Change the Culture

As we will argue extensively in the concluding chapter of this book, the hypermasculine, entitled, sex-segregated culture of SportsWorld needs to shift. We recognize that the kind of culture shift we are talking about will not come easily or quickly. The locker room rituals we described are evidence of that. That said, the locker room is a powerful place, and coaches and captains have a tremendous amount of influence. If leaders would be brave enough to demand a culture shift, we believe it could have a tremendous impact on reducing GBV. Central to this culture shift is redefining masculinity and femininity such that women are no longer valued only for their sexuality and men are valued for an identity that is strong and self-assured on its own and does not rely on degrading the feminine, and by extension women or gay men. As with so many other recommendations, this too, applies to every institution we interrogate.

Somewhat unique to SportsWorld is the culture of entitlement. In some ways its elimination may prove a more difficult task because of the degree to which entitlement has become so central to SportsWorld. Athletes are deemed of such high value that the colleges, universities, and professional teams they play for will literally do anything to keep them. This type of culture shift is also made more challenging by the sheer dollar value of SportsWorld. The benefits of being a college athlete are tremendous, including the opportunity to earn a college degree at no cost, but the benefits of being a professional athlete are enormous. Minimum salaries in the NFL and the NBA hover at nearly half a million dollars per year, and stars have multimillion-dollar *annual* contracts that run into the double figures ($20 million *per year*). Under these conditions, it is not surprising that athletes feel a sense of entitlement. We have told them that they are special, and we have shown them that they are special. Unless we can reign in SportsWorld from its outrageous sense of elitism, there is not much hope in shifting the culture of entitlement that contributes to GBV.

As is clearly evidenced in the case of Jerry Sandusky, this sense of elitism is a powerful tool for an abuser. We see this same tool being used all over SportsWorld, even in such modest quarters as Little League teams or AAU travel teams. As long as SportsWorld continues to be overvalued by our society, child molesters will be able to harness tools of privilege as they troll for potential victims and keep them from reporting the abuse.

## Reduce Black Men's Exposure to Violence

Black men in SportsWorld are more likely to perpetrate GBV than their white counterparts for a variety of reasons. One of the reasons that has not received enough attention in the media is the fact that Black men in our culture are more likely to be *exposed* to violence—both in their homes and in their communities—that predisposes them to perpetrating it. This does not mean that young Black men should be removed from SportsWorld. In fact, we suggest just the opposite. SportsWorld and the mentoring that takes place inside of it can create an opportunity for the lessons of violence to be *unlearned*. Black men who have been exposed to violence can receive appropriate interventions, therapy, and re-socialization that will reduce the likelihood that they will engage in violence in their own lives. We argue that in the midst of all of the darkness of SportsWorld, this is a ray of light, of possibility. But it will require the leaders of SportsWorld to recognize this phenomenon and to be open to the recommendation that it is worth investing in these young men in ways that are not directly related to winning and losing but that, in the end, will actually improve their play. Why? Because they will no longer be in trouble! Literally, every moment they spend fighting an accusation or a suspension is time they are not lifting weights or running drills. Of course, we will never know the answer to this, but we wonder if New England Patriot Aaron Hernandez would have avoided a sentence of life in prison at the age of twenty-four had he been held accountable and received appropriate interventions when he found himself in trouble for engaging in violence in Gainesville, Florida.

Violence against women affects all of us; we are all impacted by the ways in which this violence spills into our lives through family members, friends, people we work with, and in our own relationships. We must, as a society, begin to have honest conversations about the root causes of violence against women and develop real strategies for reducing and hopefully eliminating this violence.

Let us be clear, we in no way think that the violence against women perpetrated by athletes is unique; men from all walks of life abuse women. However, the hypermasculinity of athletics, the hero worship that allows us to overlook their misbehavior and fail to hold them accountable, and the sense of entitlement we build into them by passing them through high school and college and paying them millions of dollars a year creates an environment that is ripe for violence against women. The fact is that what goes on in SportsWorld holds a great deal of influence over people, especially young men, which means that SportsWorld is particularly situated to make a difference. If leaders in SportsWorld could be convinced to take violence against women seriously, then perhaps not only would violence against women by athletes decline but treating women with respect could become a behavior to be emulated by young men who look to these athletes as role models.

We are quite certain that this will not happen on its own. We challenge the leadership of SportsWorld—both collegiate and professional—to take this issue seriously before more young men are lost to their own self-inflicted violence as both Jovan Belcher and Aaron Hernandez were.

## FINAL THOUGHTS

We end this chapter perplexed. We are perplexed by the fact that in SportsWorld, as in no other part of life, Black men who sexually assault, abuse, and rape white women are protected and shielded from the law. In contrast, when Black men who can't carry a football, score a touchdown, or dunk a basketball are accused of violence against white women, they are significantly more likely to be arrested and convicted and they are given significantly longer sentences. *In all other parts of American life*, when a white woman identifies a Black man as her rapist, the wheels of justice move quickly, often so quickly that important mistakes are made and innocent men are sent to prison for crimes they did not commit. Indeed, for hundreds of years, the number one rationale for the lynching of tens of thousands of Black men was the accusation that they had raped a white women, accusations that almost never proved true.

The incredible power SportsWorld holds in American life is no better illustrated by the fact that Black male athletes are shielded by coaches and owners and universities and professional teams when they are accused of the same thing for which their fathers and grandfathers and great-grandfathers could be lynched.

# 7

# THE CATHOLIC
# CHURCH

[Pope Francis is] obviously a likeable, warm, humble, compassionate man. But many of us who were molested can say the very same thing about the priests who molested us, and the bishops who rebuffed us. . . . It takes not symbolic action, but real courage to say, "I'm demoting you, or kicking you out, because you put kids in harm's way."

—David Clohessy, national director of Survivors Network of Those Abused by Priests (SNAP)[1]

Of all of the issues we interrogate in this book, the child sex abuse scandal in the Catholic Church broke the earliest and has been both the most widespread and the most enduring. The epigraph that opens this chapter was uttered in 2014. At the time we are putting the final touches on this book, in the early fall of 2018, Pope Francis has just been accused of knowing about the sexual abuse perpetrated by Cardinal McCarrick, who served in Washington, D.C., and resigned in July 2018. There is speculation, based on an eleven-page memo released on August 26, 2018, by Archbishop Carlo Maria Vigano, that Pope Francis may also have known something about the widespread sexual abuse by Catholic priests across Pennsylvania, which hit the news cycle in August 2018. The hope and optimism that was expressed when Pope Francis was elected by the College of Cardinals has dimmed throughout 2018 as more and more allegations of child sexual abuse have surfaced. Though many were surprised, we were not, and the reasons why are a result of conducting the research, over more than a decade, to write this chapter.

Since the child sex abuse scandals came to light in the late 1990s and into the current century, the Vatican, while it did punish some priests (only a small fraction), failed to systematically address the problems. Here we focus on the widespread nature of the abuse. If it were a priest here, a priest there, that would be one thing. But this scandal is massive. It reaches every corner of the globe where there are Catholics, and while we confine our analysis to the United States, the problems in the Catholic Church are global in reach.

One of the most troubling aspects of the scandal is that the abuse was well known among the leadership of the Catholic Church yet they chose remedies that continued to put children in harm's way—for decades. The late former priest Father Eugene Kennedy, a licensed psychologist who studied his colleagues, issued warnings, saying that many priests that he studied were "emotionally undeveloped and incapable of forming healthy, trusting, nonsexual relationships."[2] He argued in his 1972 book *The Catholic Priest in the United States: Psychological Investigations*, considered by many to be an early warning sign of the trouble brewing in parishes all over the United States, that the hierarchical structure of the church prevented it from addressing long-standing problems, including sex abuse by priests.[3] It is hard to understand why the early warning signs about a possible epidemic like child sex abuse were not heeded, especially coming from a priest like Eugene Kennedy. And this is precisely the focus of this chapter. The cover up of the sexual abuse was deliberate, and thousands paid the consequences.

A caveat: When we teach classes in which we include a discussion of the sex abuse scandal in the Catholic Church, we often face a number of points of resistance. First, not surprisingly, many Catholics feel deeply about their religious identity, and perhaps many feel defensive and protective toward their church and their religious leaders. Others are deeply saddened by the scandal and would simply rather not talk about it. Second, Catholics and non-Catholics alike are quick to point out that sex abuse happens in all faiths, in all organized religions, and to limit our discussion to the Catholic Church is somehow biased. As we will demonstrate in this chapter, our focus on the Catholic Church is deliberate, not only because as the scandal has continued to unfold we are awed by its enormity, but also because there are specific practices and policies in the Catholic Church that are unique to its structure and that allow priests who sexually abuse children to continue doing so, often for decades.

## HISTORICAL OVERVIEW OF THE CATHOLIC CHURCH

Christianity was founded by Jesus Christ in the first century. Catholics believe, based on the New Testament writings of the Apostles, that Christ was born to a Jewish family and that his virgin birth is the result of a union between God and the Virgin Mary. He is considered by all Christians to be the Son of God. This belief is in contrast to those held by Jews and Muslims, who believe that Jesus was a prophet but not the Son of God.

Scholars of Catholic history argue that for the first few centuries after Jesus's death, the apostles and their followers were writing the books that comprise the New Testament and that they were sharing these Gospels with their communities, primarily by speaking or preaching. By the second or third century the communities had grown in size—both through population increases and expanding territories—and Christianity needed to codify not only its teachings but also its governance, and thus emerges the Roman Catholic Church.

### Women in the Early Catholic Church

One of the premier feminist scholars of the early church, Karen King, argues, based on her research of scrolls discovered in the late twentieth century buried in the sands of Egypt, that in the early years of the Catholic Church women held leadership roles alongside of men. Her research on the structure of the early Catholic Church forms the basis of her analysis. For example, King notes that for the first several centuries the church was a community of believers who met in homes because they couldn't afford to build structures or houses of worship. Women then, as now, were prominent figures in the home and, King argues, may have even made up the majority of believers. But it is the hidden texts, among them the Gospel of Mary, that offer insight into the roles that women played in the early church. King believes that in the early centuries of the Catholic Church women's gospels were held in the same esteem as men's, and it is not until the Catholic Church moved its center to Rome that women's status changed.

The Roman Empire, centered in Rome, was a society based on hierarchies and the stratification of power by gender, age, and other statuses as well, including slaves. King believes that as the Church moved to Rome and became institutionalized, among other things, it selected the gospels that would be officially included in the New Testament. Women's voices were all but erased. King's 2003 book, *The Gospel of Mary of Magdala: Jesus and the First Woman Apostle*, tells the story of Mary Magdala, whose gospel was discovered and analyzed by King.

According to King, this gospel provides evidence not only of Mary Magdalene's status as one of the favored disciples of Jesus, but also of other women, some of whom were removed from the gospels codified in the New Testament so as to erase them entirely from the history of the Catholic Church. All of this is important because the rationale for restricting leadership and especially ordination in the Catholic Church to men is based on the belief that, according to the gospels included in the New Testament, Jesus chose only men to be his disciples, and therefore his intent was for men to be the leaders of the church. To acknowledge women disciples and leaders, like Mary Magdalene, would be to undermine the very basis of gender stratification in the Catholic Church.

## The History of Celibacy in the Catholic Church

We include a discussion of celibacy in the Catholic Church for two reasons: first, because we argue it is another way in which women are excluded, and second, because it is often and *wrongly* assumed to be the cause of child sexual abuse. Let's begin with the second issue, the belief that celibacy is the cause of child sexual abuse. We hope that this book will enlighten the reader about many important issues, but one that we wish to emphasize is that *celibacy is in no way a cause of or connected to child sexual abuse.* The vast majority of pedophiles have sexual relationships with adults.

Returning to the first point, the celibacy requirement for priests is important to our discussion because it definitively removes women from any power they might have had as a spouse of a priest and launches the consolidation of power and wealth exclusively in the hierarchy of the Catholic Church and away from families and communities. According to documents available on the Vatican website,[4] it is clear from the gospels that at least one Apostle (Peter) had been married and that deacons and church leaders in the first centuries of the Catholic Church were married and had families. The first legislative expression of celibacy does not appear until the year 314, and it's not until the Second Lateran Council in 1139 when celibacy is mandated for priests, which is then reaffirmed in the Council of Trent in 1563.

Why does celibacy become important and how is it justified? During the eleventh and twelfth centuries, sex comes to be defined as something that is worldly rather than Godly, and therefore priests, who are human incarnations of God, must not participate in sex anymore than they should participate in any other worldly behaviors. But, the celibacy vow is much more powerful than its restriction on sexual behavior. The vow of celibacy is really about preventing priests from having families, who might then have a claim on property and wealth at the time of the priest's death. The Catholic Church also requires priests to take a vow of poverty for the same reason; material things are of the world and not of the sacred. The vow of poverty not only consolidated wealth in the coffers of the Church rather than in the individual pocket, but it allowed the Church to uphold the ideology expressed in the New Testament favoring spirituality over material goods—priests were poor—while simultaneously *amassing tremendous wealth*. In other words, priests are to be poor, but the institution, the Catholic Church, need not be.

## The Holy See and the Vatican City State

Unlike any other religious institution, the Catholic Church is a political state, the Holy See, which is located in Vatican City (in Rome, Italy), from where it oversees the worldwide Catholic community. Vatican City is ruled by a monarch, the pope. In addition to the pope, the Holy See has a secretary of state and ambassadors installed in embassies around the world. As we shall see, the decision to politicize the Catholic Church by obtaining the status of a political state is brilliant. As a political state, the Catholic Church is not under the control of any other political state; the Catholic Church does not have to file financial records, pay taxes, or be subjected to the laws of any other political state. This unique status not only facilitates the ability of the Catholic Church to amass wealth, but also allows the Catholic Church to govern itself, including when its leaders are accused of behaviors, like child sexual abuse, that are illegal in most other political states.

It is very difficult to estimate the vast wealth of the Catholic Church because the Vatican is not required to file financial records that other institutions, like publicly held companies, are required to file. Kristopher Morrison, who has been studying the wealth of the Catholic Church, notes that regardless of the actual figure, the Catholic Church is most likely the wealthiest institution in the world, in large part because of its vast collection of priceless art, buildings, and real estate. The Vatican owns just under three hundred thousand square miles of property around the world, including apartment buildings in London and Paris, not to mention magnificent structures like St. Patrick's Cathedral in downtown New York City. It has a reported $10 billion in foreign investments, owns $22 million in gold (1 metric ton), and reportedly has approximately $86 million in Peter's Pence, its cash or liquid assets, which are largely generated by weekly giving by the millions of Catholics all around the world. According to Morrison, much of the real estate and art was "acquired" during the Holy Wars or Crusades of the eleventh and twelfth centuries and later when Spain and Italy were colonizing the Americas, the Caribbean, and Africa.

## THE CATHOLIC CHURCH AS A TOTAL INSTITUTION

Like other institutions we have interrogated in this book, the Catholic Church is not a purely total institution, especially not for its members. For the average Catholic, the Catholic Church exerts very little control over daily life. In survey after survey, for example, Catholics indicate support for birth control, and most Catholic women report using birth control during some periods of their reproductive lives, despite the fact that the Catholic Church forbids it. Catholics report similar levels of sex outside of marriage as members of other faith communities. But, when it comes to priests and other members of the Catholic hierarchy, the Catholic Church more closely resembles a total institution.

Unlike many other religions, those ordained in the Catholic Church—priests, bishops, cardinals, and the pope—are required to dress in a manner appropriate to their station. Those who have attended a Catholic Mass in person or watched televised ceremonies will be familiar with ceremonial robes. For example, the pope wears a white robe, cardinals wear red, and bishops and priests wear black. Ritual or ceremonial dress also includes headwear and jewelry, which is distinct for the various ranks in the Catholic hierarchy. What non-Catholics may not be aware of is the fact that, in general, Catholic priests are required to wear the equivalent of a black suit and a white (Roman) collar, unless there is a good reason to deviate, perhaps for a church picnic. Even in the case of a church picnic the priest will generally wear more comfortable and appropriate clothing but will typically include a black button shirt with the collar. A constant visual reminder of his status.

The Catholic Church functions as a total institution in other ways as well. Priests may express an interest in various professional pathways, but they serve at the pleasure of the pope and thus an individual priest must work (and live) in the parish to which he is assigned and must do the work that he is given, which might include teaching in the local Catholic school or serving in a pastoral capacity in the local Catholic hospital in addition to working as a parish priest. Finally, should a priest choose to leave the priesthood, he is never allowed to work in a Catholic institution again. For example, a priest who leaves the priesthood and goes to medical school may not work in a Catholic hospital upon earning his medical degree. In short, Catholic priests may express preferences, but the vast majority of their daily lives—from what they wear, to the work that they perform, to where they live and work—is determined by their superiors.

## POWER AND HIERARCHY WITHIN THE CATHOLIC CHURCH

One of the points of contention during the Protestant Reformation was the relationship among believers, leaders, and God. The Catholic Church is the most hierarchical of all religious institutions, and like most hierarchies, power is concentrated at the top. In this hierarchal structure, there are clear distinctions in rank and power—who can make decisions, who can set church doctrine—and key to this hierarchy is knowledge and access to God. Based on the model of the New Testament, in which Jesus was surrounded by apostles and disciples, the Catholic Church hierarchy reserves the power of knowledge and access to God to those who have been ordained as priests.

Unlike in many Protestant churches in which anyone can assume the mantel of the preacher as long as he or she can convince others to join a congregation, priests have enormous power in the day-to-day lives of Catholics that is unique. For example, up until 1962 and the Second Vatican Council, the Catholic Mass was celebrated in Latin, and the priest faced the altar rather than the Sanctuary. The rationale for this was the requirement of weekly attendance at Mass for Catholics; when Catholics were traveling the world they would be able to attend Mass anywhere and understand what was going on.

In reality, even though the prayers and rituals were translated in the missals into the native languages of the congregants, few Catholics were fluent in Latin, and as a result this practice was a way of concentrating power in the hands of the priest, for only he knew *exactly* what the sacred words meant. Today,

**Figure 7.1. Hierarchy of the Catholic Church.**

when Mass is celebrated in the native language of the congregation, the priest is still the interpreter of the sacred texts. For example, though lay members of the church are allowed to read from the Old Testament during Mass, only the priest is allowed to read from the Gospels. This is in stark contrast to mainline Protestant religion in which the primacy of spirituality is the relationship between the believer and Jesus Christ; Protestants talk for example about their "personal relationship with Christ." Preachers are considered more like guides, but believers are encouraged to actively read the Bible and enter into conversation with Jesus on their own.

## THE SACRAMENTS

Another illustration of the hierarchical nature of the Catholic Church comes from the sacraments, and especially the sacrament of confession or what is formally known as penance. There are seven sacraments in Catholicism: Baptism, Eucharist, Penance, Confirmation, Matrimony, Anointing of the Sick, and Holy Orders. Administering of the sacraments is restricted to those who have been ordained, including priests, bishops, cardinals, and the pope. Again, this is in contrast to the structure of many Protestant churches in which a preacher with no formal training may baptize or perform marriages for believers. Another important distinction between Protestant beliefs and Catholicism is "Communion." In Protestant faiths, Communion is a reminder of the Last Supper, when the followers of Jesus came together as a community to share a meal. In Catholicism, Communion refers to the receiving of the Eucharist, which is the body and blood of Christ literally transformed from bread and wine to be consumed by Catholics, a way for Catholics to be "in body" with Jesus. The sacrament of the Eucharist is the most critical part of the Mass and, as noted, is required at least weekly of Catholics. Exceptions are made only in the cases of illness that prevent the body and blood to be consumed safely, for example, if one is suffering a bout of the flu or in more serious cases is undergoing chemotherapy or some other treatment.

Let's consider matrimony as an example. In the United States, marriage is a civil contract that two people make with each other and the state. Marriages are performed by someone deemed eligible by the state, who may or may not have any religious affiliation, for example a Justice of the Peace or your next-door neighbor who has completed an online certificate program. It is the marriage certificate that is produced in order to have a spouse added to one's insurance package, for example. And when marriages fail, it is a judge, not a minister, who presides over the dissolution of the civil contract. For Catholics, however, because matrimony is more than a ceremony performed in a church, it is a sacrament, it has requirements that supersede the civil contract. Catholics who seek the sacrament of marriage must be married by a priest (or bishop or cardinal or the pope), and the marriage must take place in a Catholic church—no beach or mountain weddings allowed. If the civil union is dissolved through divorce, the only way that a Catholic who has received the sacrament of marriage may be released from the union is by the process of annulment. Without an annulment, Catholics who are divorced are prohibited from marrying again in the Catholic Church (one may of course marry civilly), and they are prohibited from receiving any of the other sacraments as well, including receiving the Eucharist at weekly Mass. This exclusion from participating in the Eucharist is significant. Not being able to participate in the sacrament of the Eucharist is to be denied the opportunity to be in communion with the body of Christ, and as a result, one is alienated from God.

One of the most powerful sacraments in the Catholic Church is the sacrament of penance. Catholicism requires that believers confess their sins and receive absolution of their sins at least annually, before the celebration of Easter. Catholics are encouraged to go to confession as often as they feel they need to, in other words, every time they believe they have committed a sin. In fact, the sacrament begins with the penitent indicating the last time they participated in the sacrament and detailing the sins they have committed since that last confession. "Dear Father, it has been several weeks since my last confession, and since then I have yelled at my child, taken the Lord's name in vain, and told a lie when I told my supervisor I was sick when in fact I really just needed a day off to take care of things at home." The sacrament of penance is extremely powerful in Catholicism because it is only in this act that sinners can receive Jesus's absolution for their sins. Again, in contrast to Protestant religions in which believers are encouraged to pray to God and seek forgiveness, Catholics cannot receive forgiveness on their own; it can only be obtained through the sacrament of penance. This underscores for Catholics the power of the priest. In the case of confession, the priest is believed to be literally acting as the human embodiment of Christ. This gives priests incredible power. They literally stand between an individual Catholic and a state of alienation from God—and one cannot go to heaven if they are alienated. But it also reinforces for Catholics that priests are not just individuals with religious training, as other ordained ministers are; priests are the physical embodiment of Jesus Christ, a status that cannot be overstated.

# SEX SEGREGATION IN THE CATHOLIC CHURCH

Often when we first begin describing the various institutions that are analyzed in this book, people raise their eyebrows and seem especially skeptical when we mention that one institution we are analyzing is the Catholic Church. Obviously the Catholic Church is a gender-diverse institution. And, yes, the Catholic Church is very gender diverse in its membership. In fact, women are more likely to regularly attend church than are men.

However, as we discussed, women are excluded from all ordained positions in the Catholic Church. The only option for a woman who seeks to serve Jesus and the Church is to become a nun. Nuns do incredible work in local parishes, hospitals, and among the poor, but nuns are not allowed to hold any power in the Catholic Church; they are not even allowed to administer the sacraments. In fact, there is a similar status for men, Catholic brothers. Nuns and brothers, although they are not able to administer the sacraments, are required to take the same vows of poverty and chastity as priests do, and their daily lives are as tightly controlled. They live in gender-segregated communities; they wear a habit, which varies by the denomination to which they consecrate their lives; and they must work in the jobs they are assigned to and live in the communities to which they are assigned, regardless of their individual preferences or professional goals. Most nuns and brothers work as teachers in Catholic schools and nurses in Catholic hospitals.

Though this may seem insignificant at first glance, the Catholic Church has historically segregated even the most minimal lay positions as well, and most important among them to our discussion of child sexual abuse is the altar server. Altar servers assist the priest during the saying of Mass. Servers escort the priest in and out of the sanctuary, light the candles on the altar, perform a hand-washing ritual, and hold the book that the priest reads from when he is performing the transformation of the Eucharist. Up until very recently, the 1990s, this position was exclusively reserved for boys. Even today, individual pastors can set the policy for their churches, and although the Catholic Church does not explicitly prohibit girls from being altar servers, there are still many parishes that do not allow girls to serve in this capacity. Thus, at every level, including in rituals that involve the entire congregation, what one can and cannot do is explicitly regulated by one's gender. And the message could not be more clear that men have *all of the power*, even the opportunity to be altar servers, and women's roles are regulated to serving priests—as housekeepers and cooks—and to serving the Church in traditionally gendered occupations, like teaching and nursing.

Women's voices are simply not present in any significant way, and they are not allowed into any discussions. As the child sex abuse scandal began to gain momentum in the 2000s, we were among many who suggested that the inclusion of women in the conversations and in the leadership may have made a difference in the way the scandal unfolded. This is not to suggest that priests wouldn't have sexually abused children, and certainly we know women are often complicit when the sexual perpetrator is their husband or boyfriend, for example Dotty Sandusky, and when the victims are her children, but overall, women are far more critical of sexual abuse of all kinds, and their voices might have impacted the manner in which reports of abuse were handled.

## THE FRATERNITY OF THE PRIESTHOOD

Men who intend to become priests begin by entering a period of training, which takes place in a seminary. In the United States a college degree is required, although some seminaries allow for the completion of the college degree while in seminary. Seminary training is not only focused on training around the theology and laws of the Catholic Church but also on socializing seminarians into the norms of behavior expected of priests. According to the website for the Office of Vocations in Baltimore, "The seminary is the place where a man is formed mind, body, and soul *into the image of Jesus Christ.*"[5]

In addition to the burden that this vocation demands, including vows of poverty and chastity, and the responsibilities of living the life of Christ, it's not hard to imagine the power that a priest must feel once he is ordained as the physical embodiment of Jesus. As is the case with all of the other institutions we have analyzed in this book, the priesthood is an exclusive club whose members are superior to others and they can use that power to influence the lives of individual Catholics. Certainly, the majority of Catholic priests are honest, authentic men who feel the calling to serve God. But those who choose to abuse their power, whether in influencing politics, the misuse of financial resources, or abusing the vulnerable, have opportunities to do so.

Not only does the Catholic Church function as a total institution for the men ordained as priests and those who advance to the status of bishops and cardinals, but in many ways it also functions as a fraternity. Men live together, eat together—in homes with female housekeepers—socialize together, even take vacations together. They also make decisions together. And, though we would never argue that all men think the same way or hold the same perspectives, there is an abundance of research that suggests that diversity in perspective is a key to successfully navigating challenges to the organization. Segregation also tends to produce a sort of group-think mentality in which one perspective grows to dominate simply by its reinforcement over and over again by people with similar backgrounds and training. For example, in fraternities, young men, isolated from other perspectives, can come to hold beliefs they otherwise never considered, and these beliefs tend to intensify over time. It is not surprising that fraternities often get into trouble when they behave as a group in public, for example, shouting "no means no, yes means anal" as they marched past women's residence halls on the Yale campus.

Similarly, when men who occupy the priesthood have very limited regular contact with people who think differently from them or who live different lives—women, members of other religious organizations—they can develop this kind of group-think mentality as well. And, something that would otherwise seem inappropriate or unreasonable can come to be viewed differently when everyone else around you expresses a common sentiment.

Bryon Cones, in his 2010 essay, describes his experience in seminary as much like basic training in the military or pledging in a fraternity:

> In effect, a Roman Catholic priest is made in a way similar to a U.S. Marine. Candidates are sent away to "basic training" for an extended time, share an intense experience in a strict hierarchical system, and are encouraged to form bonds of brotherhood in that system, in fact, to draw their identity from it. Precious few non-priests are involved in the day-to-day formation of seminarians, and personal contact with parishioners, especially women, is limited and infrequent. One result of such formation is a certain loyalty to the priestly institution, such that priests identify first with their brothers rather than with those they are ordained to serve. (I still detect that tendency in myself though I was never ordained.) One product of such group loyalty has been a systemic failure among priests and bishops to report clerical child sexual abuse, some cases of which are so monstrous they should be labeled rape and torture.

Cones's description sounds eerily similar to the process of pledging and initiation that we describe in our analysis of fraternities; the bonds to the other priests and the loyalty to the institution are the most important in one's life.

The Catholic Church is one of the most hierarchical institutions, and certainly the most hierarchical of any of the world's major religions. Like the military, this hierarchy, as Cones notes in his essay, is an integral part of the training in the seminary. As is the case with any significant hierarchy, those with little power have the least ability to raise questions or concerns. And, when those in the upper ranks of the hierarchy hand down an order or even an opinion, those of lesser "rank" are required to follow that order or invoke that opinion even if it is in opposition to what they believe. This is critical when we think about the child sexual abuse scandal in the Catholic Church. Priests learn early on that one cannot disagree publicly with the church hierarchy. A priest who does so can be defrocked and ex-communicated from the Church. And there are plenty of examples of this in cases involving seemingly far less troubling issues. In 2012 Father Roy Bourgeois was ex-communicated from the Catholic Church for ordaining women. Clearly, ordaining women would violate the very basic tenets of the Catholic Church. But it is hard to imagine that the ordination of a few women by Father Bourgeois warrants ex-communication yet the sexual abuse of dozens, hundreds or even one child does not. It is not hard to imagine that the message to young priests is clear: If you take a suspicion of inappropriate behavior, including child sexual abuse, to your supervisor, and he tells you to leave it alone, the report you are making will simply die in that conversation. To pursue it would be to risk being defrocked, in essence losing your profession, and being ex-communicated, or losing your religion and your pathway to heaven. The costs are simply too great.

The fraternal nature of the priesthood is similar to fraternities in another important way that facilitates sexual abuse, specifically a house with bedrooms. In modern-day Catholic communities, the priests live communally in a rectory or house that is typically near the church. This is distinct from Protestant churches, for example, where the parsonage is reserved for the pastor and his family. The absence of women and other family members makes it easier to engage in behavior that is undetected—though the case of Jerry Sandusky confirms what we already know that much child sexual abuse takes place underneath the noses of wives and girlfriends—and much like a fraternity house, the mere presence of bedrooms with doors that can be locked further facilitates abuse to go on undetected.

The seminary, much like the pledging process in fraternities, is designed to develop a strong sense of brotherhood among priests as well as a loyalty to the Church. In addition to the sense of brotherhood that the priests develop with each other, which is maintained through living together, traveling together, and so on, the ordained Catholic Church is also an elitist group. Priests are members of a club that denies access to all women and to men who are unwilling to forgo a traditional family life. Men who become priests are different from other people; they are special, they are elite, and they are loyal to each other and to their fraternity. Just as we see in the military and in fraternities, brothers always have their brothers' backs. This type of fraternal bond and loyalty is an important element in the child sexual abuse scandal in the Catholic Church. When priests were accused of child sexual abuse, their peers and their superiors tended to close ranks in order to protect their "brother," which further reinforces the perspective that the allegation is false or that it was simply a misunderstanding. We are not sure how any sexual activity between a priest and a child could be a misunderstanding, but that's a different matter.

## COMPARING THE CATHOLIC CHURCH TO OTHER CHRISTIAN RELIGIONS

The Catholic Church is very different from any of the other world religions, specifically in terms of its structure. The Catholic Church is sex segregated; it functions as a total institution, at least for ordained priests, bishops, cardinals, and even the pope; and its hierarchy is universal. The pope oversees the entire community and dictates the policies and protocols that are to be followed. The pope is also charged with the vision of Catholicism, and no one in the ranks is allowed to express any difference of opinion without risking ex-communication. As noted, Father Bourgeois was ex-communicated for ordaining women, people who wanted nothing more than most men seeking ordination want, a chance to serve God in the capacity that makes sense to them. In the Catholic Church, the perspective on ordaining women is not a guideline, it's a ban. The belief that homosexuality is a sin is not an interpretation, it is a fact. Catholics are not given the privilege or responsibility, as Christians in many mainline Protestant faiths are, to interpret the Bible or Catholic doctrine on their own. In fact, individual priests are not even allowed this privilege or opportunity. Nor are bishops or cardinals, except in their capacity as advisors to the pope. It is the pope and the pope alone, the person who most embodies the material expression of God and Jesus, who can dictate doctrine. Complete obedience is required of all Catholics, as congregants as well as ordained members of the Church.

We cannot emphasize enough the power that this hierarchical structure has, particularly when it is combined with the belief that the pope, and by extension all ordained cardinals, bishops, and priests, represents God and Jesus in the material world. The child sex abuse scandal in the Catholic Church can only be understood in this context, one of absolute power and no avenues for disagreement. When a child accuses a priest of sexual abuse, an entire system of internal justice is activated that virtually guarantees that the offender will not be held accountable and he will be free to abuse others.

## CRIMEN SOLLICITATIONIS AND CATHOLIC CHURCH PROTOCOLS

It is clear in studying just a brief history of the Catholic Church that for at least the last eleven hundred years, since the Second Lateran Council in 1139, which instituted mandatory celibacy, that the pope and a variety of councils, have been concerned with the sexual behavior of priests. It should come as no surprise, then, that in 1962 the Vatican developed a protocol for dealing with what was considered to be one of the most egregious acts: soliciting sexual acts in the context of confession. Unlike other religious traditions, the priest alone can absolve one's sins, and thus there is no place more powerful than the confessional for soliciting sex in exchange for absolution. The protocol developed by the Vatican in 1962, Crimen Sollicitationis, Latin for "criminal solicitation," makes it clear that soliciting sex in the context of the confessional violates the official doctrines of the Catholic Church, otherwise known as Canon Law. The document also dictates that rather than go to the police or report the solicitation, even when it involves a minor, the accusation should be handled *internally*. The accused has the right to have his case heard by the Apostolic See—a phrase which refers to the authority of the Catholic Church—that is in the same territory in which the accused resides. In other words, the accused has the *right* to have his case heard and administered by *his* pastor or by the bishop overseeing the diocese to which *he* is assigned.[6] Crimen Sollicitationis mandates that the accused, already suffering from his own conscience, be counseled and evaluated. And, if necessary, he may be removed from some of his ministry or transferred to another assignment.

According to Crimen Sollicitationis the "confessional" is broadly defined and can be in any place someone felt they could confess, for example, in a pew in the church, in the sacristy, in the rectory, in the priest's office, or anywhere else one felt was appropriate. Though many of the child sexual abuse lawsuits do not denote that the sexual abuse took place in the context of a formal confession, the reliance on Crimen Sollicitationis by leaders in the Catholic Church implies that they understood the accusations to fall under this doctrine.

An interesting, but perhaps not so surprising, turn of fate is that the architect of Crimen Sollicitationis was a man named Joseph Ratzinger. Forty years after he authored the policy that was utilized to protect the Catholic Church from the tens of thousands of allegations of child sexual abuse, on four continents, Cardinal Joseph Ratzinger was elected by his colleagues to serve as pope. He took the name Pope Benedict. Clearly, the Catholic Church rewarded men whose loyalty lay first and foremost with the Church. In addition to being loyal, these men also engaged in a form of spiritual abuse by putting the Church above the victims of such horrible crimes.

There is some debate over the degree to which Crimen Sollicitationis is the policy that explicitly resulted in the pastors and bishops moving priests who have been accused of child sexual abuse to other parishes, or if Crimen Sollicitationis is merely a scapegoat for other factors that contributed to the covering up of child sexual abuse, or to what degree Crimen Sollicitationis applies to the majority of child sex abuse which may or may not be taking place in the context of confession. What we know is that the over many decades, beginning at least in the early 1960s, hundreds of Catholic priests were accused of sexual abuse and almost all of the cases were handled internally. Priests were asked to confess; they were urged to pray; and then they were simply moved to another, often less visible, parish filled with children who were even more vulnerable.

In personal communication with a former Catholic priest and Canon Law scholar, we were cautioned that Crimen Sollicitationis ought not to become a scapegoat in our analysis, that other factors also contributed to the mishandling of sexual abuse allegations that resulted in the cover-up.

## Counseling and Forgiveness amid a Cover-Up

According to our source, the early 1960s, the same time period when Crimen Sollicitationis was adopted, was a time of transformation and modernization in the Catholic Church. The Second Vatican Council, under the leadership of Pope John Paul XXIII, which convened in 1962, the same year that Crimen Sollicitationis was adopted, sought to open up the Church and make it more accessible to the average Catholic. Among other things, the Council instituted celebrating Mass in the language of the congregation, rather than in Latin, and opening up opportunities for laymen and women to be involved not only in the Mass itself but also in the day-to-day workings of parishes, schools, and hospitals. John Paul XXIII advocated for a more humane Church that focused on forgiveness rather than punishment as well as a Church that embraced rather than rejected science. The reader will recall that it was the Catholic Church that administered the Spanish Inquisition, which, among other things, excommunicated Galileo for his scientific discovery that the Earth was not the center of the universe. According to our source, this transformation in the 1960s opened up the possibility that psychologists and others would be consulted in order to help develop policies and practices for evaluating priests accused of child sexual abuse and providing appropriate interventions for them.

As social scientists we certainly embrace the fact that the Catholic Church opened up enough to include scholars and experts in the development of these policies and practices. The problem is that the science of the early 1960s and well into the 1980s viewed pedophilia as a disease that could be treated by counseling and in some cases behavior modification programs and that successful completion of a treatment program would result in a priest (or any pedophile) being able to return to positions in which he worked closely with children. Coupled with Pope John Paul XXIII's call to forgive rather than punish, allegations of child sexual abuse were handled by meeting with the accused, asking him to pray for forgiveness, and possibly referring or requiring him to attend counseling in a *Catholic based program*. This practice is in clear violation of best practices developed by researchers who treat pedophilia: "[Review of] predictors of treatment outcome conclude that pedophilia is extremely difficult to treat and that effective treatment needs to be intensive, long-term, and comprehensive, possibly with lifetime follow-up."[7] As the cases of child sexual abuse in the Catholic Church reveal, even priests who received treatment and returned to the ministry, which the vast majority did, continued to sexually abuse young children.

Our "informant" also cautioned us, based on his own experience, about the widespread understanding of Crimen Sollicitationis among local priests. Our informant noted that in order for Crimen Sollicitationis to be one of the strategies used to cover up child sexual abuse by priests, those charged with making decisions—pastors, bishops, even cardinals—would have to have knowledge of the doctrine. In his experience in the priesthood, and based on his conversations with fellow priests who had studied at the North American College, an elite seminary for Americans in Rome, he noted that very few priest have any significant training in policies like Crimen Sollicitationis and therefore they may not have been explicitly following it when they hid cases of child sexual abuse and moved abusive priests around from parish to parish. This is an important consideration and certainly reinforces the other explanations we have laid out in this discussion. Priests charged with investigating allegations of child sexual abuse may have believed the child was lying and may have chosen to hide the allegations in order to protect their brother priest and out of loyalty to the church—believing that doing so was protecting the best interest of the church. And in cases where they did believe the allegations, they followed the customs and norms of the post Vatican II proclamations and counseled the accused to seek forgiveness and attend counseling so that he might return to his ministry. When all else failed and allegations continued, decision-makers moved abusive priests around, perhaps intentionally trying to cover up the abuse, and perhaps hoping that a change of scenery and distance from the target of his abuse might quell his behavior. As we know from the psychological research and the lawsuits, pedophiles don't stop abusing just because they are moved from one community to another. Instead, they begin grooming a new community and searching for new victims, as Malcolm Gladwell describes in his 2012 essay. We encourage the reader to return to the section on child sexual abuse in our discussion of SportsWorld on pages 133–137 in order to review the definitions of child sexual abuse and the typical grooming strategies used by pedophiles. Regardless of the intentionality of individual pastors and bishops who may have intentionally or unintentionally handled child sexual abuse by covering it up and moving pedophile priests from one parish to another, their actions harmed thousands of innocent children.

## STATISTICS ON CHILD SEXUAL ABUSE IN THE CATHOLIC CHURCH

The scope of the child sex abuse scandal in the Catholic Church is nothing short of overwhelming. We start by acknowledging that the vast majority of Catholic priests are not child sex abusers. However, just because most priests are not child sexual predators does not in any way minimize the enormity of the scandal. Church should be a safe place for everyone, including children. What makes the child sex abuse scandal in the Catholic Church so damaging is that *tens of thousands of young children were not safe in church.*

Though most priests are not pedophiles, one of the most disturbing aspects of the child sex abuse scandal is its universality. On every continent where there is a reasonable Catholic presence, including Europe, the Americas, Latin America, and Australia, thousands and thousands of victims have come forward claiming Catholic priests sexually abused them. And just as in the United States, on every other continent where allegations have been made, abusive priests were moved around in an attempt to cover up their crimes. Child sexual abuse and the cover-up are not limited to one priest, one parish, one bishop, not even to one country or continent. This is the most profound evidence that the strategy to deal with allegations of child sexual abuse was systematic, for all of the reasons we lay out here, including the official policies contained in Crimen Sollicitationis.

The U.S. College of Catholic Bishops commissioned researchers at the John Jay College of Criminal Justice to examine the data and the cases of allegations of child sexual abuse in the United States. The John Jay report covers the years 1950 to 2002. As contained in the report, researchers uncovered that a total of 4,392 priests were accused of abusing 10,667 children under the age of eighteen for the period 1950–2002, *just in the United States*. One of the more startling findings in the John Jay College report is this:

> The majority of priests (56%) were alleged to have abused one victim, nearly 27% were alleged to have abused two or three victims, nearly 14% were alleged to have abused four to nine victims and 3.4% were alleged to have abused more than ten victims. The 149 priests (3.5%) who had more than ten allegations of abuse were allegedly responsible for abusing 2,960 victims, thus accounting for 26% of allegations. Therefore, a very small percentage of accused priests are responsible for a substantial percentage of the allegations.[8]

Drilling down into the numbers, in the period from 1950 to 2002 there were 4,392 reported cases of Catholic priest child sex abuse. During the period from 2004 to 2014, approximately another 3,400 cases were reported, and 401 cases were reported in 2013 alone. Since 2004, some 848 priests have been defrocked, and over 2, 572 have been given lesser sentences because of age or illness. The *overwhelming majority* never set foot in a courthouse, let alone a prison.

We imagine that one might take comfort in knowing that only a small percentage of accused priests (3.5 percent) were responsible for approximately one-third of the child sexual abuse. We actually find this to be extremely troubling. Why? For two reasons. First, it confirms the claim that these abusive priests were pedophiles. Sexual abuse was not a single act; it was not a single mistake. These were serial rapists. Second, this confirms the cover up. It would be impossible for any priest to sexually abuse as many victims as these 3.5 percent did without being discovered. How would no one notice a priest like Fr. Geoghan sexually abusing hundreds of children? Rather, this evidence strongly confirms our argument that when allegations were made, supervisors engaged in inappropriate, in fact, *illegal*, strategies for addressing the abuse—providing inadequate counseling, encouraging confession, and forgiveness—and when the abuse continued, moving the abuser to increasingly remote parishes.

Frankly, we find this behavior unforgivable. When sexual predators are not held accountable, not only are thousands of children put at risk for child sexual abuse, but by moving abusers to remote locations, they are less supervised and thus more able to engage in abuse. Moving priests to remote locations may seem like a strategy to reduce the potential number of future victims by reducing the number of available children, but in fact, what happens instead is that priests sexually abused significant proportions of the children in their midst. In St. Michael's, Alaska, 80 percent, nearly *every* child in a single generation was sexually abused.

Finally, we ask how priests, men of God, sent to guide humanity in the ways of Jesus toward eternal salvation, went to bed at night knowing they were harboring criminals who were committing what even prisoners say is the most heinous crime. And, even if only a small number of all priests were sexually abusing children, we still find it hard to believe that most priests knew nothing about it.

Numbers are, of course, very important when we talk about any phenomenon like the child sex abuse scandal in the Catholic Church, just as they are when we talk about rape on college campuses or in prisons or in the military. But often more powerful than the numbers are the stories of the victims that reveal the power of the experience and the impact on their lives. For most victims of sexual abuse—children and adults—looking only at the numbers appears to reduce their experiences to a single moment in time, when, as we know, the impact of sexual abuse lasts a lifetime. Ideally, with appropriate intervention and treatment, the impact of the abuse lessens with time, but it never goes away, and even among those who are "healed," the experience continues to influence the way they interpret the world and make decisions. For the victims of child sexual abuse at the hands of a priest, the impact is often more severe because the victims almost always held the "secret" for a long time, and as a result of not telling anyone, they didn't receive appropriate and timely therapy and treatment. They often tried to self-medicate and thus developed problems with drugs and alcohol. Many male victims struggled with their sexual identity. All the while, the abuser continued to move freely through the community, loved by everyone.

One of the most tragic aspects of child sexual abuse in the Catholic Church is the spiritual abuse that priests waged on the souls of young children. Beyond simply using the confessional as a vehicle for perpetrating sexual abuse, pedophile priests took advantage of the Catholic ideology that they are the embodiment of Jesus Christ. Many pedophile priests invoked their special status when they preyed on victims, claiming, for example, "This (sexual activity) will make us closer to God," or "This (sexual activity) is a way to show special love to Jesus." Not only were pedophile priests abusing the trust that children had in them, they were committing spiritual abuse. The trauma of the spiritual abuse magnifies the impact of the sexual abuse—first, because the abuser uses the victim's faith to force them into sexual acts; and second, the Church further abuses victims by protecting abusive priests and refusing to take the allegations of victims seriously. As a result, victims were traumatized not only by individual priests, but by the entire institution of the Catholic Church.

## CASE STUDIES OF CHILD SEXUAL ABUSE IN THE CATHOLIC CHURCH

We could write entire volumes on the cases of child sexual abuse in the Catholic Church. More than ten thousand victims means more than ten thousand individual stories. And, of course, we know that this figure is likely a gross underestimate of the actual number of children sexually abused by Catholic priests. We chose just a few cases in order to illustrate the wide-ranging impact of child sexual abuse in the United States Catholic Church.

### Boston, Massachusetts

Perhaps the most widely publicized case of child sexual abuse by a Catholic priest is that of Father Geoghan of Boston. His case is widely known for a number of reasons, because the case in Boston broke open the scandal in the United States, because of the number of victims, and because he ultimately went to prison and was killed shortly into his incarceration.

Father Geoghan was a priest who served in six different parishes in the diocese of Boston across thirty years, from 1962 to 1993, when he retired. Over the course of his thirty-year career he was accused of sexually abusing 130 boys. For a variety of reasons, including the expiration of the statute of limitations and victims being reluctant to testify, Father Geoghan was tried on only one count of sexual abuse, for a case in 1991. He was defrocked by Pope John Paul II in 1998 and sentenced in 2002 to nine years in prison. In August 2003, he was murdered in prison by an acknowledged white supremacist already serving a life sentence.

We choose this particular case not only because of the fact that Father Geoghan's case is so well known but also because this particular case provides such a clear illustration of so many of the patterns that we see in child sexual abuse cases. Father Geoghan targeted vulnerable families and was revered in the community; no one believed the allegations. We know from examining a variety of sources that during his thirty-year career, Geoghan admitted to molesting dozens of boys and was sent to at least five different treatment facilities. What we also know from the civil settlements against the Archdiocese of Boston, is that not only did Geoghan have more than one hundred victims, but there were a total of 895 victims in Boston alone. The Archdiocese will not release the names of all of the priests who have been credibly accused, but it is clear that there were likely dozens if not more than one hundred priests who were accused of child sexual abuse. This case illustrates the profound impact of the cover-up, the moving of accused priests from one parish to another, never providing appropriate interventions. As a result of this cover-up, hundreds more children were subjected to sexual abuse, because Cardinal Law, who oversaw the Archdiocese of Boston refused to remove perpetrators completely from the ministry until they could demonstrate that they were in fact "cured," which, as we noted, is a state that is very unlikely to be achieved.

The Boston case served as a watershed moment in the Catholic Church child sex abuse scandal. In the years since the scandal broke in Boston, hundreds of priests in dozens of diocese around the world have faced accusations by tens of thousands of victims. Beginning with the case in Boston, courts have ruled that the bishops and archbishops who knew about the accusations and allowed priests to be moved from parish to parish were responsible for this complicity. In some of these cases the bishops and archbishops have resigned, as was the case with Cardinal Law in Boston, who resigned in 2002, after admitting that for decades under his leadership the Archdiocese of Boston dealt with accused priests like Geoghan without a full understanding of the nature of pedophilia. *None have gone to prison for their role in facilitating child sexual abuse in the Catholic Church.*

## St. Michael, Alaska

One of the most remote communities in which allegations of child sexual abuse against Catholic priests have been made is the parish of St. Michael, Alaska. In contrast to Boston, St. Michael is a remote fishing village in western Alaska. It is accessible only by boat or by air. According to the United States Census, the small village has fewer than four hundred residents, living in ninety households. The median household income is $34,000 per year, approximately $15,000 below the national average, and one in four people living in St. Michael lives below the poverty line. The economy of St. Michael centers on subsistence fishing, hunting, trapping, and gardening. It is without a doubt a very poor and isolated community. The complexities of power are self-evident in the child sex abuse in St. Michael. White men with power sexually and spiritually abused the most vulnerable: poor Alaskan native children. And, though there is evidence that Church officials knew about the abuse taking place in St. Michael, no one could be bothered to lift a finger for these incredibly vulnerable victims.

Catholic missionaries came to St. Michael, Alaska, in 1899, just thirty years after the United States government purchased Alaska. Father George S. Endal arrived in St. Michael in 1936 and across a forty-plus-year career, he moved in and out of St. Michael and other remote Alaskan villages. In 1949 he met Joseph Lundowski, a non-ordained volunteer in Catholic parishes and communities across rural Alaska. Posted together in St. Michael, from 1961 to 1987, between them *these two men sexually abused nearly an entire generation of children in St. Michael, nearly 100 victims, both boys and girls.* More troubling is the fact that there is evidence of communication between parish priests and the vicar dating back to as early as 1965 warning about accusations of sexual abuse by Endal, Lundowski, and the then famous Father Jim Poole, who was allegedly known for having a penchant for taking girls into his bedroom.[9]

According to the details laid out in a lawsuit and reported in the *Los Angeles Times*, not only is there evidence for a cover up, but for the systematic movement of pedophile priests into the most remote and vulnerable communities:

> A dozen priests and three missionaries were accused of sexually abusing Eskimo children in 15 villages and Nome, [Alaska] from 1961 to 1987. The flood of allegations led to accusations that the Eskimo communities were a *dumping ground* [emphasis ours] for abusive priests and lay workers affiliated with the Jesuit order, which supplied bishops, priests and lay missionaries to the Fairbanks diocese.[10]

Even one victim of child sexual abuse is too many. But the case of St. Michael forces us to ask the question: What is the impact of this degree of child sexual abuse on an entire community? As noted, St. Michael is already a very poor community populated by one of the most marginalized people in the United States: Alaskan Natives. As the *Frontline* documentary *The Silence* makes clear, the aftermath of the child sexual abuse in St. Michael is a story of alcoholism, unemployment, and domestic violence. What responsibility does the Catholic Church have for not only allowing the child sexual abuse to continue, but for purposively placing known pedophiles in this community? How many children might never have been sexually abused if the Catholic Church had taken the allegations seriously? How many social problems facing St. Michael would never have been born had priests not abused an entire generation of its residents?

Just as we were putting the final edits to this book, the child sex abuse scandal in the Catholic Church broke open, again, in what will perhaps become its biggest case yet, covering the entire Commonwealth of Pennsylvania.

On August 14, 2018, several media outlets, including the *Washington Post*, released the findings of the Grand Jury of Pennsylvania. Titled, *40th Statewide*

*Investigating Grand Jury Report 1*,[11] the report details the results of the long eighteen-month investigation of child sexual abuse by priests in six Pennsylvania dioceses, including Allentown, Erie, Greensburg, Harrisburg, Pittsburgh, and Scranton, The 1,400-page report revealed that the massive and deliberate cover-up resulted in more than one thousand victims who were abused by at least three hundred priests identified in the report. Some of the victims were as young as seven years old and some as old as 83. Because of the cover-up, many of the cases have extended past the state's statutes of limitation, but according to the Pennsylvania Attorney General's Office, they will pursue prosecution of as many cases as they can, hoping to get justice for at least some of the victims.

## CIVIL LITIGATION

As we have detailed throughout this chapter, it has been nearly impossible to get justice for the victims of child sexual abuse at the hands of Catholic priests. Despite combing through the data and reports, it is difficult to get an accurate estimate of the number of priests who have been convicted and sent to prison, but it is clear that the number is low. In many cases, dioceses avoided criminal prosecution of accused priest by retiring them and moving them into retirement communities, many of which are quite luxurious, with the hope that by removing them from any access to children, they would stop sexually abusing children. What an ironic twist of fate that priests who took a vow of poverty get to retire in upscale communities while their victims get no justice, legal or financial. And, nowhere in these cases is there any mention of requiring these retired priests to undergo appropriate treatment for pedophilia; they are simply hidden away from public view.

In terms of seeking justice, a far more successful strategy that many victims have pursued has been to sue individual dioceses for both the sexual abuse perpetrated by member priests, but also for the cover-up that bishops and archbishops engaged in that allowed the abusers to prey on more victims. The cost to the Church has been enormous. Between 2004 and 2011, somewhere in the neighborhood of $3 billion to $5 billion has been spent to settle lawsuits and at least eight dioceses in the United States alone, have had to declare bankruptcy, including Portland, Tucson, Spokane, Davenport, San Diego, Fairbanks, Wilmington, Milwaukee, and the Archdiocese of Saint Paul and Minneapolis.

The largest payout to date has been in the Los Angeles Archdiocese, which settled clergy sex abuse cases among 508 victims for $660 million. Second is the case in the state of Minnesota, where the Archdiocese of St. Paul and Minneapolis has agreed to pay a $210 million settlement to 450 victims of clergy sexual abuse. It is one of the largest payouts to date in the Catholic Church sexual abuse scandal in the United States.

Examining cases outside of the United States, for example in Australia and at the Vatican, illustrates the enormity of the outcome of not handling child sexual abuse and allowing perpetrators to move from one community to another to abuse more and more children. In Australia, in 2018, Archbishop Philip Wilson of Adelaide was found guilty of hiding child sex abuse by fellow priests that dated back to the 1970s. Wilson is the senior-most Catholic cleric ever to be charged with concealing abusers. He is not alone.

In Rome, treasurer for the Vatican Cardinal George Pell is, at the time of this writing, under investigation for child sex abuse he allegedly perpetrated in the 1970s and 1980s. All of these cases together illuminate a *pattern* unfolding from Boston to Rochester, Minnesota, to California, to Australia straight up to the door of the Vatican! To argue that the cover-up is not systematic, is not informed by Vatican doctrine, is nothing short of naive or ridiculous.

Although it has taken many, many decades, we have to acknowledge the hard work of victims, their families, and savvy attorneys who have fought legal battle after legal battle with one of the richest institutions in the world, in the quest to have their day in court. It is estimated that the Catholic Church—which, of course, has a tax free status—is worth between $15 and $50 billion dollars, and yet, with all that money, the Catholic Church continues to fight victims' attempts to claim resources (mainly money) for the years of abuse by the very priests who vowed to "serve" their parishioners.

A nonprofit organization, Bishopaccountability.org,[12] has as its mission exposing the sexual abuse in the Catholic Church. This organization culls public records and provides information on every case of alleged child sexual abuse, details about the accused, as well as the outcomes of civil lawsuits. We caution the reader that not all cases of alleged child sexual abuse can be factually demonstrated, and thus using the database as a tool in a witch hunt would be dangerous. That said, the database paints a vivid picture of the breadth and depth of child sexual abuse by priests. We find it most useful as a clearinghouse for data on the lawsuits. What is evident in the data is that many dioceses, not just the one's we feature here, involved dozens of priests who were moved around from parish to parish by bishops and archbishops who had received sexual abuse allegations multiple times, often across several decades. As a result of their unwillingness or inability to handle allegations of sexual abuse properly, thousands of children were needlessly sexually abused by priests.

And, though these financial settlements have brought some relief to the victims, and a small number of dioceses and archdioceses have been forced into bankruptcy, $5 billion in settlements is but a tiny fraction of the wealth of the Catholic Church. We wonder when the cost—financial, shame, declining membership—will be great enough for the Catholic Church to take child sexual abuse by their priests seriously.

## A TALE OF NO ACCOUNTABILITY:
## CARDINAL TIMOTHY DOLAN

The child sex abuse scandal in the Catholic Church is deeply disturbing. But what is perhaps most troublesome is the fact that some bishops and archbishops who not only covered up allegations of child sexual abuse but oversaw strategies for more effective cover-ups were promoted through the ranks of the Catholic Church. Cardinal Timothy Dolan, now the president of the US Council of Catholic Bishops and the most prominent leader in the Catholic Church in the United States, in his term as archbishop of the Diocese of Milwaukee hid money to protect it from lawsuits and devised a plan to pay priests accused of sexual abuse to leave the priesthood. Cardinal Dolan expressed concern to then Cardinal Ratzinger that the child sex abuse scandal could rock the Catholic Church. Ratzinger who is the architect of Crimen Sollicitationis, was charged by the Vatican to handle allegations of child sexual abuse for decades, from the early 1960s through his election in 2005 as pope, when he took the name Benedict. "Cardinal Dolan told Cardinal Ratzinger that 'as victims organise and become more public, the potential for true scandal is very real.'"[13] Dolan did his very best to protect the diocese of Milwaukee from the financial burden associated with compensating victims of child sexual abuse. Records were released as part of bankruptcy hearings for the diocese of Milwaukee:

> The documents provide new details on Cardinal Dolan's plan to pay some abusers to leave the priesthood and move the $57 million into a trust for "improved protection" as the Milwaukee archdiocese prepared to file for bankruptcy amid dozens of abuse claims. A Vatican office approved the request to move the money.[14]

How can one make sense of Dolan's, or for that matter Raztinger's, participation in the cover-up and his rise to the highest position in the Catholic Church in the United States? It is difficult to imagine such a professional climb if the

Vatican were truly interested in addressing the child sex abuse scandal and eradicating child sexual abuse perpetrated by its priests. On the other hand, Dolan's promotion is quite logical if he is being rewarded for his expertise in protecting the Catholic Church and its assets. Whether it is explicit policies or loyalty to the fraternity of the Catholic Church, these documents suggest that Cardinal Dolan was well aware of the consequences of the child sex abuse scandal and chose to protect the Church rather than hold pedophile priests accountable and protect the children of Milwaukee.

It can be very difficult to have any optimism at the end of reading a chapter such as this one, which details such horrific crimes being perpetrated by religious leaders upon the most vulnerable in their care. And, as many have noted in their discussions of the child sexual abuse scandal in the Catholic Church, though only a tiny fraction of priests have perpetrated child sexual abuse, the scandal has shaken the faith of many in this institution. We add that it should shake our faith in this institution because far more damaging than the acts of this small number of abusive priests is the complicity of the institution in their abuse by failing to hold them accountable and thereby exposing future victims to thousands of acts of sexual abuse. The child sex abuse scandal in the Catholic Church worldwide is quite simply the direct result of specific and systematic policies and practices that placed the interests of the Catholic Church above the needs of its most vulnerable members. This is not the case of a few bad apples spoiling the barrel, but rather of the barrel being designed to protect the bad apples.

## WHAT CAN BE DONE?

### Use Internal Hierarchy for Good

If there is anything to be optimistic about, it is the fact that the hierarchy of the Catholic Church could be transformed to eradicate child sexual abuse rather than facilitate it. With the right kind of leadership by the pope, the loyalties of all of the thousands of priests who support the Church, the bishops who supervise them, and the cardinals who advise the pope, the hierarchy could be transformed and refocused on rooting out pedophile priests, holding them accountable, and protecting the youngest and most vulnerable members of the Catholic community worldwide. Unlike the lack of hierarchy in the other world religions, the very hierarchy that is distinct in the Catholic Church could be turned from evil to good. And this is where our optimism lies.

On June 9, 2015, Pope Francis established the office of Congregation for the Doctrine of the Faith that would address sexual assault issues in the priesthood but especially—for the first time—deal with bishops who have not addressed these difficult issues with their priests, especially those who simply moved abusive priests from parish to parish. This new development is significant in that it is the power that the bishops have, especially to move priests from one parish to another, that was never addressed as the church fought to find ways to skirt pedophilia in the ranks of priests.

For all of the optimism that might be had from this move by Pope Francis, in the summer of 2017, Pope Francis's handpicked senior financial advisor, Cardinal George Pell, was charged in Austrian court with child sexual abuse. We have to ask the question, how can Pope Francis meet his obligation to the billions of Catholics worldwide if he can't even keep his own house in order?

## Demand Accountability and Prosecution

It is obvious that the best way to prevent any crime is to remove the perpetrators from the community. Just as rapists must be removed from college campuses and from military duty, priests who perpetrate child sexual abuse need to be removed from the priesthood, and their criminal prosecution should be supported rather than blocked by the Catholic Church. Going one step further, child sexual abuse is a crime that requires mandatory reporting. When a pastor or bishop receives an allegation of child sexual abuse, he is legally mandated to call child protective services, who will begin an investigation. Pastors and bishops who knowingly moved pedophile priests around should be legally culpable for ignoring their obligations as mandatory reporters.

## IMPROVE RECORD KEEPING AND BACKGROUND CHECKS

Any comprehensive strategy for preventing child sexual abuse must include other recommendations as well. For example, according to Jennifer Haselberger, who spent five years as Archbishop John Nienstedt's archivist and top adviser on Roman Catholic Church law, found that the Church had chaotic record keeping practices that contributed to the ease in hiding pedophiles. In her audit she discovered that despite requirements to conduct background checks, seminaries in the United States stopped conducting background checks in the early 1990s.[15] Quite clearly, Haselberger's recommendations to keep accurate records and to conduct background checks would prevent some pedophiles from coming into the priesthood to begin with and would prevent perpetrators from moving on their own from one location to another as Joseph Lundowski did in St. Michael across several decades.

## Provide Education to Priests-in-Training

The seminary provides another opportunity for training future priests in ways that reduce child sexual abuse and encourage appropriate interventions when it is reported. In addition to training future priests about proper ways to detect and report sexual abuse, the seminary also provides an opportunity to train young men to establish close relationships with each other and with the families whom they seek to support in ways that are healthy and not in any way abusive. We do want to be clear: Celibacy is not the cause of child sexual abuse and it is absolutely wrong to conflate the two. That being said, celibacy is not a choice devoid of sexuality, it is a choice about sexuality, and it must be central in seminary training.

The majority of men who enter the seminary are young. One of the challenges the Catholic Church has faced is criticism, specifically in the wake of the child sex abuse scandal, that sexuality training has been inadequate in preparing men for a life of celibacy. There are many accounts online of priests reflecting on the training that was mandated in the 1950s and 1960s and the training that is required since the child sex abuse scandal broke. Most recall that in the 1950s and 1960s sex was rendered to that category of things never to be talked about. And, celibacy was believed to be a matter of prayer, self-control, and rules. For example, in the 1950s and 1960s, when a priest rode in a car with a woman, even his mother, one must be in the front seat and one in the back seat. When a priest met with a woman in his office, the desk must be between them and the door must be open. What we know about sexuality in general is that rules rarely work. And, that what is most effective in impacting sexual behavior is education; for example, the age of first intercourse increases by one year when teenagers receive comprehensive sex education in comparison to when they are not given any sex education or when the only education they receive is abstinence only.

Seminarians, who are often teenagers or young adults, are, like most people in that age group, experiencing a sexual awakening. Rather than ignoring their emerging sexuality, pretending that they will simply *just be* celibate, what they need is education and training around sexuality. They also need *strategies*, not rules, to aid them in living a celibate life. One of the things we know is that priests often engage in sexual abuse, of adults and of children, when they feel socially isolated. The abuse can, among other things, be a way for them to make a personal connection, as abusive as that may be, with another person. Seminarians need strategies that will help them develop close personal, nonsexual relationships so that they don't feel isolated and pursue abusive strategies as a salve for social isolation. Seminarians need to be trained to seek help when they need it and to form relationships of trust in which they can share their feelings and struggles with regards to their sexuality. Whether a priest is considering pursuing a sexual relationship with an adult or sexually abusing a child, priests who are experiencing the desire to express their sexuality by abusing children might be detected earlier and provided with appropriate mental health interventions that can prevent them from ever acting on their pedophilic urges.

## PROVIDE EDUCATION TO LAYPEOPLE AND CHILDREN

The Catholic Church should also be providing its members with information about child sexual abuse so that they are better able to identify warning signs, so that they know how to report their suspicions, and so that they can talk to their children about appropriate and inappropriate touching, which will empower them to report anything that doesn't feel right and that may be potentially abusive. One of the barriers to effectively empowering children about child sexual abuse is that the grooming process can make it difficult to identify the moment when one should be concerned. By teaching children what is appropriate and not appropriate when it comes to touching by adults, experts believe that a significant amount of child sexual abuse can be interrupted before it really starts. Children can be taught, for example, that an adult putting a hand on their thigh or brushing up against their genital areas is never OK and should be reported to a parent or other trusted adult as soon as possible. Far too often, children and their parents are afraid of making a mountain out of a molehill, so to speak, and the abuse becomes significantly more serious before it is ever reported.

## FINAL THOUGHTS

Lastly, to Catholics and non-Catholics alike, to priests and teachers and police officers and school nurses, and most of all to parents: Children almost never lie about being sexually abused. We need to shift our culture so that children are believed. When we empower our children to speak the truth and when we believe them, we not only interrupt the abuse but we provide the beginning of a healing process that will reduce the impact of the abuse on them. We call on the

Catholic Church to hold the leadership accountable at all levels and to employ any means necessary—policy changes, reporting strategies, seminary training, and prevention programs—to eradicate child sexual abuse and make the Church safe for everyone, especially its littlest members. Their spiritual health is in your hands.

# 8

# HOLLYWOOD, WASHINGTON, DC, AND THE #METOO MOVEMENT

I was confused and at a loss because I could not believe that anyone would believe me over Bill Cosby.

—Margie Shapiro

Although sexual harassment and assault, as well as intimate partner violence, have always been part of the entertainment industry and United States politics, beginning in the summer of 2017, a new social movement, #MeToo, flooded our Facebook, Twitter, and Instagram accounts, and more than one hundred women accused well-known, in some cases iconic, men in entertainment and politics with sexual harassment, sexual violence, and intimate partner violence. Many things felt different about the #MeToo movement; among the most striking was the speed at which companies, corporations, and Congress acted. Often within days of being accused, senators, including Al Franken, and Oscar Award–winning actor Kevin Spacey were forced to resign or had their characters written out of popular and ongoing, TV and Netflix series.

We decided to treat these two institutions together, rather than separately, for a variety of reasons, but primarily because of their co-emergence in the #MeToo movement. Interestingly, although women have accused men in other industries with sexual or intimate partner violence or harassment under the hashtag #MeToo, these are the two industries that have received the brunt of the attention, it is these accusations that have been made most public, and it is these institutions that have acted most swiftly.

The Time's Up and #MeToo movements are finally exposing the sexual harassment and assault women have experienced in their professional entertainment careers for decades. Tarana Burke founded the "MeToo" movement in 2006 to raise awareness of the pervasive sexual assault faced by women in society. The #MeToo hashtag soared to popularity when actress Ashley Judd used it on twitter to expose Harvey Weinstein's sexual abuse. The Time's Up movement was founded in response to the Weinstein scandal and the #MeToo movement as a way to protect women from sexual assault, provide support to victims, and offer opportunities for legal remedies. Time's Up includes a large legal defense fund and hundreds of volunteer lawyers.

Hollywood is no stranger to sexual assault. In fact, the power held by entertainment bigwigs creates a hotbed for toxic masculinity and sexual harassment, a "locker room" climate according to businessman Donald Trump. In 2017, comedian Louis C. K. was accused of masturbating in front of women he had worked with, something his male colleagues were aware of years before accusations were made public.[1]

In January 2018, allegations against comedian Aziz Ansari surfaced when an anonymous woman accused him of sexual assault. She decided to share her story after watching Ansari receive an Emmy while wearing a #TimesUp button. The woman said that Ansari had repeatedly pressured her for sex while at his apartment after she made it clear she did not want to engage in any sexual acts. While they did not have intercourse, the woman believed Ansari had groomed her to perform sexual acts she did not wish to engage in. The fallout of this accusation has been mixed. Many supporters of Ansari responded that she could have left at any point and chose not to do so. For them, the encounter was one of regret, not assault. Feminist writer Jessica Valenti's response to the Ansari accusations presented a different perspective:

"A lot of men will read that post about Aziz Ansari and see an everyday, reasonable sexual interaction. But part of what women are saying right now is that what the culture considers 'normal' sexual encounters are not working for us, and [are] oftentimes harmful."[2]

## ENTERTAINMENT AND POLITICS AS "TOTAL INSTITUTIONS"

The world of United States politics is in no way a total institution. But, much like the military, the system of politics in the United States is highly regimented, bureaucratic, and hierarchical, and at the federal level, it has its own, internal system of justice. We focus our attention here on national politics because, of all levels of government, this level functions the most like the other institutions we interrogate in this book and because this is where the #MeToo movement has had the most impact.

Membership in the United States Congress is highly coveted and those rare 545 people who serve in any given year are under intense public scrutiny, especially by the news media, which cover their every move. As they should. In the age of "fake news," many have commented on the importance of a free press in the democracy. In response, the United States government, a body not fond of scandals, has developed a tight set of rules and regulations that govern members' behavior. Unlike private citizens, members of the federal government are public servants, and as such, they are required, by law and tradition, to comply with a variety of rules and policies that, to the private citizen, would seem very personal, invasive, and controlling. Only a small number of these are related to sexual and intimate partner violence and harassment. Googling "Congress rules" reveals a website where one can download the Members' Congressional Handbook. The handbook details everything from the use of volunteers and interns to the types of things that a member of Congress can have reimbursed from their "Member's Representational Allowance," or MRA. And, the rules are very clear. For example, a member of Congress can use their MRA to pay (or be reimbursed) for their "travel to a parade" but they may not use their MRA to pay or be reimbursed for any other expenses associated with a parade. And if they use their MRA to pay or be reimbursed for travel to a parade, "then no campaign activity or materials are permissible at the parade." Members of Congress are highly restricted in terms of when they can send direct campaign mail, which cannot be sent fewer than 90 days before an election, including primaries. Aides are able to log on to a website that has a map with each state detailing the last day for mailing. Members of Congress face limits on the types of gifts they can receive (absolutely no gifts from lobbyists), including a detailed set of rules surrounding invitations to attend events for free. Members of Congress cannot engage in any activities that would constitute a conflict of interest, and neither can their staff. For example, no staffer earning more than $25,000 can serve as a consultant (including medical, real estate, or legal services). Government does not rise to the level of a total institution, but the regulations and rules that members are required to abide by certainly constrain member behavior.

Of all the industries we examine in this book, the entertainment industry has perhaps the fewest qualities of a total institution. Similar to SportsWorld in many ways, what is absent from the entertainment industry is a governing body like the NCAA or professional organizations like the NBA or the NFL. The entertainment industry is a loosely connected set of private corporations that produce the majority of audiovisual entertainment consumed in the United

States and marketed abroad. At its beginning, film companies like 20th Century Fox "owned" actors and actresses, whom they signed to long-term contracts and whose development they invested in so they could cash in on their "star power." Today, however, because of agents who are able to negotiate lucrative terms for their clients, rather than long-term contracts, film companies have significantly less control over individual actors. Thus, in no way do they replicate a total institution. That being said, film companies and their powerful owners and stars operate like the "star" fraternity on a premiere college campus.

## THE FRATERNITY OF THE INSTITUTION

Both Hollywood and the government can be described as fraternal, they are bastions of "old boys networks" that serve to restrict opportunities to men, and to white men in particular, while simultaneously helping to ensure a code of silence and protection when members are challenged. For example, Bill Cosby was, up until the end, defended by dozens of people in Hollywood. This even after he was ultimately convicted in the spring of 2018 on three counts of sexual assault of one victim, Andrea Constand, and, according to an article published by *USA Today* on the date of his conviction, was accused by a total of sixty women who came forward alleging various kinds of sexual violence ranging from sexual harassment to rape.[3] Why? Because Hollywood is a closed society, where social connections matter more than anything. Where to burn a bridge is to risk losing a part in the next blockbuster film. The power that is derived from this type of fraternal system requires silence. Especially when the accused is as powerful as Bill Cosby or Harvey Weinstein—what an interesting, perhaps unintentional, outcome of the movement away from film company contracts. Though contracts restricted the work opportunities for actors signed to contracts, they also simultaneously protected their livelihood. Without contracts, Hollywood actors not only cannot afford to make an accusation of sexual violence, they also cannot afford not to rally around the accused. Ironically, as quoted in a 2018 piece about Bill Cosby in the *Atlantic*, "in 2009, during the allegations against Roman Polanski, Harvey Weinstein publicly supported Polanski: 'Hollywood has the best moral compass, because it has compassion,' a cultural power player noted in 2009. It was Harvey Weinstein, staging an impassioned defense of his friend Roman Polanski."[4] Much like sorority women will often defend the fraternity party norms that put them and their sisters at risk for sexual violence, women in Hollywood are too afraid to speak out as accusers, and too afraid to support accusers over the accused because they fear for their livelihood.

Politics is equally as fraternal, and success in this sphere is equally as reliant on social networks and support. Fictional accounts like the popular Netflix series *House of Cards* and *Scandal* have plot lines that are built around loyalty and quid pro quo arrangements of all kinds. Powerful characters often ask each other what they need to close the next deal or make the next scandal go away. Though there is an official new member orientation, the fraternal nature of Congress is developed less formally, through a series of caucuses and committee working groups. Many people characterize Congress as an "old boys network," a place where it is difficult for women and minorities to obtain a foothold. Women and Black congresspersons have formed their own caucuses that cross party lines, because Congress is still so segregated by race and gender, these caucuses are rarely able to accomplish anything meaningful on their own. Rather, they use the caucus as a "block," both in terms of fundraising and voting, that can be courted by other members and caucuses. Like so many other institutions we interrogate in this book, there are serious consequences for "whistle-blowing," and thus members who are engaged in sexual harassment or violence are shielded by the code of silence so often prevalent in fraternal groups.

## HYPERMASCULINE CULTURE OF THE INSTITUTION

Both Hollywood and politics can be characterized as bastions of hypermasculinity. Men in both of these institutions subscribe, at least in their public personas, to the core tenets of hypermasculinity, power, and sexuality. Though Donald Trump may be an outlier of sorts, he is by far not the first man in government to extol the virtues of his sexuality. He is not the first man serving in the federal government to admit, typically under pressure, of extramarital affairs, and to have married multiple times. We need look no further in the past than the public relationship between President Kennedy and Marilyn Monroe, or the more recent presidential bids of Gary Hart and John Edwards that were derailed by accusations of infidelity. Although no president in recent memory has served in the military—indeed the same privilege that protected men like Donald Trump and George W. Bush from the draft, helped them to get elected—in general, men with military experience are over-, rather than underrepresented in our federal government. Not only must this experience in the military seep into their lives as politicians, but it helps to explain the frequency of war metaphors in campaigns and political banter.

Tom Cruise, George Clooney, Will Smith. Hollywood stars like these exude hypermasculinity. They have it all, both personally and on screen: money, power, lots of beautiful women. Though more recently gay men have been able to find a place in Hollywood, hypermasculinity is key even to their success. Kevin Spacey, for example, didn't come out as gay until he was accused of sexual harassment. His on- and off-screen personae were characterized by oozing sexuality and power. Not only is hypermasculinity a staple of Hollywood but its companion, hyperfemininity, is as well. The critique of the Hollywood female specimen runs deep and wide. Women in Hollywood, with few exceptions are required to conform to very narrow images of beauty: white, thin, tall, and sexual. Angelina Jolie, as powerful as she may be in her charitable work, is, in part, successful because she is able to manage her image to not only conform to normative standards of beauty but to push the limits of being both feminine and hypersexual.

Like the fraternity and sorority culture on college campuses, the deep and pervasive nature of sexual harassment in Hollywood is facilitated by the culture of sex. Women's roles in Hollywood are primarily limited to the role of sex object, and thus, in order to win roles, it's reasonable to assume that they may perform the role as part of being cast. We are not suggesting that women seeking movie parts be required to have sex with the likes of Harvey Weinstein. What we are suggesting is that Harvey Weinstein's predatory practices are made easier and more difficult to detect or call out because of the sexualized nature of Hollywood, much as the hookup culture of college campuses, and Greek life in particular, facilitates rape in fraternity houses.

## HOLLYWOOD AND POLITICS ARE GENDER-SEGREGATED INSTITUTIONS

What is sexual consent, and what role does power, like that held by a famous person, play in consent? The power held by men, and especially white men, in Hollywood and in politics is clear. In fact, it is overwhelming.

In the top 100 films of 2017, the presence of women was scarce, with women only representing 8 percent of directors, 10 percent of writers, and 14 percent of editors. And, according to the research of the Center for the Study of Women in Television and Film,[5] a clearing house for data on Hollywood, only one woman *has ever* won the Academy Award for Best Director. In addition, between 2000 and 2011, only 6 percent of Hollywood films were directed by Black men, and less than 1 percent were directed by Black women.[6] Not only are they less likely to direct a film, but the average budget for a Black directed movie is 28 million dollars, whereas the average budget for a white directed movie is 46 million.[7]

The presence of minorities on screen is scarce as well. In the top 100 films of 2016, 25 did not feature a single black character in a speaking role, with 47 featuring no black women at all.[8]

When it comes to politics, men, and white men in particular, remain fully in charge. Despite a great deal of hope on the part of many women, especially young women, and despite having, in 2016, the most viable woman candidate in the history of the United States, we, in the United States, have still never elected a woman president. And, though that might not seem to be such a big deal, this failure makes us unique among our "peer countries," many of whom have elected women more than once. For example, the United Kingdom has elected two women prime ministers, Margaret Thatcher and Theresa May, and Germany has elected a woman, Angela Merkel, to four successive terms.

When it comes to Congress, women have been far more successful in the House of Representatives than in the Senate, a pattern that holds for other minorities as well, including Blacks. As we detail in our book *African American Families Today: Myths and Realities*,[9] which explores the impact of the election of Barack Obama on contemporary Black families, we argue that women and minorities are more successful in winning house seats because congressional districts are often relatively small and less heterogeneous than the larger states in which they exist. Convincing a smaller group of people, whom candidates may be more likely to know personally, to elect them seems to be a much more successful route to Capitol Hill than securing enough support from an entire state, with its larger and more diverse voting populace. The election of Donald Trump seems to have been a catalyst for women to run in the 2018 midterm election as well as for local seats. In 2018, women comprise only 20 percent of Congress, 19 percent of the House (84 of 435 members) and 23 percent of the Senate (23 of 100 members). And, it's even worse when it comes to governorships, only six of fifty state governors (12 percent) are held by women.

## STATS ON RAPE IN THE INSTITUTION

Unlike many of the other institutions we have interrogated in this book, neither Hollywood nor the government is required to keep statistics on sexual or intimate partner violence. Therefore, what we know is purely anecdotal. We do know that we have no reason to believe that either Hollywood or politics is populated by men less likely to engage in sexual or intimate partner violence than men in any other realm of social life. Just like fraternities or SportsWorld, both institutions are populated by men with power and fame. Thus, it's reasonable to assume that rates of sexual and intimate partner violence are high among men who rise in Hollywood or politics for all of the same reasons they are high among high-prolife athletes or campus leaders. The power and prestige the men hold gives them access to potential victims and protects them when accusations are made. The fraternities of politics and Hollywood are so powerful that thanks to the #MeToo movement, we know now that men like Bill Cosby and Harvey Weinstein and John Conyers and Al Franken faced accusations by multiple women. Even President Donald Trump has been accused by sixteen women. In each case, it's clear that others in the men's orbits facilitated the sexual violence by recruiting potential victims, covering up for unusual circumstances, and, in the case of Cosby, even filling prescriptions for drugs he used to incapacitate his victims. In each case, the institutions to which they belonged, including the halls of Congress, hid them, protected them from the law, and even used taxpayer funds to pay out hush money or legal settlements. It's clear that these men could never have engaged in this volume of predatory behavior with this many different victims had the institutions not valued them more than the lives of those they were harming.

## THE CASE OF HARVEY WEINSTEIN

So, who is running the show? For decades, one major player was Hollywood producer Harvey Weinstein. Weinstein cofounded the entertainment company Miramax, where he produced mega hits such as *Pulp Fiction, Good Will Hunting,* and *Shakespeare in Love.* After leaving Miramax, Weinstein founded The Weinstein Company with his brother Bob. Over the span of more than three decades, Weinstein made a name for himself in Hollywood. Weinstein's films have had tremendous success, resulting in more than three hundred Academy Award wins. An analysis of Academy Award acceptance speeches from 1966 to 2016 found that Weinstein was thanked or mentioned thirty-four times, the same number of times as God.[10] Despite earning a reputation for being ruthless, aggressive, and having a short temper with those he worked with, Weinstein cultivated a public image of supporting women and espousing a liberal ideology, supporting the Democratic Party and advocating for women's rights.[11] Weinstein rubbed shoulders with the Obamas and other powerful political players. This aggressive and influential man had taken advantage of his extremely powerful position for over thirty years.

In October of 2017, actresses Ashley Judd and Rose McGowan came forward with allegations against Weinstein. An article in the *New York Times* detailed the sexual assault both Judd and McGowan experienced at the hands of Weinstein. One of Weinstein's favorite tactics? Promising to boost the careers of young actresses if they provided sexual favors. In a memo exposing the assaults faced by countless women over the years, Lauren O'Connor wrote, "I am a 28 year old woman trying to make a living and a career. Harvey Weinstein is a 64 year old, world famous man and this is his company. The balance of power is me: 0, Harvey Weinstein: 10."[12]

After the *New York Times* article broke, more than eighty women, including superstars like Angelina Jolie and Gwyneth Paltrow, came forward with stories of Weinstein's long history of sexual exploitation. Judd took to twitter to discuss Weinstein's abuse where she utilized the #MeToo hashtag, spurring a rapid explosion of sexual assault survivors all across the world sharing their own personal stories.

Among the first accusations to come out publicly were that Weinstein forced women to watch him naked, forced them to watch while he masturbated, and forced women to massage him while he was naked. Soon after these initial accusations, Weinstein was fired from the Weinstein Company and suspended from the British Academy of Film and Television Arts (BAFTA) and the Academy of Motion Picture Arts and Sciences. Upon further investigation, it was found that Weinstein and his associates had a long history of covering up sexual assault and abuse allegations, including several made against Amazon Studio chief, Roy Price. As more women came forward, it was revealed that Weinstein had raped several women over the course of his career, though his legal team denied all rape accusations. On the day of his arrest, Weinstein's lawyer, Ben Brafman, noted that Harvey "didn't invent the casting couch." Weinstein would invite women, mostly young, who were trying to break into the entertainment business, to his hotel room under the guise of work-related meetings, only to proposition them. Part of his "script" included answering the door naked. Several actresses, including Rose McGowan, turned down more than $1 million to be silent about the sexual violence they experienced at the hands of Harvey Weinstein.

Account after account demonstrated clearly Weinstein's pattern of sexually abusive behavior. He used his incredible power in the industry to take advantage of as many women as possible, and to only advance the careers of women he was able to sexually abuse. One of Weinstein's victims, Laura Madden, said, "It was so manipulative, you constantly question yourself—am I the one who is the problem?"[13]

On May 25, 2018, Weinstein turned himself in to the police in New York, where he was charged with rape and several accounts of sexual abuse. He posted $1 million dollars in bail, surrendered his passport, and agreed to wear an electronic monitoring anklet until his trial.

## THE CASE OF BILL COSBY

William Henry (Bill) Cosby Jr. was born in Philadelphia, Pennsylvania, in July of 1937. Never fond of school, he dropped out in 1956 to join the United States Navy. After leaving the military, Cosby worked in New York where he began doing stand-up routines at clubs around the city. Cosby released his first album in 1963 titled *Bill Cosby Is a Very Funny Fellow . . . Right!* for which he won a Grammy Award. Cosby continued to release comedy albums that were instant hits, earning him five more Grammys.[14]

In 1965, Cosby costarred in the TV show, *I Spy*, where he became the first Black actor to star in a dramatic series on American TV. In this roll, Cosby also became the first Black actor to win an Emmy. He won two more subsequent Emmys for *I Spy*. Following his rapid rise to stardom, Cosby began a comedy residence in Las Vegas. From 1969 to 1971, Cosby starred in *The Bill Cosby Show*, a variety show that won Cosby another Emmy. Bill Cosby was quickly becoming a massive name both in comedy and the entertainment industry. Cosby continued to land roles in major projects, including his first feature film *Man and Boy*, and the children's show *Fat Albert*. In 1977, a star on the Hollywood Walk of Fame was dedicated to Bill Cosby. He continued to act in several box-office hits, including *Uptown Saturday Night*. Cosby was amazingly charismatic, which led to him serving as the pitch person for many products. Perhaps most famously, he served for twenty-five years as the Jell-O spokesperson.

Modeled after his real-life family, *The Cosby Show* debuted in 1984 and was an instant hit, eventually earning Cosby a Golden Globe. *The Cosby Show* ran for eight years, during which Cosby also became a best-selling author. Ironically, in 1990, he published a book entitled *Love and Marriage*. Hindsight is certainly 20-20 but we wonder what people today would say about his expertise to offer advice in this area.

Bill Cosby's career continued to thrive. In 1991, Cosby was inducted into the Television Academy Hall of Fame. Cosby earned many notable awards for his work, including the 2002 Presidential Medal of Freedom. Bill Cosby was regarded as an outstanding family man. He was America's Dad.

This picture of him began to slowly change in 2005 when Andrea Constand reported to police that Cosby had drugged and sexually assaulted her.[15] She sued Cosby, and thirteen other women came forward to anonymously testify as witnesses and to share their own stories of abuse at the hands of Cosby. Unfortunately, the case was dismissed, and not much attention was paid for another decade.

Cosby continued in his career as a public figure, doing stand-up and writing children's books. In October of 2014, comedian Hannibal Buress did a stand-up routine in which he accused Cosby of raping women. The routine went viral, and soon after allegations began flooding in. In 2015, Cosby was charged in criminal court with sexually assaulting Constand. During his deposition, Cosby admitted to buying Quaaludes for the specific purpose of drugging women for sex.[16] At that time, there were nine additional lawsuits, specifically related to sexual assault, pending against Cosby.

In the 2015 trial, only Andrea Constand was allowed to testify. This didn't stop other women from sharing their eerily similar stories with the media. In July 2015, the *Atlantic* magazine published the cover story entitled "Cosby: The Women," featuring the black-and-white images of thirty-five women who had accused "America's Dad." Prophetically, they included an empty chair in the cover image. As if to say, there are more, or, who will be next?

Based on the dozens of depositions and stories that women shared in media accounts, Cosby, like Weinstein, had a system; he methodically planned assaults. The scenario goes something like this: Cosby would offer a drugged drink, or a special pill to alleviate pain before sexually assaulting his victims. Cindra Ladd was visiting Cosby in 1969 when she complained of a headache. Cosby offered her a pill that he promised would instantly provide relief. Ladd woke up the next morning naked, while Cosby wore a bathrobe. "It was obvious that he had had sex with me," Ladd said.[17]

Some victims remembered the attacks, like Barbara Bowman, who testified in court saying, "I was screaming and crying and yelling and begging him to stop."[18] Some women did not remember the particulars of what had happened. PJ Masten recalled the 1979 assault saying, "I took two sips and the next thing I remember I woke up naked with him next to me naked. I was bruised, battered and hysterical. This was not a sexual encounter, this was an extreme act of violence. There was blood involved."[19]

Nearly all of the women were afraid to come forward with their stories. Kathy McKee was raped by Cosby in 1971. She recalled, "[He] just assumed, I'm Bill Cosby, I'm the number 1 star in the world. I can do what I want, take what I want. That's the way it's been in this business."[20]

The reaction from the public regarding the allegations was mixed. Bill Cosby was an American institution, he was *America's Dad*, and many people did not believe he could be the violent abuser these women alleged him to be. Hollywood stars like Whoopi Goldberg and Raven-Symoné publicly defended Cosby during his trial. Cosby's wife, Camille, released a statement in which she accused the women and the media of conducting a smear campaign. Cosby himself had spoken out about the accusations, saying racism could be a factor in the judgment, still fiercely denying any wrong doing. The Bill Cosby case was difficult to digest for those who had loved him for so long. Cosby had broken many barriers for Black entertainers and Black entertainment. Jewel Allison spoke out about her complicated feelings regarding her assault. "I didn't tell because I didn't want to let Black America down."[21]

A mistrial was declared in the 2015 trial when the jury could not come to a consensus. A second trial took place in April 2018, and this time the prosecution petitioned for nineteen additional victims to be able to testify against Cosby. In April of 2018, Cosby was found guilty of three counts of aggravated indecent assault against Andrea Constand. In September of 2018, Bill Cosby was sentenced to 3–10 years in prison. At the time of this writing he is incarcerated at SCI, Phenix in Pennsylvania.

Controversy continued even after his trial. Again, his wife defended him, claiming that the guilty verdict was more than a witch hunt, more than a smear campaign; it was a modern day lynching! Mrs. Cosby compared the treatment of her husband, who was accused by more than sixty women of sexual assault, to the murder of Emmett Till. She also invoked, ironically enough, a case of wrongful conviction in which a Black man, Darryl Hunt, served twenty years in prison for the brutal rape and murder of a white woman in Winston-Salem, North Carolina, in the mid-1980s. Darryl Hunt was a friend of ours. We worked with him. We profile his case in our book *Policing Black Bodies: How Black Lives Are Surveilled and How to Work for Change*. Bill Cosby is nothing like Darryl Hunt. Darryl was a poor, Black kid who the prosecutors wrongly accused and who was convicted by an all-white jury. Darryl was finally exonerated, but after little more than a decade out of prison he committed suicide. The demons he carried, having been incarcerated for a lifetime for a crime he didn't commit, was simply too much to bear. Comparing the sexual predator Bill Cosby to an innocent, broken man, Darryl Hunt is disgusting. Any shred of respect or pity we had for Camille Cosby was erased the moment she invoked Darryl's name.

## REPORTING, ESPECIALLY IN CONGRESS

As the #MeToo movement swept through the halls of Congress, some were quick to point out how relatively few sexual harassment claims were made in comparison to the number of people employed. Those with knowledge of the sexual harassment protocol in Congress were quick to point out that the low rates of reporting did not necessarily mean low rates of sexual harassment. Rather, it pointed to an arcane reporting system that seriously reduces reports and disadvantages victims.[22] And, as we will demonstrate, costs taxpayers money!

Step 1: File a claim! Once an incident of sexual harassment takes place, a victim has 180 days to file a claim with the Office of Compliance. One the one hand, this type of timeline is not unusual in claims that involve the federal government. For example, the Lilly Ledbetter Act, better known as the equal-pay act, requires that women file a complaint within 180 days of the first incident of unequal pay. But, herein lies the problem: When it comes to equal pay, women may not learn they are making less than their male counterparts within the first six months of the job. Similarly, a person who has experienced sexual harassment, or racial harassment for that matter, may not be 100 percent sure that what was experienced was harassment or if it rose to the level of being worthy of filing a claim. This experience, by the way, is a form of gaslighting, whereby harassers minimize the experiences of their victims, even suggesting they made it up or were overly sensitive. All of this can lead to the closing of the 180-day window before the victim is even sure they have in fact experienced harassment and are willing to take the risk of reporting it. But, let's say that the victim is clear that the experience was harassment and that they want to file a claim.

Step 2: Get counseling and wait. Upon filing a claim, victims are required to attend thirty days of mandatory counseling with the Office of Compliance before they can move forward with the claim. This feels much like waiting periods that many states require for women to access an abortion. This mandatory counseling does not include trauma-informed counseling or therapy, but rather functions to require victims to weigh all of the costs and benefits of filing a complaint. Though, of course, we want people to think carefully before they accuse anyone of anything, this cooling-off period has a chilling effect. Many complainants never make it through this period to file a claim, not because the claims aren't grounded, but because the waiting period serves as another form of minimizing the victim's experience. So you survived the thirty-day mandatory counseling, what's next?

Step 3: Decision time. Victims who complete the thirty days of mandatory counseling have fifteen days to decide whether to go to mediation. "Decision" implies that victims can choose mediation or something else. But not when one is accusing a congressperson of sexual harassment. This decision is a "constrained" choice, a one and done. Go to mediation or forget this ever happened.

Step 4: Mediation. Mediation is such a pleasant word. It implies fairness, an opportunity for both sides to tell their story. A goal of finding common ground, coming up with a solution that both parties can live with. Except in sexual harassment claims in Congress. In this mediation, unlike, let's say, in divorce proceedings, the victim has to continue to work in the toxic environment, with the person they have accused, while a lawyer *representing the congressperson's office, paid by taxpayers*, conducts the mediation. It seems unlikely, if not flat out impossible, to get a fair hearing in this setup. No wonder no one files sexual harassment claims! This process is reminiscent of the process we outlined in the military, whereby a victim of sexual harassment or violence is often abused by the very person they would report the abuse to. Or his very close friend.

Step 5: Settle. For the few who go through mediation process, the next stage is to settle the claim. Settlement typically requires that the parties sign a nondisclosure agreement (or NDA, an acronym that became a household term when adult film star Stormy Daniels spoke out about her "affair" with Donald Trump). NDAs are documents stating that victims can't talk about their experiences in any way; they can't warn potential new hires (potential future victims) or share their experiences with others in the office who may also be victims of the congresspersons' abuse. Oh, and by the way, the financial reparations of the settlement are paid not by the congressperson but by the taxpayer! You and me.

Step 6: Cool-down period. If the parties are not able to reach a settlement, victims must wait thirty days before they can file a lawsuit. The Office of Compliance indicates that the reason for the "cooling-off" period is so that victims can assess their legal strategies before moving forward. I guess for those who had already lined up Gloria Allred and have paid her a retainer, who are as ready as one can possibly be, are out of luck. How patronizing that an office, and not a complainant and their attorney, decide how soon they can pursue litigation. Again, this mimics the waiting period for an abortion, which is not determined by a woman's doctor, but imposed by a state legislature.

Step 7: Litigation. Should a complainant survive the previous six steps, they are "free" to file a lawsuit or seek an administrative hearing. That being said, *though they too are an employee of the federal government*, just like the congressperson they are accusing, once they reach this stage, they are on her own. Hope they hired Gloria Allred.

## WHY VICTIM'S DON'T REPORT

Victims of sexual abuse in Hollywood and politics don't report for the same reasons that victims in other institutions we've interrogated here don't report.

Shame, humiliation, having one's abuse routinely minimized by the abuser and other members of the institution. But in both the cases of Hollywood and politics, victims also don't report because, like victims in the military, their livelihood depends upon their silence. Both Hollywood and politics are lands of the elite, islands of power and vast wealth, where only the very lucky few will ever get a chance to pursue their dreams with the hopes of making a career and a living. As the cases of Harvey Weinstein in Hollywood and congresspersons like John Conyers reveal, literal access to work depended upon both submitting to sexually harassing, even violent, behavior and shutting up about it. Those who complained found that movie roles vanished in Hollywood, and political capital sank into the Washington swamp. Others watched what happened to the victims who reported—which further silenced them.

Of all the institutions we investigate in this book, Hollywood is perhaps the most unique in that sex and sex appeal are baked in. Victims of sexual harassment and violence at the hands of folks like Harvey Weinstein or Bill Cosby may have trouble defining their experiences as problematic because they may have consented to other sexualized practices or behaviors, for example, taking nude photos as part of a "screen test." The blurred lines between what women have consented to and what they have not consented to may leave women reluctant to report and it makes prosecuting perpetrators all the more challenging.

What's so insidious about sexual harassment and violence in the workplace is quite simply that it prevents people from simply doing their jobs and pursuing their dreams, something that all United States citizens are entitled to by the constitution.

The power of Hollywood and politics is just that—power. These spaces of rarified air, in which men hold all of the power, facilitate high levels of sexual harassment and violence, which, among other things, function to preserve extreme gender segregation and to concentrate men's power.

## WHAT CAN BE DONE?

First and foremost, we must start by believing. When someone tells us a story of sexual harassment or violence, especially at the hands of a powerful man, we should start by believing them. If they're making it up, a thorough investigation will determine that. What we know from the data is that victims seldom make it up, and a much more serious problem is underreporting.

One the most obvious things we uncovered in doing the research for this chapter is the sexual harassment reporting system in Congress. Though this will take time and effort, revising the reporting structures in Congress is not only critical to creating a safe workplace for all, but also a logical next step. Sexual harassment is not only wrong, but it's illegal, and our government, from the president, to Congress, need to set a zero-tolerance policy.

Power in Hollywood needs to be diluted if we have any hope of reducing sexual harassment and violence in this institution. As we noted in the beginning, Hollywood, unlike the other institutions we examine here, is a loosely connected set of private corporations. Forcing these private companies to diversify their power is difficult. This is where the #MeToo movement is so important. If Harvey Weinstein is convicted, film companies may be afraid of giving too much power to a few men at the top. The #MeToo movement may also encourage film companies to establish, as other private corporations have, strict sexual harassment policies that victims can access, confidentially, with a guarantee of being treated fairly. This will not be easy, but just as we have this expectation set for college campuses, we argue that it's reasonable to hold all private businesses to the same high standard.

## FINAL THOUGHTS

As we noted in the Preface, #MeToo is not only an incredibly powerful moment in the history of sexual and intimate partner violence, but it was also a blessing in disguise for this book. #MeToo opened up the conversation around sexual and intimate partner violence across all kinds of settings, but especially in Hollywood and politics. Why? Because unlike in the other institutions we interrogate here, the names of the accused are well known. We caution that there can be a danger in focusing too much on the household names; it can draw attention away from the abuse that is happening right under our noses, in our schools and houses of worship and in the locker rooms where our children are supposed to be safe. In the final chapter we "go deep" in our discussion of the interconnectedness of sexual and intimate partner violence and child sexual abuse and we offer practical things that we can each do to make our families and communities safer.

# A CALL TO ACTION

A minority of men, who demonstrate their manhood in hostile ways, create a general fear of men in our culture. As a result, women often need to be afraid of the men whom they meet and with whom they develop intimate relationships.

—Paula Gilbert and Kim Eby[1]

I stand unhesitatingly and unwaveringly with the women. Not out of virtue, or integrity, or high moral outrage—as much as I'd like to say so—but because late in life, I met one extraordinary woman with a particularly awful story to tell, who introduced me to other extraordinary women with equally awful stories.

—Anthony Bourdain[2]

Nearly forty-four million women in the United States have been raped and perhaps an equal number have experienced violence at the hands of men who claim to love them. If forty-four million men in the United States were the victims of these same kinds of violent crimes, it would be a national emergency and resources would be made available to protect men from becoming victims. Shelters for victims would be on every corner. Prisons would be full of the perpetrators. And educational programming designed to prevent rape and intimate partner violence would begin in kindergarten. That's how we know we live in patriarchy, a society in which men's lives matter and women's (and children's) are devalued.

The data presented and the arguments made in this book can be overwhelming. One of the reasons we believe that our society is so tolerant of sexual and intimate partner violence and child sexual abuse is because we don't think about it long and hard enough to be able to really feel the impact. We rush through the stories, quickly moving past the words themselves so that we don't have to think about the woman whose rape is so violent that she bleeds for three days from both her vagina and her rectum, as Jon Krakauer describes in his book *Missoula: Rape and the Justice System in a College Town.*[3] We don't want to visualize the child forced to perform oral sex on Jerry Sandusky in the locker room shower in the football complex at Penn State University. Because, if we did have to hold those images in our head and heart for very long we would be so angry and disgusted that we would have no other choice than to seek impactful consequences for those perpetrating these atrocities. If we are not overwhelmed, then either we aren't brave enough to hold these images in our heads and hearts or we have become numb to them.

We'd like to believe that as common as sexual violence, intimate partner violence, and child sexual abuse are, that the average person doesn't really understand how significant the impact of this behavior is. We'd like to believe this because the alternative is unthinkable, that people do know how terrible such violence and abuse are and they choose to look away and do nothing. We do believe that one barrier that victims face to receiving justice is that people find it particularly difficult to think about rape and battering and child sexual abuse, and thus they move away as quickly as possible, not really listening to victim's accounts and failing to fully investigate cases when the accused individuals indicate that the sex was consensual, or the fight was mutual, or perhaps it was a misunderstanding. In Jon Krakauer's thorough investigation of the Missoula Police Department, he documents this scenario repeatedly, confirming our own experience on many college campuses over decades. We are frankly stunned at the number of cases we are aware of in which the victim reports the assault to campus police and endures a rape kit exam at the emergency room, yet when the police question the accused and he says that he didn't do anything or that the sex was consensual, the allegation is considered unfounded, and they close the case without ever talking to a single witness, including the nurses who conducted the rape kit.

Gender-based violence and child sexual abuse are epidemic for two key reasons: (1) we live in and perpetuate a rape culture that devalues women and anything feminine and (2) we fail to hold the perpetrators accountable, which allows them to commit more acts of violence. For every rapist we take off a college campus, we save at least six future victims. For every sexually abusive Catholic priest that the Church removes, perhaps a dozen children will be spared this violence, or in the case of priests like Father Geoghan, literally hundreds of children could have been spared. What is perhaps most discouraging is the fact that across the last thirty years or so since we, as a society, started talking about these issues, very little has changed. Women and children face as much violence on college campuses, in the military, in prisons, by athletes, by Hollywood producers, by politicians, and in the Catholic Church as they always have. One main reason we have failed to make any progress in reducing GBV and child sexual abuse is that we have not addressed the rape culture that protects perpetrators and fails to hold them accountable. When we fail to hold perpetrators accountable, we all pay a hefty price.

## THE COSTS OF THE EPIDEMIC

The epidemic has costs: to individuals, to communities, and to our society. The economic costs of sexual violence and intimate partner violence combined are over $130 billion annually, including lost wages, lost tuition, lower productivity, health care costs, mental health costs, the costs of addiction, not to mention the costs associated with investigating crimes and prosecuting them. How much, we wonder, was the total bill to the Commonwealth of Pennsylvania for prosecuting Bill Cosby, or to the state of Michigan for prosecuting Larry Nassar? And, the costs to individual institutions are extremely high. For the Catholic Church, not only has membership and attendance declined, but the Church has paid out billions of dollars globally in settlements to victims of child sexual abuse. As did Penn State University in the wake of the Jerry Sandusky trial. Penn State was fined $50 million by the NCAA and most of the victims were awarded multimillion-dollar settlements by the courts. In the wake of Larry Nassar's convictions of molesting upwards of two hundred fifty children, Michigan State has agreed to pay out $500 million in settlements. On college campuses, victims are more likely to drop out or transfer, and the cost to replace them by recruiting new students is significant. We can also speculate that even those who do graduate are less likely to donate as alumni. Why? Because the violence they experienced on campus often taints their sense of belonging. These are lost dollars to the university. In the military, service members who are raped are less likely to recommit after their contracts end. And, the cost to recruit and replace members is significant, especially when those members who leave have been highly trained; it is not just the cost of replacing the body, but of investing in training new people. When politicians are accused of sexual harassment we all pay the price. Every taxpayer.

And, of course, there are the human costs. Victims of sexual abuse—adults and children—have more difficulty in intimate relationships and in parenting. Men and women become alienated from each other. When women are afraid of their supervisor, of the handyman, of the metro driver, and of their husband, they perform below their capacity. In other words, even the "good guys" lose.

## STRUCTURES THAT FACILITATE GENDER-BASED VIOLENCE

Each of the institutions we analyzed in the book has at least some qualities of a total institution, and these structures facilitate gender-based violence and child sexual abuse in several keys ways: (1) by controlling the environment, (2) by having the power to compel behavior, and (3) by having internal systems of justice.

### Controlling the Environment

When we consider the various institutions we have analyzed in this book, one of the interesting points of variation involves the control over the environment. In both the military and in prisons, the environment is controlled by the institution itself. States build prisons and configure them in particular ways and the branches of the military engage in similar practices, building bases and ships and submarines and other installments where members live and work. In prisons and in the military, those in power—corrections officers or commanders—control nearly every aspect of the environment, including assignment to cells or housing units, work assignments, and so forth. In both cases, those with power demand absolute obedience.

In the other institutions, the Catholic Church, fraternities, Hollywood, politics, and in SportsWorld, it is the men who control the environments into which women and children are invited. The Catholic priest or the fraternity brother or the director who invites a victim into the special space of the sacristy or the fraternity house or his hotel suite equipped with a "casting couch" has total control over that environment, which gives him the power to sexually abuse his victims. First and foremost, he controls access to the space, and he will threaten a victim with no longer having access to the space—which is special and desirable—if the victim resists or reports the abuse. In the case of the fraternity house, the message may be a bit more subtle, but it is still clear: If women want to attend fraternity parties, which are *the social center* of the college campus, then they must behave in the ways that they are expected to. Second, the perpetrator is familiar with the space and the victim often is not. We cannot underestimate the kind of power that is associated with knowledge. For example, potential victims who enter the space for the first time or only very rarely may not have a clear understanding of the norms of the space. A college woman attending her first fraternity party in late August or early September may not know what to expect in terms of the proscribed roles for men and women, the noise level, the norms around alcohol, and so on. A new visitor to the sacristy or locker room would likely not understand norms around changing clothes, for example. In the sacristy, the altar server may not be sure how much he is supposed to (or not) help the priest take off and put on priestly garments. The boy new to the Penn State locker room may not be sure if showering with the coach is typical or unusual. The teenage girl seeking treatment from the official team physician may not know what to expect a typical exam to include. Is he supposed to touch her "private parts" in order to stretch out her hamstring? This lack of knowledge gives the perpetrator significant power over the victim and is a key to facilitating sexually abusive behavior. In the case of fraternities, the brothers rely on the women they bring to the house not knowing where they are, whose bedroom is whose, and how to get out. It is the brothers who control the flow of alcohol, the volume of the music, and the ratio of men to women, all of which are associated with determining if a fraternity is high or low risk for sexual assault.

## Ability to Compel Behavior

Very clearly, in prisons and in the military those with power have absolute power to compel behavior. Neither an inmate nor a service member can ignore an order, be it an order to have one's personal items inspected, to submit to a strip search, or to shoot at an enemy. One of the main goals of basic training in the military is the establishment of this hierarchical relationship; when one defies orders, as Jack Nicholson's character notes in the popular film *A Few Good Men*, people die. In this context then, neither inmates nor service members can refuse to perform a sex act if they are ordered to; to resist is to risk punishment as well as the loss of privileges.

Catholic priests also have tremendous power that they can leverage to compel behavior. Priests control a Catholic's access to forgiveness, which is a requirement for entrance into heaven after death. The confessional, then, becomes a powerful space in which the priest may solicit sexual acts in exchange for forgiveness. Catholic priests are also considered to be the literal embodiment of Jesus Christ, and as we noted, they will often groom their victims by telling them that their relationship is special and that engaging in sex acts will bring them closer to God. We cannot underestimate the power the Catholic priest has to compel behavior.

In the cases of fraternities and SportsWorld, the ability to compel behavior is less about power and more about entitlement. Fraternities, and by extension their members, control the social life on the college and university campuses where they exist. Students who want to be popular and have social outlets must participate in the fraternity, either as members (for men) or as partygoers (for women). Not only do young men desire to become fraternity members, seeing it as the only route to the dictates of masculinity—access to alcohol and sex—but during the pledging and initiation process, the brothers have the total capacity to compel the behavior of new members, some of which is nothing short of sexual and physical violence, "endured" as a route to the benefits of fraternity membership.

Both fraternity members and athletes can compel women to engage in sexual behavior by controlling access to status. Though athletes do not control the social life on campus or in their communities if they are professionals, they do have the ability to control access to status. Many wives and girlfriends of college and professional athletes stay with abusive or sexually promiscuous partners because of that status they gain by being on the arm of a famous athlete. Many of our own students report that high-profile student athletes take advantage of their status by compelling young women to do their academic assignments, their laundry, and service their sexual needs. We can speculate with a great degree of certainty that the same is true for professional athletes. Thus, women may be coerced into engaging in sexual acts that they do not want to engage in order to retain access to a status they cannot otherwise attain. In a patriarchy, women's status is defined by the men in their lives, first their fathers and later their partners. Athletes are simply taking advantage of a system men created and have exploited for centuries.

In Hollywood and in Washington, D.C., powerful men control access to work, to a professional life, literally to one's livelihood. Men like Bill Cosby, Harvey Weinstein, and John Conyers were able to sexually abuse their victims by promising them an opportunity to break into an industry that is highly elite and super competitive. Similar to the star power that athletes can also offer, these men in Hollywood and Washington, D.C., could offer something even greater—job opportunities, a way to make a living, a way to access professional success. The question for their victims has always been, is this price too high simply to pursue a career? Of course it is.

### Internal Systems of Justice

Each of the institutions that we have analyzed in this book has an internal system of justice and, perhaps more importantly, each institution does everything in its power to handle accusations of gender-based violence and child abuse internally. We have discussed the issue of internal systems of justice at length, and though we can and did make an argument that on college campuses and in the military there may be a case to be made for some claims being handled internally, in general we argue that internal systems of justice rarely result in justice or even in fair treatment for the victims. Overall, be it abusive priests or commanders or fraternity men or congressmen or athletes, internal systems of justice are designed to protect their members. Catholic priests are provided counseling and then moved to less conspicuous, remote, rural parishes, like St. Michael's, Alaska. Out of sight out of mind. Conduct boards on college campuses hold hearings on felonious sexual assault often with limited training and almost always applying standards of "beyond a reasonable doubt" rather than "preponderance of evidence." On both college campuses and in the military, even when perpetrators are found responsible, the punishments are minimal and may be limited to fines, reduction of rank, or even research papers. Our research and that of ESPN's *Outside the Lines* reveals that both college and professional athletes receive preferential treatment by law enforcement, and cases are often deferred back to the college or, in the case of professional athletes, to a governing body, such as the NFL, which protects the athlete from criminal prosecution. Much like the military, it imposes fines and suspensions from play rather than removal from the institution. When politicians sexually harass or abuse their staff, not only are the allegations handled internally, but we, the taxpayer, foot the bill—not only for the investigation but also for the settlement.

So, what is the message being sent to victims and perpetrators in each of these institutions? The messages are crystal clear. Rape and child sexual abuse are not taken seriously, and most perpetrators will never suffer any consequence for their behavior, even when they are found responsible.

## INTERSECTIONALITY

Despite little progress being made to address GBV and child sexual abuse, it has not been for a lack of trying. PREA, the Prison Rape Elimination Act, despite its shortcomings, was the result of years of advocacy by prison reformers. Between 2012 and 2014, Senators Claire McCaskill and Kirsten Gillibrand attempted to address rape in the military; specifically, they recommended that rape investigations be conducted externally, by local law enforcement. Despite much support throughout the Senate for McCaskill and Gillibrand's recommendations, the highest-ranking military officials "assured" the Senate they had rape in the military "under control." That point is debatable. Even though not much has been done to meaningfully impact sexual and intimate partner violence and child sexual abuse, we remain optimistic, and we are committed to identifying strategies that would, if implemented, reduce both GBV and child sexual abuse in the military, prisons, fraternities, the entertainment industry, politics, SportsWorld, and the Catholic Church.

As sociologists, we are not satisfied by simply describing a problem; we are interested in analyzing it and understanding how it operates in a society steeped in inequalities and structured by systems of race, class, and gender. Gender-based violence and child sexual abuse can only be understood through the lens provided by intersectional theory.

Intersectionality is a theoretical paradigm and, perhaps more importantly, an analytic tool that exposes systems of power that produce privilege and oppression. In the United States several systems of oppression have operated independently and in a reinforcing matrix of domination such that rewards and privileges are distributed and made available primarily to white, heterosexual, upper-middle-class men, and everyone else, including white women and Black men, and folks in the LGBTQ community, is left to fight over the few scraps that fall from the table. Those without privilege experience oppression and a lack of access to the opportunity structure, such that over time disadvantages accrue to the members of these groups and their communities. Despite making up 50 percent of the United States population, and voting at higher rates than men, women still only make up 20 percent of the United States Congress. What that means practically is that very few districts have women representing them. No woman has ever been elected to the presidency. Women cannot be priests. Women are not represented in all ranks of the military, especially not in the elite units or in any positions of power. There are very few women who are producers or directors in the entertainment industry. In fact, in Hollywood, the quickest route to success for women remains being naked.

Intersectionality is about power and power relations—the ability to determine whose bodies have value and whose can be abused. Women and children are the vulnerable, especially if they are poor or Black or brown or LGBTQ, because their voices are almost always unheard. The bodies of the child victims of

Jerry Sandusky and the thousands of pedophile priests were simply discarded, disposable, while Penn State and the Catholic Church protected the predators. CeCe McDonald was locked in solitary confinement to "protect" her while the correctional officers who raped her were allowed to continue collecting their paychecks. The women victims of Bill Cosby's violent, predatory sexual violence were left to put the pieces back together, while Cosby continued to amass a fortune and win awards for his work.

Intersectionality is also about social justice. At its most basic level, the goal we set out to achieve in writing this book was to shine a light on a set of policies, practices, and lived realities that were often not seen as connected but which, in fact, alone and in combination, deliberately create environments in which sexual and intimate partner violence and child sexual abuse are common, and perpetrators' lives have more value than victims'. Only when we can describe and analyze a set of problems can we begin to design remedies and solutions. Intersectionality is just this type of analytical tool if used with the express goal of dismantling all forms of inequality and delivering the promises of the Declaration of Independence, the Constitution of the United States, and the United Nations Declaration of Human Rights.

## WHAT CAN BE DONE?

Throughout each chapter's concluding sections, we identified the ways in which the power of the institution could be harnessed to reduce gender-based violence and child sexual abuse. Ironically, the very features of a total institution or quasi-total institution that create climates where gender-based violence and child sexual abuse can flourish are the very same features that can be harnessed to address the problem. Institutional leaders have the power to uphold an existing culture or to change it. Because of their immense power to compel behavior, if they were to choose to change the cultures of the institutions they lead, and if they were to hold perpetrators accountable, we are quite certain that rates of gender-based violence and child sexual abuse would drop dramatically. This is where we are optimistic. Unlike reducing rates of gender-based violence in an entire society, the structures of these institutions can facilitate rapid change. And, because these institutions are powerful in our society, and because millions of people belong to or participate in them, reductions in the rates of gender-based violence and child sexual abuse would drop significantly in the wider United States society as well. We propose several strategies.

## More Women in Leadership

Though all of the structures of these institutions are important in creating a climate ripe for gender-based violence, the entire analysis we have presented in this book is built on one fundamental feature: gender segregation. As is the case with the concept of a total institution, these institutions vary in the degree to which they are gender segregated, but at a minimum all can be characterized by two features: a gender segregated leadership and limited roles for women, none of which involve power or even allow for egalitarian interaction.

We feel quite strongly in our assertion that gender-based violence and child sexual abuse would be far less common in the military, in Washington, in Hollywood, and the Catholic Church were women in leadership positions. First, as noted, because women are far less likely to perpetrate gender-based violence and child sexual abuse, the simple shift in ratio of men to women serving as commanders or directors or majority whips or as priests would reduce the number of potential perpetrators. Second, because women are far more likely to believe accusations of rape and child sexual abuse, reports in the Catholic Church and the military and in the hills of Hollywood or on Capitol Hill would be investigated and appropriate punishment would be administered to perpetrators who are found responsible. Third, as is well documented by anthropological research, in societies where women are allowed to hold leadership roles, gender equity is highly correlated with reductions in gender-based violence. We can't imagine why the military or the Catholic Church or Hollywood or Congress would be any different.

## Reduce Gender Segregation

All of the institutions we have interrogated here have been deliberate in creating gender-segregated environments. In some cases, this may remain necessary, such as in housing incarcerated people. But, in most of the institutions that we detail here, some gender integration is possible and would likely reduce the high levels of sexual and intimate partner violence that is present. Perhaps men and women will never compete on the same athletic teams in college or professional athletics. But, that doesn't prohibit women from holding leadership roles, as coaches, trainers, athletic directors, and owners. The presence of women with power equal to or greater than men would likely impact men's perceptions of women as more than cheerleaders or bodies designed for sexual conquest. The same argument could be made for fraternities, which could, in fact, go even further and fully integrate, as some service and professional fraternities already do.

When it comes to politics, the United States is woefully behind our sister nation-states. Political economies like the United Kingdom and Germany have women prime ministers and equal representation in their legislative houses. This past year, as the #MeToo campaign was erupting, we had the opportunity to be interviewed for a German television station. We asked the young woman intern about the impact of Angela Merkel on gender politics in Germany, and she paused and noted that because Angela Merkel was elected before she was born, in her world the prime minister had always been a woman. That was important, she said, in shaping her own sense of self and the professional opportunities she could pursue. Much like the impact of the presidency of Barack Obama on young Black children, we can't overstate the potential impact a woman in the "oval" would have. Most importantly, gender integration has the power to transform a culture of hypermasculinity to one of equality, a space in which there is no room for rape culture or victim blaming of any kind, a space in which the only kind of sexual encounter is one that is consensual.

## Stop Blaming Victims

Let us be crystal clear. There is absolutely nothing a child does that makes them in any way responsible for the sexual abuse they experience. Nothing. Not becoming an altar server or going with Jerry Sandusky into the Penn State locker room. And though drinking too much or agreeing to leave a club or a bar to go to a man's home may be risk factors for being raped, *nothing the victim does makes her responsible for rape*, any more than carrying a wallet makes a mugging victim responsible for being mugged. It's not as if a woman can leave her vagina at home or put a lock on it when she decides to have a drink or trust a man. One of the most essential keys to both reducing rape to begin with and holding perpetrators accountable is eliminating rape culture and the beliefs and ideologies and myths it perpetuates.

## Believe Victims while Maintaining Due Process

Despite the fact that rape, child sexual abuse, and intimate partner violence have rates of false reporting that are no higher than any other crime, in the range of 2–4 percent, there is a disproportionate amount of concern by investigators that women and children are predisposed to making false allegations. The concern over false reports is disproportionate in two ways: because false allegations are very rare in these cases and because there is no similar response to other crimes. When victims report a mugging, or an assault, or car accident, or a burglary, the police rarely if ever ask if what they are reporting really happened. When they interview the person suspected of committing the crime—a mugging or a burglary—they rarely if ever settle for an explanation like "I didn't do it" or "it was consensual" or "she must be mistaken." In fact, it turns out that 96 percent of the time when women report a rape it is true, and more than 90 percent of the time the person who raped her has raped or will rape other women. In no other situation, including the scientific standards for analysis of data, do we automatically reject a claim that is true 96 percent of the time. In fact, it's quite the opposite. Anything true 96 percent of the time, like water boiling at 212 degrees Fahrenheit is considered to be true. And indisputable. Clearly, then, the only explanation for the obsession people have with false accusations is rape culture.

> Rape is unique. No other violent crime is so fraught with controversy, so enmeshed in dispute and in the politics of gender and sexuality. . . . And within the domain of rape, the most highly charged area of debate concerns the issue of false accusations. For centuries it has been asserted and assumed that women "cry rape," that a large proportion of rape allegations are maliciously concocted for the purposes of revenge or other motives.[4]

Let us be clear. We are not arguing that the due process rights of the accused be in any way weakened. As scholars who have also written about exoneration, cases in which citizens who are innocent have spent decades of their lives in prison for crimes they did not commit, we are highly concerned about "getting it right." In fact, as we have argued elsewhere, in addition to the problems associated with incarcerating someone for crimes they did not commit, when we incarcerate the wrong person, the real perpetrator is free to continue committing crimes, and in the case of rape and child sexual abuse, this is exactly what happens. So, we care deeply about getting it right, for the accused, for the victim, and for all future victims. We believe that we can protect the rights of the accused to be innocent until proven guilty while simultaneously believing victims and conducting appropriately rigorous investigations of the facts in order to make a determination of guilt or innocence in a court of law, or in rendering an accused responsible when internal systems of justice are invoked. And we are confident, based on the thousands of other cases that do not involve gender-based violence or child sexual abuse that we get right every year, that if investigators didn't rely on their own rape myths to evaluate a victim's story and if the same rigorous standards of investigation were applied in rape cases as they are to muggings and burglaries and drug deals and plagiarism, we would see justice for victims and the rates of gender-based violence and child sexual abuse would automatically decline because the perpetrators would be removed from the community, the college campus, or Capitol Hill.

## Hold Perpetrators Accountable

Based on the research of Diana Scully, who interviewed convicted rapists, and Jackie Campbell's studies of rapists on college campuses,[5] as well as the civil cases brought against Bill Cosby, the Catholic Church, Jerry Sandusky and Penn State University, and Larry Nassar, who alone had more than two hundred fifty victims, the evidence is clear: the majority of rapes and instances of child sexual abuse are perpetrated by serial abusers. The average rapist is purported to have raped six or seven victims. Simply put, the most efficient way to reduce the rates of rape and child sexual abuse in any of the institutions we have analyzed in this book is by holding the perpetrators accountable, including removing them from the institution if necessary. In fact, one of the upsides to the fact that each institution has an internal system of justice is that all of this can be done without even engaging any law enforcement systems. Colleges and universities can suspend and/or expel those who are found responsible for sexual violence. The military can dishonorably discharge members found responsible for sexual or intimate partner violence. The Catholic Church can defrock priests found responsible for child sexual abuse. Prisons can assign inmates found responsible for sexual violence to solitary confinement, and they can fire guards found responsible for sexual violence and child sexual abuse. When athletes commit violence against women, if they are college students, they can be suspended or expelled, just as any other college student can be. And professional athletes can be suspended or fired from their jobs. As can politicians and men in the entertainment business. In fact, if Hollywood and Washington are any indication, 2017 and 2018 saw many men swiftly removed from their jobs, including Harvey Weinstein, Matt Lauer, Charlie Rose, Al Franken, Kevin Spacey, and many more. Again, let us be clear. We are not advocating for the removal of allegedly perpetrators without due process. We are suggesting that when there is evidence of sexual or intimate partner violence or child sexual abuse being perpetrated, institutions can and should hold perpetrators accountable, including by removing them from their jobs and positions of power.

## Revise the Investigation and Adjudication Processes

There seems to be a tremendous amount of reluctance in each of these institutions to hold perpetrators accountable. More than one hundred ten thousand women are raped each year on our college and university campuses, and yet the average campus doesn't expel a single student a year. And, among the colleges and universities that do expel students for sexual misconduct, the numbers are small, representing only a tiny fraction of the cases reported by student victims. In the military, nearly twenty thousand service members report being raped every year, and yet fewer than 7 percent of perpetrators found responsible receive any punishment at all, and only a fraction of those are dismissed or confined. The majority are assessed fines, have their rank reduced, and/or have their work reassigned. In the Catholic Church, of all of the hundreds of priests who have faced claims of child sexual abuse, only a tiny fraction have been defrocked. Many of the most egregious offenders were graciously allowed to retire to luxury retirement communities, never facing any consequences for their behavior. Every day in SportsWorld, men who have admitted to or been convicted of sexual and intimate partner violence run up and down courts and fields, representing the university for which they play or being paid millions of dollars by professional teams who hold their contracts. We can guarantee that if Baylor University adhered to the policies laid out in Title IX, they wouldn't be facing accusations by fifty-two victims who were raped by thirty-one football players. One doesn't have to have a PhD in math to understand what these numbers make clear: There are serial rapists on the Baylor football team.

## Dismantle Rape Culture

Dismantling rape culture requires far more than simply educating people about rape. Fundamental to dismantling a rape culture is a simultaneous shifting of ideologies of gender. Imagine a world, as Judith Lorber writes, "without gender." A world in which men and women are not defined by their bodies or by assumptions about masculinity and femininity, a world in which physical strength is valued as equally as emotional strength and that children of all genders are encouraged to develop and embrace both. In a world in which we valued women's contributions beyond their sexuality, they would be free to forgo their reliance on men for approval. Fraternity parties could become places for equal socializing, where students of all gender identities could enjoy each others' company. Feminists argue that in this world, gender-based violence would decline precipitously, and so would child sexual abuse, because in this world it becomes very difficult to "other" the victim and dehumanize them. In this world, there is no need to police feminine bodies, of any gender, or to police women who are attempting to pursue the same opportunities as men, as ordained leaders in the Catholic Church or as helicopter pilots in the military or as legislators on

Capitol Hill or as actors in the next Netflix series or as competitors and coaches and trainers in SportsWorld.

As we noted in our discussions of the military, and we extend this to SportsWorld, we are not suggesting that strength and power be devalued. What we are suggesting is that physical strength and power be *decoupled* from hyper-masculinity. Service members can be trained for combat while simultaneously being trained for respect, especially of their peers. Service members would no longer fear going to the bathroom or being alone on the deck of an aircraft carrier, and in being released from this fear they would be healthier and stronger and able to reach their capacities.

Practically speaking, then, how can we being this work today? As we noted earlier in this chapter, the leaders of these institutions can take a lead in setting the tone. Many scholars and observers of the epidemic note that leaders can make a significant difference in the culture of an institution by not being afraid to hold perpetrators accountable, but also by going further and demanding shifts in attitudes that engender inequality. We believe that men are not born being violent but rather that violence is learned over a lifetime of being socialized into the standards and expectations of hypermasculinity. Thus, we are intrigued by comprehensive sex education programs, beginning in kindergarten, that teach young children about respect and consent and that have been successful in reducing teen dating violence and sexual assault where they have been adopted. We encourage the reader to examine the program in the Netherlands; we believe it has incredible potential if adopted in the United States.[6]

Three of the institutions that we have analyzed in this book—fraternities (college campuses), the military, and SportsWorld have attempted to reduce gender-based violence by requiring new members to undergo some sort of antiviolence training. In our own experience on college and university campuses, and based on the research we cited in our discussion of fraternities, one-shot programs that the majority of college and universities rely on are woefully inadequate in shifting attitudes. Research, including a project completed by one of our students, documented that the only factor that significantly shifted student attitudes about rape culture was completing a course in women and gender studies. As the director of a women and gender studies program Hattery would, of course, endorse a requirement like this being built into college and university curricula, just as basic English and Math courses are. However, we do not believe that the course has to be taught in a women and gender studies curriculum, what we do believe is that a semester-long course with an emphasis on gender inequality would be far more effective in shifting the attitudes and climate among students than a few hours of training during orientation. And, we believe this model could be adapted fairly easily to the military, to Catholic seminaries, and even to prisons. In the balance, the cost of providing even a semester-long educational program is dwarfed in comparison to the cost of GBV and child sexual abuse. Certainly, not all men go to college, but the majority of men who play professional sports, serve in political office, and hold power in Hollywood do. And, so do men who work as physicians, like Larry Nassar, and coaches like Jerry Sandusky. Training in college would not reach all men, but if combined with training in the military it would reach millions.

## FINAL THOUGHTS

We opened the book by arguing that one of the tensions each of these institutions faces is between their moral obligation to protect their members and the desire to keep the institution alive and growing. When confronted with a rape accusation, colleges and university administrators, military commanders, fraternity chapters, bishops, coaches, and athletic directors all fear that the accusation itself will lead to such a dramatic decline in the reputation of the institution that as a result the institution will fail. Crippled by this fear, institutions respond by hiding the rape allegations, which automatically results in a failure to investigate the allegation and hold the perpetrator accountable. Of course, the problem of rape only grows when the perpetrators are not held accountable and removed from the institution. Thus, on Capitol Hill, in the military, among fraternities, in the global Catholic Church, in Hollywood, and in college and professional athletics there is suddenly a crisis that no one can quite figure out where it came from. We argue that certainly there is a short-term risk in admitting that rapes happen—at ridiculously high rates—and in dismissing perpetrators who have had due process. The institutions risk hits to their reputations and they lose people with value—commanders with combat experience, men who can dunk a basketball and might lead the team to a championship and a windfall of cash to coaches, players, owners, and even college presidents. But we argue that if these institutions can look past the short-term risk, there is guaranteed long-term gain. For every rapist dismissed from the military, each of his victims is likely to remain in the service, the value of their experience retained and the cost to replace them reduced. For every rapist expelled from a college campus, the women he would have raped will be spared, which is obviously of benefit to them, but also of benefit to the university which will see its rates of rape decline and its women students graduate and go on to successful careers. They will give back to their alma mater because they felt they mattered. For each Catholic priest removed from the priesthood, not only are dozens of children spared the horrors of child sexual abuse, but millions of dollars would be saved in lawsuits. This is the gamble that some in Washington and in Hollywood took in the fall of 2017 and the spring of 2018. Only time will tell whether men like Matt Lauer or Charlie Rose will be hired again, whether their firing will cause other men who are engaged in sexually harassing behavior to change the way they interact with women, whether women will find their workplaces to be safer. Like many others, we are sitting on pins and needles!

Institutions will change only when it is in their best interest to do so, out of shame, to preserve their reputation, or because it becomes too costly not to. We argue that the time is now. Each of the institutions we have analyzed in this book has a rape epidemic and each is facing significant scrutiny in the court of public opinion. If they are to survive, colleges and universities, the fraternity system, SportsWorld, the military and even prisons must follow the lead of Hollywood and Congress, and take the short-term risk for the long-term gain. In doing so, they will be able to eliminate the moral tension, treating their members with the dignity they deserve and preserving their reputation in the public eye.

We wrote this book to draw attention to some of the worst sexual abuse that is being perpetrated against women, children, and men and to challenge our readers to become more aware and to be moved to some action. In the appendix you will find a list of resources and organizations to which you can donate your time and/or your money toward easing the impact of sexual and intimate partner violence and child sexual abuse and eradicating it for our next generation.

If each of us doesn't do our part, if we aren't willing to look victims in the eye and believe them and hold some of their pain, if we aren't willing to hold perpetrators accountable, even when they are our heroes, our scout leaders, and coaches and sports idols and representatives we will raise another generation of children who will grow up with sexual and intimate partner violence as part of their landscape. We leave you with a really simple challenge: What will you do? How will you be the change? What kind of world do you want to leave for the next generation?

# APPENDIX

## End Rape on Campus (EROC)

End Rape on Campus (EROC) works to end campus sexual violence through direct support for survivors and their communities; prevention through education; and policy reform at the campus, local, state, and federal levels. http://endrapeoncampus.org/

## Guttmacher Policy Review

Explanation and a breakdown to understanding what intimate partner violence is and how it has led to a United States public health crisis issue. It also discusses the rights women have and how to handle a situation where intimate partner violence is involved. https://www.guttmacher.org/gpr/2016/07/understanding-intimate-partner-violence-sexual-and-reproductive-health-and-rights-issue?

## House of Ruth: Hope Starts Here

Since 1976, this organization has been providing homes and helpful resources to those affected by sexual abuse or severe trauma to gain independence and safety, and be provided with food and shelter. Both donations and volunteering are available here. https://houseofruth.org

## Hope Haven

This purpose of this program is to provide education, safe housing, and resources within their community to survivors of intimate partner violence and sexual abuse or harassment. Both donations and volunteering are available. https://www.hopehavenofcasscounty.org

## National Coalition against Domestic Violence (NCADV)

An organization acting as a voice for those who have survived any kind of domestic abuse or intimate partner violence. This website has an entire source list packed with resources and hotline numbers for survivors. Both becoming a member of this organization and donations are available on the website. https://ncadv.org/

## Family and Youth Services Bureau (FYSB)

With the Family Violence Prevention and Services Program being the primary funding for this organization, a network of resources, safe living spaces, and job opportunities are available to those families who have survived sexual abuse domestically. https://www.acf.hhs.gov/fysb/resource/help-fv

## Stop It Now!

A guidance in how to be observant of warning signs of sexual abuse when dealing with a child or adolescent. Both donations and volunteering are available here. http://www.stopitnow.org/

## Kid Power: Take Charge of Your Safety

An organization dedicated to teaching children how to prevent sexual abuse with videos, books, and helpful resources to educate the youth community on how to protect themselves. Both opportunities to mentor children and donate are available through this organization. https://www.kidpower.org

## Childhelp

To help children already impacted by sexual abuse and to help it from happening in the future. Donations are available to be made on the website. https://www.childhelp.org/

## National Council of Juvenile and Family Court Judges (NCJFCJ)

Donations made by this website help fund the field of juvenile and family law and protective services under those survivors of intimate partner violence, family sexual abuse, or sexual abuse. http://www.ncjfcj.org

## Time's Up

Time's Up is an organization that insists on safe, fair, and dignified work for women of all kinds from the factory floor to the floor of the Stock Exchange. They provide a comprehensive website with resources, ways to donate, and links to legal assistance. https://www.timesupnow.com/

## SurvJustice

This is a D.C.-based national nonprofit organization that offers sexual violence survivors legal assistance. It also advocates for policy changes and institutional training. Founded in 2014, it is still the only national organization that provides legal assistance to survivors in campus hearings across the country. http://www.survjustice.org

## Know Your IX

A survivor- and youth-led project of Advocates for Youth that aims to empower students to end sexual and dating violence in their schools. Their work draws upon Title IX as an alternative to the criminal legal system to respond to the educational, emotional, financial, and stigmatic harms of violence. https://www.knowyourix.org

## Love Is Respect

The first twenty-four-hour resource for teens who were experiencing dating violence and abuse and still the only teen helpline serving all of the United States and its territories. In 2011, the Hotline entered into a strategic partnership with Break the Cycle, another national leader in preventing dating abuse, and also launched twenty-four-hour text services in addition to phone and live chat services. https://www.loveisrespect.org

## One Love Foundation

An organization formed in response to the killing of Yeardley Love by her boyfriend. They place their efforts in educating young people and addressing unhealthy and dangerous kinds of relationship behaviors. https://www.joinonelove.org

## SNAP

SNAP (Survivors Network of Those Abused by Priests) is an independent peer network of survivors of institutional sexual abuse and their supporters who work to support survivors through email, a hotline, and support groups nationwide. They advocate for stronger laws to protect children and for reform of statutes of limitation, and they work to expose predators and educate communities about the effects of abuse. http://www.snapnetwork.org

## National Coalition against Violent Athletes

An organization supporting survivors of athlete violence through counseling services, legal services, and advocacy services. They work to ensure that a survivor receives as much information as possible in order to make informed decisions and remove the elements of fear in moving forward. http://www.ncava.org/survivors/

## 1in6

The mission of 1in6 is to help men who have had unwanted or abusive sexual experiences both in childhood and as adults, providing information and support resources on the web and in the community. http://1in6.org

## Hotlines

RAINN (the national sexual assault hotline): 1-800-656-HOPE www.rainn.org

Love Is Respect: Chat at www.loveisrespect.org Text loveis to 22522* Call 1-866-331-9474

National Domestic Violence Hotline: 1-800-799-7233

National Dating Abuse Hotline: 1-866-331-9474

National Child Abuse Hotline/Childhelp: 1-800-422-4453

Darkness to Light: End Child Sexual Abuse: 1-866-367-5444

National Suicide Prevention Hotline: 1-800-273-8255

National Resource Center on Domestic Violence: 1-800-537-2238

National Center on Domestic Violence, Trauma, and Mental Health: 1-312-726-7020 (extension 2011)

Childhelp USA/National Child Abuse Hotline: 1-800-422-4453

Hope Haven: 816-380-4663 (24 Hour Hotline)

National Council on Juvenile and Family Court Judges: 1-800-527-3233

Americans Overseas Domestic Violence Crisis Center: 1-866-879-6636 (Toll-free and 24/7 Hotline)

D.C. Victim Hotline: 1-844-443-5732


## RECOMMENDED FILMS

### Child Sexual Abuse

The Silence: *Frontline Season #29* (2012)

Examines a little-known chapter of the Catholic Church sex abuse story: decades of abuse of Native Americans by priests and church workers in Alaska. (http://www.pbs.org/wgbh/pages/frontline/the-silence/)


*Happy Valley* (2014)

The town of State College, the home of Pennsylvania State University, has long been known as Happy Valley, and its iconic figure for more than forty years was Joe Paterno, the head coach of the school's storied football team. But then, in November 2011, everything came crashing down. Assistant football coach Jerry Sandusky was indicted on fifty-two counts of child molestation.


*Spotlight* (2015)

True story of how the *Boston Globe* newspaper uncovered the decades-long cover-up of child abuse within the local Catholic Archdiocese.


*Doubt* (2008)

In a Bronx, New York, Catholic school in 1964 a popular priest's ambiguous relationship with a troubled twelve-year-old Black student is questioned by the school's principal. The subject involves the suspicions of a nun eager to seize on any reason for ridding the parish of Father Flynn, whom she accuses of an immoral act with a young Black altar boy. (http://www.imdb.com/title/tt0918927/)

*Sleepers* (1996)

Four young white males in New York's Hell's Kitchen are punished for a prank gone wrong and sent to the Wilkinson School for Boys reform school. While there they are mistreated at will by a cadre of sadistic guards. Once released they seek revenge. The film has many stars, including Kevin Bacon, Robert De Niro, Dustin Hoffman, and Brad Pitt. (http://www.imdb.com/title/tt0117665/)

## Sexual and Intimate Partner Violence

*Sin by Silence* (2009)

Instead of fighting a system that does not fully comprehend the complexities of abuse, the Convicted Women against Abuse (CWAA) led an initiative to help educate the system. Through careful orchestration of letter-writing campaigns, media coverage, and Senate hearings, a movement was born and laws for battered women were changed.

*The Accused* (1988)

In the film, Sarah Tobias (Jodie Foster), a young waitress, is gang-raped by three men at a local bar; she and district attorney Kathryn Murphy (Kelly McGillis) set out to prosecute the rapists as well as the men who encouraged them. A plea deal is made. Sarah is enraged by the deal, as there is no acknowledgment on the record that the men raped her. Based on a true story.

*The Burning Bed* (1984)

The plot follows the trial of Francine Hughes (a housewife) for the murder of her husband, James Berlin "Mickey" Hughes. Francine sets fire to the bed he was sleeping in at their Dansville, Michigan, home after thirteen years of physical domestic abuse at his hands. Based on a true story.

*Enough* (2002)

The movie is based on the 1998 novel entitled *Black and Blue*, by then *New York Times* op-ed writer Anna Quindlen. It stars Jennifer Lopez as Slim, an abused wife who learns to fight back against repeated domestic violence.

*Sleepers* (1996)

See under "Child Sexual Abuse" above.

# NOTES

**CHAPTER 2**

1. Rebecca Maria Loya, "Economic Consequences of Sexual Violence for Survivors: Implications for Social Policy and Social Change" (PhD Dissertation Brandeis, University, 2012, ProQuest 3540084).

2. Michael Messner, "Bad Men, Good Men, Bystanders: Who Is the Rapist?" *Gender and Society* 30, no. 1 (2016): 57–66. doi: 10.1177/0891243215608781.

3. Patricia Hill Collins and Sirma Bilge, *Intersectionality* (New York: Polity Press, 2016).

4. Angela Browne, *When Battered Women Kill* (New York: Free Press, 1989). See also Angela Hattery, *Intimate Partner Violence* (Lanham, MD: Rowman and Littlefield, 2008).

5. Centers for Disease Control. Racial and Ethnic Differences in Homicides of Adult Women and the Role of Intimate Partner Violence — United States, 2003-2014. *Weekly* / July 21, 2017 / 66(28);741–746. https://www.cdc.gov/mmwr/volumes/66/wr/mm6628a1.htm?s_cid=mm6628a1_w

6. Dennis Reidy et al., "Masculine Discrepancy Stress, Teen Dating Violence, and Sexual Violence Perpetration among Adolescent Boys," *Journal of Adolescent Health* 56 (2015): 623.

**CHAPTER 3**

1. Elahe Izadi, "'Princeton Mom' on CNN: 'What We're Really Identifying as Rape Is a Clumsy, Hook-Up Melodrama," *Washington Post*, December

12, 2014, http://www.washingtonpost.com/news/post-nation/wp/2014/12/12/princeton-mom-on-cnn-what-were-really-identifying-as-rape-is-a-clumsy-hook-up-melodrama/.

2. Peggy Reeves Sanday, *Fraternity Gang Rape* (New York: New York University Press, 1997), 7.

3. Nicholas L. Syrett, *The Company He Keeps: A History of White College Fraternities* (Chapel Hill: University of North Carolina Press, 2009).

4. Syrett, *The Company He Keeps*, xi.

5. Sofi Sinozich and Lynn Langton, *Rape and Sexual Assault Victimization Among College-Age Females, 1995–2013*, NCJ 248471 (Washington, DC: Bureau of Justice Statistics, 2014).

6. Jacquelyn Campbell, "Campus Sexual Assault Perpetration: What Else We Need to Know," *Journal of the American Medical Association Pediatrics* 169, no. 12 (2015): 1088–89. Retrieved July 13, 2015. doi:10.1001/jamapediatrics.2015.1313.

7. John D. Foubert, Johnathan T. Newberry, and Jerry L. Tatum, "Behavior Differences Seven Months Later: Effects of a Rape Prevention Program," *Journal of Student Affairs Research and Practice* 44, no. 4 (2007): 728–49.

8. Sigma Alpha Epsilon, "Fraternity Mission," http://www.sae.net/page.aspx?pid=753.

9. Sigma Alpha Epsilon, "Our Creed: 'The True Gentleman,'" http://www.sae.net/page.aspx?pid=753.

10. Sanday, *Fraternity Gang Rape*, 77.

11. Sanday, *Fraternity Gang Rape*, 168.

12. Sanday, *Fraternity Gang Rape*, 174.

13. Sanday, *Fraternity Gang Rape*, 69

14. Juliet Lapidos, "Sororities Should Throw Parties," *New York Times*, January 20, 2015, http://www.nytimes.com/2015/01/21/opinion/sororities-should-throw-parties.html?_r=0.

15. Sanday, *Fraternity Gang Rape*, 72.

16. Sanday, *Fraternity Gang Rape*, 89.

17. Sanday, *Fraternity Gang Rape*, 133.

18. Sanday, *Fraternity Gang Rape*, 111.

19. Sanday, *Fraternity Gang Rape*, 65.

20. Erica L. Green and Sheryl Gay Stolberg, "Campus Rape Policies Get a New Look as the Accused Get DeVos's Ear," *New York Times*, July 12, 2017, http://nyti.ms/2gW7PbO.

21. Nancy Chi Cantalupo, *Five Things Student Affairs Professionals Should Know about Campus Gender-Based Violence* (Washington, DC: NASPA, 2015),

https://www.naspa.org/images/uploads/main/5Things_Gender_Based_Violence.pdf.

22. Charlene Y. Senn, Misha Eliasziw, Paula C. Barata, Wilfreda E. Thurston, Ian R. Newby-Clark, H. Lorraine Radtke, and Karen L. Hobden, "Efficacy of a Sexual Assault Resistance Program for University Women," *New England Journal of Medicine* 372 (2015): 2326–35. http://www.nejm.org/toc/nejm/372/24/, doi: 10.1056/NEJMsa1411131

23. "Greek Life Statistics," The Fraternity Advisor, http://thefraternityadvisor.com/greek-life-statistics/.

24. Cantalupo, *Five Things*, 15.

25. Patricia Yancey Martin, *Rape Work: Victims, Gender, and Emotions in Organization and Community Context* (New York: Routledge, 2005).

**CHAPTER 4**

1. Megan Chuchmach, "Female Soldier More Likely to Be Raped Than Killed in Action, Says Rep," ABC News, September 10, 2008, retrieved May 1, 2015, http://abcnews.go.com/Blotter/story?id=5760295.

2. Scott Kirsch and Colin Flint, *Reconstructing Conflict: Integrating War and Post-War Geographies* (Burlington, VT: Ashgate, 2011), 307.

3. Kirsch and Flint, *Reconstructing Conflict*, 307.

4. Melissa Healy, "Pentagon Blasts Tailhook Probe, Two Admirals Resign," *Los Angeles Times*, September 25, 1992.

5. Adam Nossiter, "Woman Who Left the Citadel Tells of Brutal Hazing Ordeal," *New York Times*, February 18, 1997. Retrieved July 4, 2015, 1997. http://www.nytimes.com/1997/02/18/us/woman-who-left-the-citadel-tells-of-brutal-hazing-ordeal.html.

6. US Department of Defense, *Annual Report on Sexual Assault in the Military* (Washington, DC: US Department of Defense, 2018), http://sapr.mil/public/docs/reports/FY17_Annual/DoD_FY17_Annual_Report_on_Sexual_Assault_in_the_Military.pdf.

7. Heather Hlavka, "Normalizing Sexual Violence: Young Women Account for Harassment and Abuse," *Gender & Society* 28 (2014): 344. doi: 10.1177/0891243214526468.

8. Holly Kearl, "Military Sexual Assault: Betrayal and Retaliation for Service Members," *Women's Media Center*, May 20, 2015. http://www.womensmediacenter.com/feature/entry/military-sexual-assault-betrayal-and-retaliation-for-service-members.

9. Human Rights Watch, *Embattled: Retaliation against Sexual Assault Survivors in the Military* (New York: Human Rights Watch, 2015), 4, http://bit.ly/1BZgIpv.

10. Human Rights Watch, *Embattled*, 7.

11. Kearl, "Military Sexual Assault."

12. "Army Employs Video Game to Help Curb Sex Assaults; Critics Call It 'Affront,'" NBC News, April 10, 2013, http://usnews.nbcnews.com/_news/2013/04/10/17676171-army-employs-video-game-to-help-curb-sex-assaults-critics-call-it-affront?lite.

## CHAPTER 5

1. Ben Mathis-Lilley, "Obama Says Prison Rape Jokes Are 'Unacceptable.'" *Slatest*, July 14, 2015, http://www.slate.com/blogs/the_slatest/2015/07/14/obama_prison_rape_jokes_shouldn_t_be_tolerated_president_says.html.

2. Chris Hayes, *A Colony in a Nation* (New York: W. W. Norton, 2017).

3. Andrea Sedlak, *Survey of Youth in Residential Placement: Conditions of Confinement* (Washington, DC: Office of Justice Programs), https://www.ncjrs.gov/pdffiles1/ojjdp/grants/250754.pdf.

4. See the clip at "Brooks Was Here—*The Shawshank Redemption*" http://bit.ly/1QVuLmP.

5. Federal Bureau of Prisons, "Facility Locations" https://www.bop.gov/locations/map.jsp?region=WXR

6. Allen J. Beck, "PREA Data Collection Activities, 2015," Bureau of Justice Statistics, June 25, 2015, NCJ 248824.

7. Allen, J. Beck, Marcus Berzofsky, Rachel Caspar, and Christopher Krebs, *Sexual Victimization in Prisons and Jails Reported by Inmates, 2011–12* (Washington, DC: Bureau of Justice Statistics, 2014).

8. Beck et al., *Sexual Victimization in Prisons and Jails*.

9. David Kaiser and Lovisa Stannow, "The Shame of Our Prisons: New Evidence," *New York Review of Books*, October 2013, http://www.nybooks.com/articles/archives/2013/oct/24/shame-our-prisons-new-evidence/.

10. "NISVS: An Overview of 2010 Findings on Victimization by Sexual Orientation," http://www.cdc.gov/violenceprevention/pdf/cdc_nisvs_victimization_final-a.pdf

11. Allen J. Beck, David Cantor, John Hartge, and Tim Smith, *Sexual Victimization in Juvenile Facilities, Reported by Youth 2012* (Washington, DC: Bureau of Justice Statistics, 2013).

12. Josh Vorhees, "The Dark Secret of Juvenile Detention Centers: Nine Out of Every 10 Reporters of Sexual Abuse Are Males Victimized by Female Staffers." *Slate*, September 13, 2014, http://www.slate.com/articles/news_ and_politics/politics/2014/09/woodland_hills_youth_development_center_ the_dark_secret_of_juvenile_detention.html.

13. Beck et al., *Sexual Victimization in Juvenile Facilities*.

14. Dorothy Roberts, *Killing the Black Body: Race Reproduction and the Meaning of Liberty* (New York: Pantheon, 1997), 153.

15. Jaime M. Grant, Lisa A. Mottet, Justin Tanis, Jack Harrison, Jody L. Herman, and Mara Keisling, *Injustice at Every Turn: A Report of the National Transgender Discrimination Survey* (Washington, DC: National Center for Transgender Equality and National Gay and Lesbian Task Force, 2011).

16. *The Report of the U.S. Transgender Survey*, 2015, 15, https://www. transequality.org/sites/default/files/docs/USTS-Full-Report-FINAL.PDF

17. Valerie Jenness, Cheryl L. Maxson, Kristy N. Matsuda, and Jennifer Macy, *Violence in California Correctional Facilities: An Empirical Examination of Sexual Assault* (Irvine: Center for Evidence-Based Corrections, University of California, 2007).

18. Allen J. Beck, *Sexual Victimization in Prisons and Jails* (Supplemental Tables), Table 1, https://www.bjs.gov/content/pub/pdf/svpjri1112_st.pdf.

19. Sabrina Rubin, "The Transgender Crucible," *Rolling Stone*, July 30, 2014, http://www.rollingstone.com/culture/news/the-transgender-crucible-20140730#ixzz49bNbBmBK.

20. E. Oberholtzer, "The Dismal State of Transgender Incarceration Policies," Prison Policy Initiative, https://www.prisonpolicy.org/blog/2017/11/08/ transgender/.

21. Office of the United Nations High Commissioner for Human Rights (OHCHR), "Basic Principles for the Treatment of Prisoners," https://www.ohchr. org/en/professionalinterest/pages/basicprinciplestreatmentofprisoners.aspx.

## CHAPTER 6

1. Ann O'Neill, "'Because of You, I Trust No One,'" CNN, October 13, 2012, https://www.cnn.com/2012/10/10/justice/jerry-sandusky-victim-impact/ index.html.

2. Sonia Moghe and Lauren del Valle, "Larry Nasser's Abuse Victims in Their Own Words," CNN. January 17, 2018. https://www.cnn. com/2018/01/16/us/nassar-victim-impact-statements/index.html

3. Tony Mancuso, "A Town and University Growing with Penn State Football," *The Penn State Athletics Blog*, http://bit.ly/1gb9MM0.

4. Earl Smith, *Race, Sport and the American Dream* (Durham, NC: Carolina Academic Press, 2014).

5. Richard Majors and Janet Bilson, *Cool Pose: The Dilemmas of African American Manhood in America* (New York: Lexington Books, 1992), 4–5.

6. "Baylor University Board of Regents Findings of Fact," http://www.baylor.edu/thefacts/doc.php/266596.pdf.

7. Paula Lavigne, "Lawyers, Status, Public Backlash Aid College Athletes Accused of Crimes," ESPN, June 15, 2015, http://es.pn/1GElglf.

8. Benjamin Morris, "The Rate of Domestic Violence Arrests among NFL Players," *FiveThirtyEight*, July 31, 2014, http://fivethirtyeight.com/datalab/the-rate-of-domestic-violence-arrests-among-nfl-players/.

9. Deborah Epstein, "I'm Done Helping the NFL Players Association Pay Lip Service to Domestic Violence Prevention." *Washington Post*, June 5, 2018. https://www.washingtonpost.com/opinions/im-done-helping-the-nfl-pay-lip-service-to-domestic-violence-prevention/2018/06/05/1b470bec-6448-11e8-99d2-0d678ec08c2f_story.html?utm_term=.36df218971f6.

10. Malcolm Gladwell, "In Plain View: How Child Molesters Get Away with It," *New Yorker*, September 24, 2012, http://www.newyorker.com/magazine/2012/09/24/in-plain-view.

11. The Freeh Report is a valuable data tool for anyone interested in reading more about the case. It can be accessed online and read at, among other places, the *Chicago Tribune*: http://www.chicagotribune.com/sports/chi-freeh-report-sandusky-penn-state-20120712-pdf-htmlstory.html.

12. Tim Evans, Mark Alesia, and Marisa Kwiatkowski, "A 20-Year Toll: 368 Gymnasts Allege Sexual Exploitation," *Indianapolis Star*, December 15, 2016, http://www.indystar.com/story/news/2016/12/15/20-year-toll-368-gymnasts-allege-sexual-exploitation/95198724/.

13. Cheyna Roth, "Michigan State Reaches $500 Million Settlement over Nassar Abuse," *Morning Edition*, NPR, May 17, 2018. https://www.npr.org/2018/05/17/611869662/michigan-state-reaches-500-million-settlement-over-nassar-abuse.

14. Dan Barry, Serge F. Kovaleski, and Juliet Macur, "As F.B.I. Took a Year to Pursue the Nassar Case, Dozens Say They Were Molested," *New York Times*, February 3, 2018, https://www.nytimes.com/2018/02/03/sports/nassar-fbi.html.

15. Matt Mencarini, "Larry Nassar: 2014 Police Report Sheds Light on How He Avoided Criminal Charges," *Lansing State Journal*, January 26, 2018,

https://www.lansingstatejournal.com/story/news/nation-now/2018/01/26/larry-nassar-michigan-state-university-investigation/1069151001/.

16. Mencarini, "Larry Nassar."

17. McKayla Maroney quoted in Abigail Abrams, "'I Thought I Was Going to Die': Read McKayla Maroney's Full Victim Impact Statement in Larry Nassar Trial," *Time*, January 19, 2018, http://time.com/5109011/mckayla-maroney-larry-nassar-victim-impact-statement/.

18. Nicole Chavez, "Larry Nassar Case: Victims Say an 'Army' Silenced Them for Years,", CNN, January 23, 2018, https://www.cnn.com/2018/01/23/us/nassar-sexual-abuse-who-knew/index.html.

19. Harriet Alexander, "'I Just Signed Your Death Warrant': Larry Nassar Sentenced to 175 Years for Sexually Abusing US Gymnastics Team," *Telegraph*, January 24, 2018, https://www.telegraph.co.uk/news/2018/01/24/just-signed-death-warrant-larry-nassar-sentenced-175-years-sexually/.

20. Chavez, "Larry Nassar Case."

21. Marc Tracy, "N.C.A.A. Drops Michigan State Inquiry Over Nassar." *New York Times*, August 30, 2018, https://www.nytimes.com/2018/08/30/sports/ncaa-michigan-state-nassar.html?rref=collection/timestopic/Michigan%20State%20University&action=click&contentCollection=timestopics&region=stream&module=stream_unit&version=latest&contentPlacement=2&pgtype=collection.

22. Evans, Alesia, and Kwiatkowski, "A 20-Year Toll."

23. Patrick Redford, "Powerful Congressman Jim Jordan Accused of Knowing about Sexual Abuse as Ohio State Wrestling Coach," *Deadspin*, July 3, 2018, https://deadspin.com/powerful-congressman-jim-jordan-accused-of-knowing-abou-1827316946.

**CHAPTER 7**

1. David Clohessy, quoted in Sarah Childress, "Secrets of the Vatican: What's the State of the Church's Child Abuse Crisis?" *Frontline*, PBS, February 25, 2014, http://www.pbs.org/wgbh/pages/frontline/religion/secrets-of-the-vatican/whats-the-state-of-the-churchs-child-abuse-crisis/.

2. William Grimes, "Eugene Kennedy, a Voice for Change in the Catholic Church, Dies at 86," *New York Times*, June 10, 2015, http://nyti.ms/1KYQYv7

3. Eugene Kennedy, *The Catholic Priest in the United States: Psychological Investigations* (Washington, DC: United States Catholic Conference, Publications Office, 1972).

4. Roman Cholij, "Priestly Celibacy in Patristics and in the History of the Church," Vatican, 1993, http://www.vatican.va/roman_curia/congregations/cclergy/documents/rc_con_cclergy_doc_01011993_chisto_en.html.

5. Archdiocese of Baltimore, "Seminaries," http://www.becomeapriest.org/seminarians/seminaries/

6. Instruction on the Manner of Proceeding in Cases of Solicitation," The Vatican Press, http://www.cbsnews.com/htdocs/pdf/Criminales.pdf.

7. Lisa Cohen and Igor Galynker, "Clinical Features of Pedophilia and Implications for Treatment," *Journal of Psychiatric Practice* 8 (2002): 276–89.

8. John Jay College of Criminal Justice, *The Nature and Scope of the Problem of Sexual Abuse of Minors by Catholic Priests and Deacons in the United States* (Washington, DC: Conference of Catholic Bishops).

9. William Lobdell and Stuart Silverstein, "$50 Million for Alaskan Abuse Plaintiffs," *Los Angeles Times*, November 19, 2007, http://www.latimes.com/local/la-na-settle19nov19-story.html.

10. Lobdell and Silverstein, "$50 Million for Alaskan Abuse Plaintiffs."

11. Available from the *Washington Post* at https://wapo.st/2PrmzLZ.

12. See http://www.bishop-accountability.org.

13. Associated Press, "Top US Cardinal Timothy Dolan 'Paid Off Abusive Priests,'" *Telegraph*. June 2, 2013, http://www.telegraph.co.uk/news/world-news/northamerica/usa/10154334/Top-US-cardinal-Timothy-Dolan-paid-off-abusive-priests.html.

14. Associated Press, "Top US Cardinal Timothy Dolan."

15. Rachel Zoll, "Catholic Church Lawyer Details Cover Up Claims on Sex Abuse," *Christian Science Monitor*, July 15, 2014, http://www.csmonitor.com/USA/Latest-News-Wires/2014/0715/Catholic-church-lawyer-details-cover-up-claims-on-sex-abuse.

**CHAPTER 8**

1. Melena Ryzik, Cara Buckley, and Jodi Kantor, "Louis C. K. Is Accused by 5 Women of Sexual Misconduct," *New York Times*, November 9, 2017. https://www.nytimes.com/2017/11/09/arts/television/louis-ck-sexual-misconduct.html

2. See https://twitter.com/jessicavalenti/status/952568652066443264?lang=en.

3. Carly Mallenbaum, Patrick Ryan, and Maria Puente, "A Complete List of the 60 Bill Cosby Accusers and Their Reactions to the Guilty Verdict," *USA To-*

*day*, April 27, 2018, https://www.usatoday.com/story/life/people/2018/04/27/
bill-cosby-full-list-accusers/555144002/.

4. Megan Garber, "Bill Cosby and the Slow Death of Celebrity Impunity: The Conviction of the Actor and Comedian Is a Testament to the Power of #MeToo." *Atlantic*, April 26, 2018, https://www.theatlantic.com/entertainment/archive/2018/04/bill-cosby-conviction/559028/.

5. Center for the Study of Women in Television and Film, https://womenintvfilm.sdsu.edu/wp-content/uploads/2017/09/2016-17_Boxed_In_Report.pdf

6. Maryann Erigha, "Race, Gender, Hollywood: Representation in Cultural Production and Digital Medias Potential for Change," *Sociology Compass* 9 (1): 78–89, doi:10.1111/soc4.12237.

7. Erigha, "Race, Gender, Hollywood."

8. Lindsey Bahr, "A Star Is Not Born: New University Study Says Films Exclude Minorities Including Hispanics, as Well as Women, LGBT People and the Disabled," *The Hispanic Outlook in Higher Education* 27 (September 2017): 26–27, https://search-proquest-com.mutex.gmu.edu/docview/1949029 479?accountid=14541.

9. Angela J. Hattery and Earl Smith, *African American Families Today: Myths and Realities* (Lanham, MD: Rowman & Littlefield, 2012).

10. Ashley Rodriguez, "How Powerful Was Harvey Weinstein? Almost No One Has Been Thanked at the Oscars More," *Quartz*, October 13, 2017, https://qz.com/1101213/harvey-weinstein-is-one-of-the-most-thanked-people-in-oscars-history/.

11. Jodi Kantor and Megan Twohey, "Harvey Weinstein Paid Off Sexual Harassment Accusers for Decades," *New York Times*, October 5, 2017, https://www.nytimes.com/2017/10/05/us/harvey-weinstein-harassment-allegations.html.

12. Kantor and Twohey, "Harvey Weinstein Paid Off Sexual Harassment Accusers."

13. Kantor and Twohey, "Harvey Weinstein Paid Off Sexual Harassment Accusers."

14. "Bill Cosby Biography," Biography.com, last updated May 3, 2018, https://www.biography.com/people/bill-cosby-9258468.

15. J. Truesdell, and N. Egan, "Who Is Andrea Constand, Bill Cosby's Accuser?," *People*, April 27, 2018, https://people.com/crime/who-is-andrea-constand-bill-cosby-accuser/.

16. Truesdell, and Egan, "Who Is Andrea Constand?"

17. Kim Kyle, Christina Littlefield, and Melissa Etehad, "Bill Cosby: A 50-Year Chronicle of Accusations and Accomplishments," *Los Angeles Times*,

June 17, 2017, http://www.latimes.com/entertainment/la-et-bill-cosby-time-line-htmlstory.html.

18. Kyle et al., "Bill Cosby."

19. Kyle et al., "Bill Cosby."

20. Kyle et al., "Bill Cosby."

21. Kyle et al., "Bill Cosby."

22. Virginia Chamlee, "The Process to Report Sexual Harassment in Congress Is Actually Ridiculous," *Bustle*, November 22, 2017, https://www.bustle.com/p/the-process-to-report-sexual-harassment-in-congress-is-actually-ridiculous-5527693.

## CHAPTER 9

1. Paula Gilbert and Kimberly Eby, *Violence and Gender* (Upper Saddle River, NJ: Pearson, 2004),p. xi.

2. Sandra Gonzalez, "After #MeToo, Anthony Bourdain Stood 'Unhesitatingly and Unwaveringly' with Women," CNN, June 8, 2018, https://cnn.it/2sSzNb8.

3. Jon Krakauer, *Missoula: Rape and the Justice System in a College Town* (New York: Doubleday, 2015), 81.

4. David Lisak, Lori Gardinier, Sarah C. Nicksa, and Ashley M. Cote, "False Allegations of Sexual Assault: An Analysis of Ten Years of Reported Cases," *Violence against Women* 16, no. 12 (2010).

5. Jackie Campbell, "Campus Sexual Assault Perpetration: What Else We Need to Know," *Journal of the American Medical Association, Pediatrics* 169, no. 12 (2015): 1088–89. doi:10.1001/jamapediatrics.2015.1313.

6. Saskia de Melker, "The Case for Starting Sex Education in Kindergarten," PBS News Hour, May 27, 2015, http://www.pbs.org/newshour/updates/spring-fever/.

# BIBLIOGRAPHY

Abrams, Abigail. "'I Thought I Was Going to Die': Read McKayla Maroney's Full Victim Impact Statement in Larry Nassar Trial." *Time*, January 19, 2018. http://time.com/5109011/mckayla-maroney-larry-nassar-victim-impact-statement/.

Alexander, Harriet. "'I Just Signed Your Death Warrant': Larry Nassar Sentenced to 175 Years for Sexually Abusing US Gymnastics Team." *Telegraph*, January 24, 2018, https://www.telegraph.co.uk/news/2018/01/24/just-signed-death-warrant-larry-nassar-sentenced-175-years-sexually/.

Associated Press. "Top US Cardinal Timothy Dolan 'Paid Off Abusive Priests.'" *Telegraph*. June 2, 2013. http://www.telegraph.co.uk/news/worldnews/northamerica/usa/10154334/Top-US-cardinal-Timothy-Dolan-paid-off-abusive-priests.html.

Bahr, Lindsey. "A Star Is Not Born: New University Study Says Films Exclude Minorities Including Hispanics, as Well as Women, LGBT People and the Disabled." *The Hispanic Outlook in Higher Education* 27 (2017): 26–27. https://search-proquecom.mutex.gmu.edu/docview/1949029479?accountid=14541.

Barry, Dan, Serge Kovaleski, and Juliet Macur. "As F.B.I. Took a Year to Pursue the Nassar Case, Dozens Say They Were Molested." *New York Times*, February 3, 2018. https://nyti.ms/2N5rSk0.

Baylor University Board of Regents. "Baylor University Board of Regents Findings of Fact." http://www.baylor.edu/thefacts/doc.php/266596.pdf.

Beck, Allen "2015. PREA Data Collection Activities, 2015" *Bureau of Justice Statistics* June 25, 2015, NCJ 248824

Beck, Allen J., Marcus Berzofsky, Rachel Caspar, and Christopher Krebs. *Sexual Victimization in Prisons and Jails Reported by Inmates, 2011–12*. Washington, DC: Bureau of Justice Statistics, 2013.

Beck, Allen J., David Cantor, John Hartge, and Tim Smith. *Sexual Victimization in Juvenile Facilities, Reported by Youth 2012*. Washington, DC: Bureau of Justice Statistics, 2013.

Bill Cosby Biography. Biography.com. 2018. https://www.biography.com/people/bill-cosby-9258468.

Browne, Angela. *When Battered Women Kill*. New York: Free Press, 1989.

Campbell, Jacquelyn. "Campus Sexual Assault Perpetration: What Else We Need to Know." *Journal of the American Medical Association Pediatrics* 169, no. 12 (2015): 1088–89. doi:10.1001/jamapediatrics.2015.1313.

Cantalupo, Nancy Chi. *Five Things Student Affairs Professionals Should Know about Campus Gender-Based Violence*. Washington, DC: NASPA, 2015. https://www.naspa.org/images/uploads/main/5Things_Gender_Based_Violence.pdf.

Chamlee, Virginia. "The Process to Report Sexual Harassment in Congress Is Actually Ridiculous." *Bustle*, November 22, 2017. https://www.bustle.com/p/the-process-to-report-sexual-harassment-in-congress-is-actually-ridiculous-5527693.

Chavez, Nicole. "Larry Nassar Case: Victims Say an 'Army' Silenced Them for Years." Retrieved from https://cnn.it/2Kr2YNb.

Childress, Sarah. "What's the State of the Church's Child Abuse Scandal?" *Frontline*, February 25, 2014. http://to.pbs.org/1GY7p4H.

Cholij, Roman. "Priestly Celibacy in Patristics and in the History of the Church." Vatican, 1993. http://www.vatican.va/roman_curia/congregations/cclergy/documents/rc_con_cclergy_doc_01011993_chisto_en.html.

Chuchmach, Megan. "Female Soldier More Likely to Be Raped Than Killed in Action, Says Rep." ABC News, September 10, 2008. http://abcnews.go.com/Blotter/story?id=5760295.

Cohen, Lisa, and Igor Galynker. "Clinical Features of Pedophilia and Implications for Treatment." *Journal of Psychiatric Practice* 8 (2002): 276–89.

Collins, Patricia Hill, and Sirma Bilge. *Intersectionality*. New York: Polity Press, 2016.

de Melker, Saskia. "The Case for Starting Sex Education in Kindergarten." PBS News Hour, May 27, 2015. http://www.pbs.org/newshour/updates/spring-fever/.

Erigha, Maryann. "Race, Gender, Hollywood: Representation in Cultural Production and Digital Medias Potential for Change." *Sociology Compass* 9, no. 1 (2015): 78–89. doi:10.1111/soc4.12237.

Evans, Tim, Mark Alesia, and Marisa Kwiatkowski. "A 20-Year Toll: 368 Gymnasts Allege Sexual Exploitation. *Indianapolis Star*, December 15, 2016. http://www.indystar.com/story/news/2016/12/15/20-year-toll-368-gymnasts-allege-sexual-exploitation/95198724/

Foubert, John D., Johnathan T. Newberry, and Jerry L. Tatum. "Behavior Differences Seven Months Later: Effects of a Rape Prevention Program." *Journal of Student Affairs Research and Practice* 44, no.4 (2007): 728–49

Gilbert, Paula, and Kimberly Eby. *Violence and Gender*. Upper Saddle River, NJ: Pearson, 2004.

Gladwell, Malcolm. "In Plain View: How Child Molesters Get Away with It." *New Yorker*, September 24, 2012. http://www.newyorker.com/magazine/2012/09/24/in-plain-view.

Grant, Jaime M., Lisa A. Mottet, Justin Tanis, Jack Harrison, Jody L. Herman, and Mara Keisling, *Injustice at Every Turn: A Report of the National Transgender Discrimination Survey*. Washington, DC: National Center for Transgender Equality and National Gay and Lesbian Task Force, 2011.

Green, Erica, and Sheryl Gay Stolberg. "Campus Rape Policies Get a New Look as the Accused Get DeVos's Ear." *New York Times*, July 12, 2017. http://nyti.ms/2gW7PbO.

Grimes, William. "Eugene Kennedy, a Voice for Change in the Catholic Church, Dies at 86." *New York Times*, June 10, 2015, http://nyti.ms/1KYQYv7.

Hattery, Angela J. *Intimate Partner Violence*. Lanham, MD: Rowman & Littlefield, 2008.

Hattery, Angela J., and Earl Smith. *African American Families Today: Myths and Realities*. Lanham, MD: Rowman & Littlefield, 2012.

Hayes, Chris. *A Colony in a Nation*. New York: W. W. Norton, 2017.

Healy, Melissa. "Pentagon Blasts Tailhook Probe, Two Admirals Resign." *Los Angeles Times*, September 25, 1992.

Hlavka, Heather. "Normalizing Sexual Violence: Young Women Account for Harassment and Abuse." *Gender & Society* 28: 337–58. doi: 10.1177/0891243214526468.

Human Rights Watch. *Embattled: Retaliation Against Sexual Assault Survivors in the Military*. New York: Human Rights Watch, 2015. http://bit.ly/1BZgIpv

Izadi, Elahe. "'Princeton Mom' on CNN: 'What We're Really Identifying as Rape Is a Clumsy, Hook-Up Melodrama." *Washington Post*, December 12, 2014. http://www.washingtonpost.com/news/post-nation/wp/2014/12/12/princeton-mom-on-cnn-what-were-really-identifying-as-rape-is-a-clumsy-hook-up-melodrama/.

Jenness, Valerie, Cheryl L. Maxson, Kristy N. Matsuda, and Jennifer Macy Sumner. *Violence in California Correctional Facilities: An Empirical Examination of Sexual Assault. Irvine: Center for Evidence-Based Corrections*. Irvine: Center for Evidence-Based Corrections, University of California, 2007.

John Jay College of Criminal Justice. *The Nature and Scope of the Problem of Sexual Abuse of Minors by Catholic Priests and Deacons in the United States*. Washington, DC: Conference of Catholic Bishops, 2004.

Kaiser, David, and Lovisa Stannow. "The Shame of Our Prisons: New Evidence," *New York Review of Books*, October 2013. http://www.nybooks.com/articles/archives/2013/oct/24/shame-our-prisons-new-evidence/.

Kantor, Jodi, and Megan Twohey. "Harvey Weinstein Paid Off Sexual Harassment Accusers for Decades." *New York Times*, October 5, 2017. Retrieved from https://www.nytimes.com/2017/10/05/us/harvey-weinstein-harassment-allegations.html.

Kearl, Holly. "Military Sexual Assault: Betrayal and Retaliation for Service Members." *Women's Media Center*. May 20, 2015. http://www.womensmediacenter.com/feature/entry/military-sexual-assault-betrayal-and-retaliation-for-service-members.

Kennedy, Eugene. *The Catholic Priest in the United States: Psychological Investigations*. Washington, DC: United States Catholic Conference, Publications Office, 1972.

Kirsch, Scott, and Colin Flint. *Reconstructing Conflict: Integrating War and Post-War Geographies.* Burlington, VT: Ashgate, 2011.

Krakauer, Jon. *Missoula: Rape and the Justice System in a College Town.* New York: Doubleday, 2015.

Kyle, Kim, Christina Littlefield, and Melissa Etehad. "Bill Cosby: A 50-Year Chronicle of Accusations and Accomplishments." *Los Angeles Times*, June 17, 2017. http://www.latimes.com/entertainment/la-et-bill-cosby-timeline-htmlstory.html.

Lapidos, Juliet. "Sororities Should Throw Parties." *New York Times*, January 21, 2015. http://www.nytimes.com/2015/01/21/opinion/sororities-should-throw-parties.html?_r=0.

Lavigne, Paula. "Lawyers, Status, Public Backlash Aid College Athletes Accused of Crimes," ESPN, June 15, 2015. http://es.pn/1GElglf.

Lisak, David, Lori Gardinier, Sarah C. Nicksa, and Ashley M. Cote. "False Allegations of Sexual Assault: An Analysis of Ten Years of Reported Cases" *Violence against Women* 16, no. 12 (2010).

Lobdell, William, and Stuart Silverstein. "$50 Million for Alaskan Abuse Plaintiffs." *Los Angeles Times*, February 19, 2007. http://www.latimes.com/local/la-na-settle-19nov19-story.html.

Loya, Rebecca Maria. "Economic Consequences of Sexual Violence for Survivors: Implications for Social Policy and Social Change." PhD Dissertation. Brandeis, University, 2012. ProQuest 3540084.

Lusher, Adam. 2018. "Marilyn Monroe: Mourners at Her Funeral Were Also to Blame for Her Death, Claimed Unpublished Arthur Miller Essay." *Independent*, January 11, 2018, https://ind.pn/2s03hEx.

Majors, Richard, and Janet Bilson. *Cool Pose: The Dilemmas of African American Manhood in America.* New York: Lexington Books, 1992.

Mallenbaum, Carly, Patrick Ryan, and Maria Puente. "A Complete List of the 60 Bill Cosby and Their Reactions to the Guilty Verdict." *USA Today*, April 27, 2018. https://www.usatoday.com/story/life/people/2018/04/27/bill-cosby-full-list-accusers/555144002/

Mancuso, Tony. "A Town and University Growing with Penn State Football." *The Penn State Athletics Blog*, http://bit.ly/1gb9MM0.

Martin, Patricia Yancey. *Rape Work: Victims, Gender, and Emotions in Organization and Community Context.* New York: Routledge, 2005.

Miller, Patricia. "The Catholic Church's American Downfall." *Salon*, May 21, 2015. Retrieved June 13, 2015. http://bit.ly/1MS5FPN.

Mencarini, Matt. "Larry Nassar: 2014 Police Report Sheds Light on How He Avoided Criminal Charges." *Lansing State Journal*, January 26, 2018. Retrieved from https://on.lsj.com/2yQddWR.

Messner, Michael. "Bad Men, Good Men, Bystanders: Who Is the Rapist?" *Gender and Society* 30, no. 1 (2016): 57–66. doi: 10.1177/0891243215608781.

Moghe, Sonia, and Lauren del Valle. "Larry Nasser's Abuse Victims in Their Own Words." *CNN*, January 17, 2018. https://www.cnn.com/2018/01/16/us/nassar-victim-impact-statements/index.html.

Morris, Benjamin. "The Rate of Domestic Violence Arrests among NFL Players." *FiveThirtyEight*, July 31, 2014. http://fivethirtyeight.com/datalab/the-rate-of-domestic-violence-arrests-among-nfl-players/.

North, Anna, "#MeToo at the 2018 Oscars: The Good, the Bad, and the In Between." *Vox*, March 5, 2018. http://bit.ly/2yJ9qe4.

Nossiter, Adam. "Woman Who Left the Citadel Tells of Brutal Hazing Ordeal." *New York Times*, February 18, 1997. Retrieved July 4, 2015. http://www.nytimes.com/1997/02/18/us/woman-who-left-the-citadel-tells-of-brutal-hazing-ordeal.html.

Oberholtzer, Elliot. "The Dismal State of Transgender Incarceration Policies." Prison Policy Initiative, November 8, 2017. https://www.prisonpolicy.org/blog/2017/11/08/transgender/

O'Neill, Ann. "'Because of You, I Trust No One.'" CNN, October 13, 2012. https://www.cnn.com/2012/10/10/justice/jerry-sandusky-victim-impact/index.html.

Reidy, Dennis, et al., "Masculine Discrepancy Stress, Teen Dating Violence, and Sexual Violence Perpetration Among Adolescent Boys." *Journal of Adolescent Health* 56 (2015): 619–24.

Roberts, Dorothy. *Killing the Black Body: Race Reproduction and the Meaning of Liberty*. New York: Pantheon, 1997.

Rodriguez, Ashley. "How Powerful Was Harvey Weinstein? Almost No One Has Been Thanked at the Oscars More." *Quartz*, October 13, 2017. Retrieved from https://qz.com/1101213/harvey-weinstein-is-one-of-the-most-thanked-people-in-oscars-history/.

Rubin, Sabrina. "The Transgender Crucible." *Rolling Stone*, July 30, 2014. http://www.rollingstone.com/culture/news/the-transgender-crucible-20140730 #ixzz49bNbBmBK.

Ryzik, Melena, Cara Buckley, and Jodi Kantor. "Louis C. K. Is Accused by 5 Women of Sexual Misconduct." *New York Times*, November 9, 2017. Retrieved from https://www.nytimes.com/2017/11/09/arts/television/louis-ck-sexual-misconduct.html.

Sanday, Peggy Reeves. *Fraternity Gang Rape*. New York: New York University Press, 1997.

Senn, Charlene Y., Misha Eliasziw, Paula C. Barata, Wilfreda E. Thurston, Ian R. Newby-Clark, H. Lorraine Radtke, and Karen L. Hobden. "Efficacy of a Sexual Assault Resistance Program for University Women." *New England Journal of Medicine* 372 (2015): 2326–35. http://www.nejm.org/toc/nejm/372/24/>doi: 10.1056/NEJMsa1411131.

Sinozich, Sofi, and Lynn Langton. *Rape and Sexual Assault Victimization among College-Age Females, 1995–2013* NCJ 248471. Washington, DC: Bureau of Justice Statistics, 2014.

Smith, Earl. *Race, Sport and the American Dream*. Durham, NC: Carolina Academic Press, 2014.

Syrett, Nicholas L. *The Company He Keeps: A History of White College Fraternities*. Chapel Hill, NC: University of North Carolina Press, 2009.

Truesdell, Jeff, and Nicole Egan. 'Who Is Andrea Constand, Bill Cosby's Accuser?' *People*, April 27, 2018. Retrieved from https://people.com/crime/who-is-andrea-constand-bill-cosby-accuser/.

US Department of Defense. *Annual Report on Sexual Assault in the Military*. Washington, DC: US Department of Defense, 2018. http://bit.ly/2N9sTaC.

Zoll, Rachel. "Catholic Church Lawyer Details Cover Up Claims on Sex Abuse." *Christian Science Monitor*, July 15, 2014. Retrieved Jan 13, 2015 http://www.csmonitor.com/USA/Latest-News-Wires/2014/0715/Catholic-church-lawyer-details-cover-up-claims-on-sex-abuse.

# INDEX

"1 is 2 Many," 50
"Ask her when she's sober," 77
"beyond a reasonable doubt standard,"
   52, 205
"Don't Ask, Don't Tell," 74
"freeze frame," 103–104
"I'm a grown up kid" strategy, 134–135
"I'm the guy next door" strategy, 135
"It's On Us" campaign, 45
"preponderance of the evidence"
   standard, 52, 205
"pulling train," 39
"riffing," 37
"stealthing," 40
"Three Strikes You're Out," 99, 106
"working a 'yes' out," 37–40
#metoo, 2, 143, 183–85, 190–91, 194,
   198, 209
2002 Presidential Medal of Freedom, 192

Academy Awards, 190
Alesia, Mark, 140
Allison, Jewel, 194
Allred, Gloria, 196
Amazon, 87
Ansari, Aziz, 184
Apostolic See, 165

Arpaio, Joe, 86
Aquilina, Rosemaire (Judge in the Larry
   Nassar case), 143
Attica, 87

Baufman, Ben, 191
Baylor University, 39, 118–119, 128, 212
Beck, Allen, 92
Belcher, Jovan, 123 124, 150
Benedict, Jeff, 120
Biles, Simone, 143
Bill Cosby is a Very Funny Fellow . . .
   Right!, 192
Bill Cosby Show, The, 192
Bilson, Janet, 116–17
Bishopaccountability.org, 175
Bourdain, Anthony, 199
Bourgeois, Father Roy, 163–64
Bowman, Barbara, 193
Boyce, Larissa, 144
Briles, Art, 118
Brown, Josh, 125, 130
Bryant, Kobe, 128
Buress, Hannibal, 193
Burke, Tarana (Founder of the #MeToo
   movement), 184
Bush, George W., President, 187

Campbell, Jacquelyn, 27, 211

Campus disciplinary systems, 41–44

Canon Law, 165–66

Cantalupo, Nancy Chi, 48, 51

Cardinal Law, 172

Catholic Church: hierarchy, 157–58; sacraments, 158–59; wealth, 155

CeCe, 103, 207

celibacy, 15, 154, 160–61, 165, 179, 186. *see also* "chastity"

Champion, Robert, 26

chastity, 15, 154, 160–61, 165, 179, 186. *see also* "celibacy"

Child sexual abuse (CSA), 10–11, 130–131

Case study, Boston, Massachusetts, 171–72

Case study, St. Michael, Alaska, 170, 172–74

Case study in Pennsylvania, 173–74

Civil litigation in the Catholic Church, 174–76

chronic traumatic encephalopathy (CTE), 123 124

Citadel, the 63–64

Clery Act, 78

CRIMEN SOLLICITATIONIS, 165–68, 176, 186. *see also* internal systems of justice (Catholic Church)

Congregation for the Doctrine of the Faith, 178

Congressional Members' Handbook, 185

Clohessy, David, 151

Clooney, George, 187

Complainant, definition of, 43

Constand, Andrea, 186, 192–94

cool pose, 116–17

Cones, Bryon, 162

Conyers, John, 190, 197, 204

Cosby, Bill, 183, 186, 190, 192–94, 197, 201, 204, 207, 211

Cosby, Camille, 194

Costs of sexual and intimate partner violence, 6, 201

Costello, Carol, 23

Council of Trent, 154

Crennel, Romeo, 123

criminalization of pregnancy, 97–98

Cruise, Tom, 187

Curly, Tim, 139

Delta Kappa Epsilon, 38

Denhollander, Rachel, 142

Department of Education, 46–47

DeVos, Betsy, Secretary of Education, 46

Dolan, Cardinal Timothy, 176–77

Eby, Kim 5, 199

Edwards, Harry, 123, 126

Edwards, John, 187

Emmys, 192

Endal, Father George S., 173

Epstein, Cynthia Fuchs, 63

Evans, Tim, 140

Falkner, Shannon, 63

*Fat Albert*, 192

*fetal harm laws*, 97

Flint, Colin, 57

Florida State University, 120–121

Foubert, John, 27

Franken, Al, 183, 190, 211

fraternity, 24–25; in the Catholic Church, 88, 161–64; in the military, 60, 88; in politics and entertainment, 186–87; in prison, 88–89; in SportsWorld, 111, 114–115; initiation rituals, 29–33

Freeh Report, the 138–39

gaslighting, 195

Gelles, Richard, 19

gender based violence globally, 7

gender based violence, definition, 6–7

gender based violence statistics, 12

Geoghan, Father, 169, 171–72, 201
Gilbert, Paula Ruth, 5, 199
Gillibrand, Kirsten, 56, 79, 205–06
Gladwell, Malcolm, 132, 134, 135, 168
Goffman, Erving, 14, 85
Goldberg, Whoopi, 194
Golden Globes, 192
Good Will Hunting, 190
Goodell, Roger, 129 130
Gopnick, Adam, 84
Gospel of Mary, 153
Grooming: communities, 134–136; parents, 133–134; victims, 136–137, 179

Hardy, Greg, 129–130
Harmon, Jane, 55
Hart, Gary, 187
Haselberger, Jennifer, Archbishop John Nienstedt's archivist, 179–80
Hayes, Chris, 84
hearing board, definition of, 43
hegemonic masculinity, 25
Henry, Chris, 124
Hernandez, Aaron, 123–24, 149–50
Hill Collins, Patricia, 8–9, 225
Hlavka, Heather, 68–70
Historically Black Colleges and Universities (HBCU's), 25–26
Hollis, Mark, 144
Holy See, 155
House of Cards, 187
Human Rights Watch Report, 70–73
Hunt, Darryl, 194
hyperfemininity, 187
hypermasculinity, hypermasculine, 16–17, 21, 213; in fraternities, 25, 27–29, 32–41; in the military, 64–65, 74, 79–80; in politics and entertainment, 187–88; in SportsWorld, 111, 115–16, 146–47, 149

Indianapolis Star, 140, 142, 145
institutional power, definition of, 20
institutions, definition of, 13–14
internal systems of justice, 205, in the Catholic Church, 165–68, 176, 186; see also CRIMEN SOLLICITATIONIS in fraternities, 27, 41, 43; in the military, 66, 75, 79; in politics and entertainment, 184 in prisons, 86, 105; in SportsWorld, 11, 119, 127, 129, 146–47
intersectional theory, definition of, 8–9, 205–07
Intimate partner violence (IPV), 11–12; emotional/Psychological abuse, 12; physical abuse, 11; sexual abuse, 12; in SportsWorld, 121–22; stalking, 12
intimate partner violence homicide statistics, 13
Invisible War, the, 69–70, 72, 80
I Spy, 192

Jackson, Candice, 46
Jell-O Spokesperson (Bill Cosby), 192
John Jay Report, 168
Jolie, Angelina, 187, 191
Jones, Adam "Pacman," 124
Judd, Ashley, 184, 190–91

Kaiser, David, 92
Karpinski, Janis, 56
Karoli, Bela, 143
Karolia, Marta, 143
Katz, Jackson, 49
Kearl, Holly, 69, 73
Kennedy, Father Eugene, 152
Kennedy, John F., President, 187
King, Karen, 153
Kirsch, Scott, 57
Klages, Kathie, 141
Knight, Bobby, 5

Krakauer, Jon, 200
Kwiatkowski, Marisa, 144

Ladd, Cindra, 193
Lapidos, Juliet, 35
Lauer, Matt 211, 215
Lavigne, Paula, 120–121, 128, 146, *see also ESPN Outside the Lines,* 205
Law, Cardinal Bernard, 172
Lee, Mitch, 39
Lilly Ledbetter Act, 195
Lloyd, Odin, 124
Lorber, Judith, 212
Louis C.K., 184
*Love and Marriage,* 192
Lundowski, Joseph, 173, 179

Mace, Nancy, 64
MacKinnon, Catharine, 19, 46, 93
Madden, Laura, 191
Magdalene, Mary, 154
Majors, Richard, 116–17
*Man and Boy,* 192
Maroney, Makala, 1, 143
Masten, PJ, 193
matrix of domination, 8–9
McCarrick, Cardinal, 151
McCaskill, Claire, 56, 205–06
McCaw, Ian, 118
McCaul, Morgan, 141
McCee, Kathy, 193
McGowan, Rose, 190–91
medical amnesty, 53
Member's Representational Allowance (MRA), 185
Men Stopping Rape, 49
Mentavlos, Jeanie, 63
Mentors in Violence Prevention (MVP), 49
Merkel, Angela, 209
Messer, Kim, 63

Messner, Michael, 6–7, 225, 238
Meyer, Urban, 145
Michigan State University, 130, 140–145, 201
Mirimax, 190
Mississippi State Penitentiary 85, 87, 96–97, 101–02. *See also* Parchman
Milwaukee County Jail, 86
Monroe, Marilyn, 187
Morris, Benjamin, 122
Morrison, Kristopher, 155
McQueary, Mike, 139

Nassar, Larry, 1, 109, 130, 140–45, 201, 211, 214
*Netflix,* 213
Newberry, Jonathan T., 27
Nicholson, Jack, 203
Non-disclosure agreement (NDA), 196

Obama, Barack, President, 74, 83, 190, 209
O'Conner, Lauren, 191
Office of Civil Rights, 46–47

Palmer, Janay (spouse of Ray Rice), 124, 129, 146
Paltrow, Gwyneth, 191
Parchman, 85, 87, 96–97, 101–02. *See also* Mississippi State Penitentiary
Paterno, Joe, 138–40
Patton, Susan 23. *See also,* "Princeton Mom"
Pell, George, 175, 178
Penn State University, 33, 118, 130, 132, 135, 138–40, 143–45, 200–01, 203, 207, 209, 211
Pepper Hamilton, 118
Perkins, Kassandra (spouse of Jovan Belcher), 123
Polanski, Roman, 186

Pope Benedict, 165, 176. *See also* Ratzinger, Joseph Pope Francis, 151, 178

Pope John XXIII, 166–67

Pope John Paul II, 171

Poole, Father Jim, 173

Povilaitis, Angela (Assistant Attorney General), 142

power, definition of, 19

PREA, 89–90, 94, 205. *See also* Prison Rape Elimination Act Price, Roy (Amazon Studio Chief), 191

Princeton Mom, 23

Prison Rape Elimination, Act 89–90, 94, 205. *See also* PREA Prison Policy Initiative, 103

*Pulp Fiction*, 190

Raisman, Ali, 143

rape baiting, 38–39

rape culture, 17–18, 200–01, 209–10, 212–14; in fraternities, 25, 29, 33–35, 52; in the military, 73, 80; in prisons, 93

rape myths, 52, 210

Rand Military Workplace Survey, 65, 67–68

Ratzinger, Joseph, 165, 176. *See also* Pope Benedict Raven Symone, 194

Reagan, Ronald, President, 84, 98

resistance to Integration, 18

respondent, definition of, 43

responsible employee, definition of, 43

restricted and unrestriced reporting, 66–67

Rice, Ray, 124, 129, 146–47

Roberts, Dorothy, 97–98

Rockefeller Drug Laws, 106

*Rolling Stone*, 22, 33

Rome/Roman Empire, 153, 155, 162, 175, 178

Rose, Charlie, 211, 215

sanctions, definition of, 43

Sanday, Peggy Reeves, 2, 24, 27–29, 31–34, 37–39, 41–42

Sandusky, Dotty, 161

Sandusky, Jerry, 109, 118, 130, 132, 133–135, 137–140, 143, 145–46, 149, 163, 200–01, 207, 209, 211, 214

*Scandal*, 187

Scully, Diana, 27, 211

Seccuro, Liz, 23

Second Latern Council, 154, 165

Second Mile, 138

Second Vatican Council, 157, 166

Senn, Charlene, 49

sex segregated, 3, 7, 14, 16–18, 21, 208–09; in the Catholic church, 160–62, 164; in the military, 60–61, 64, 74; in politics and entertainment, 188–89; in prisons, 89–90, 101–02, 105; in SportsWorld, 111, 113–114, 146–48. *See also* gender segregated 16, 18

sexual assault reporting; in Congress, 194–96

sexual harassment; in the military, 62–63

Sexual Misconduct and Assault Response Teams (SMARTs), 53

sexual misconduct, definition of, 43

sexual violence, 10; in the Catholic Church, 168–170; on college campuses, 75, 77–79, 91, 94, 127; in juvenile detention centers, 94–97; in the military, 65–67; in prison, 90–94; in politics and entertainment, 189–90; in SportsWorld, 120–121; among trans people, 101–102

shackling during childbirth, 98–100

*Shakespeare in Love*, 190

Shapiro, Margie, 183

*Shawshank Redemption, The,* 86

Sigma Alpha Epsilon (SAE), 28, 30

*Silence, The*, Frontline Documentary, 173
Simon, Lou Anna, 144
Simpson, OJ, 128, 147
Sirma Bilge, 9
Smith, Will, 187
Smith, Zach, 145
Spacey, Kevin, 183, 187, 211
Spanier, Graham, 139
SportsWorld, definition of, 110
spiritual abuse, 166, 170
St. Michael, Alaska, 170–72, 205
Stallworth, Donte, 124
Stannow, Lovisa, 92
Star, Ken, 118
Stormy Daniels, 196
Straus, Murray, 19
Strauss, Richard, 145
Survivors Network of Those Abused by
    Priests (SNAP), 151,
Syrett, Nicholas, 24–25, 34

Tailhook, 62–63
Tatum, Jerry L., 27
Team Bound, 77
Television Academy Hall of Fame, 192
Thomas-Lopez, Tiffany, 143
Thomashow, Amanda, 141–42
Thomashow, Jessica, 109
Till, Emmett, 194
Time's Up, 183–84
Title IX 41–43, 45–47, 51–52, 54, 119,
    141, 212
total Institutions, 14–15, 202–04,
    207; In the Catholic church, 156,
    161–64; in the military, 57–59, 72; In
    politics and entertainment, 184–86;
    in prisons, 85–87, 105; Quasi-total
    institution, 14–16; in SportsWorld,
    111–113, 146

transgender inmates, 100–104
trauma informed interviewing, 52
Trump, Donald, President and
    candidate, 46, 184, 187, 189, 190,
    196
Tyson, Mike, 124

Uniform Code of Military Justice, 69,
    74, 78
United Nations Declaration of Human
    Rights, 107
United States, military spending, 55
University of Minnesota, 39
University of Montana, 46
University of Wisconsin-Milwaukee, 38
*Uptown Saturday Night*, 192
US Council of Catholic Bishops, 176
US Olympic Committee, 143
USA Gymnastics, 130, 140–41, 143–45

Valenti, Jessica, 1, 184
Vatican, 152, 154–55, 165, 175–77
Vick, Michael, 124
Vigano, Archbishop Carlo Maria, 151

War on Drugs, 84, 98
Weinstein, Bob, 190
Weinstein, Harvey, 15, 184, 186–88,
    190–93, 197–98, 204, 211
Weinstein Company, 190
Westerman, Scott, 144
Wilson, Philip, 175
Winston, Jamies, 120, 146–47
Woodland Hills Juvenile Detention
    Center, Tennessee, 96
World Transgender Health Standards of
    Care, 104

Yale University, 38, 46, 162